DATE DUE

HOUSING TAXATION

HOUSING TAXATION

Walter A. Morton

1955

THE UNIVERSITY OF WISCONSIN PRESS

MADISON

Published by The University of Wisconsin Press,
811 State Street, Madison, Wisconsin.

Copyright, 1955,
by the Regents of the University of Wisconsin.
Copyright, Canada, 1955.
Distributed in Canada by Burns and MacEachern, Toronto.

Printed in the United States of America
by Waverly Press, Inc., Baltimore, Maryland.

Library of Congress catalog card number 55–7899.

Contents

v

Contents

Figures

Tables

HOUSING TAXATION

1

The
Housing Tax
Problem

For more than half a century students of housing have been concerned with subnormal housing standards and their effect on health and welfare. They have exposed the slums and tenements that blighted our great cities and have proposed various means for their eradication and amelioration. In many respects, the prewar housing problem was one of poverty, poverty of national resources and poverty of groups of citizens forced to inhabit unfit homes. Although this condition still persists, in recent years attention has shifted from subnormal housing conditions of the poor to the lack of housing space for the average American citizen. As a consequence, legislation has been enacted and plans proposed for governmental aid in the construction of dwelling space, especially for veterans and for low- and middle-income groups who have hitherto found it difficult to get a roof over their heads. The great bulk of living accommodations is, nevertheless, still furnished by private capital through home ownership or rental space, and will probably continue to be furnished by these sources in the future. It is therefore not out of order to consider means of increasing the incentives to build new homes by private entrepreneurs. Taxes on homes are always a drag on private construction and this drag has not been greatly altered in recent years in spite of the admitted need for dwellings.

The main factors determining the volume of construction seem to be the number of families, the size of incomes, and housing costs. Taxes on homes, which we shall consider in

3

this volume, affect the amount of available housing because they raise the cost of rental space and of home ownership. It is generally conceded that any tax as large as the tax on houses will affect the production and consumption of the taxed article.

The tax on homes is levied as a part of the general property tax and, like all other taxes, it influences the size and distribution of disposable income. Prior to World War II, the property tax yielded more revenue than any other single source, but since then its total yield has been surpassed by federal income and corporation taxes. It remains unique, however, in respect to being the heaviest tax levied on any single commodity, except perhaps fermented spirits, tobacco, and probably gasoline. Because of its size, it is felt directly by every homeowner and renter and it affects, as well, the volume of housing and the price of shelter. It is noteworthy, moreover, that those who have justified extremely heavy excises on intoxicating liquor or tobacco have usually found it necessary to inject an appeal to the sumptuary and moral arguments purporting to show that the taxed items were superfluous or even harmful. Needless to say, such contentions are never made regarding housing; on the contrary, it is recognized both that more and better housing is eminently desirable and that any impediment to it should be removed as expeditiously as possible.

Over a period of years, the property tax has been equivalent to approximately a 25 per cent sales tax on shelter. That such a tax has persisted on a commodity necessary to the health and well-being of all citizens must, therefore, be accounted for by overpowering considerations. The chief of these is that the general property tax has been and still appears to be today the only feasible source of revenue for local governments which, by choice or by necessity, need to maintain themselves financially independent of the state and federal governments.

There is some reason to believe that the heavy housing tax is depressing to construction and is therefore among the several factors responsible for the almost continuous scarcity of dwelling space. During depression periods, income falls whereas property taxes change little and accordingly constitute a larger proportion of deflated incomes. During this period the property tax is a heavy burden on owners and renters which acts as a deterrent to new construction. Then in the next period of boom the lack of housing accommodation is keenly felt. The financial burden during depression and the scarcity of housing during the boom are not, therefore, altogether unrelated, for the absence of construction during depression causes incomes to fall at that time, and the failure to build the normal quota of houses during that period results in a scarcity of suitable shelter during the subsequent prosperity when productive resources may be fully utilized. The low construction during the 1930's, for example, was partly responsible both for the low incomes of that period and for the scarcity of housing accommodations after the war.

During the depression of the 1930's, complaint was made against the justice of the property tax, which, though it was reduced somewhat, continued to be levied regardless of the income of the taxpayer. Many consequently let their properties go delinquent, thus impairing the revenues of municipal governments and threatening their financial stability. As a result, local governments everywhere were under severe strain; their revenues were decreasing at the very time that the demands for additional expenditures were growing. Desperate taxpayers accused city governments of inefficiency, and citizens without jobs and incomes were not at all loath to join the cry that local government employees were tax-eaters who ought to be dismissed, or at least ought to have their salaries severely reduced.[1] The owners of income-producing property—factories, hotels, apartment houses—whose rentals had fallen or were uncollectible, found themselves threatened by insolvency and appealed for tax reduction commensurate with the fall in income, thus raising serious questions relating to the method of valuing income-producing property during depression.

In sum, people from all walks of life and of varying fortunes continually asked that their tax bills be reduced. The board of review in the local community that listened to their troubles, of course, had no power to alter the amount of the tax but could only change an unfair assessment. The rate was set by the council, and hence the right of the review board to diminish the tax burden of any individual was limited to its power to lower the assessment. On this point the private income of the owner, whether he was employed or jobless, was in law and in fact irrelevant. What soon became apparent was that the great trek of appellants were asking for a reduction in the assessed value of their property simply because they could not pay the existing taxes. It was only in the exceptional case that the assessment was excessive judged by current rules and procedures. Under the circumstances, the board of review, though sympathetic with the taxpayer, often an unemployed worker or an aged couple who had lost their savings, was helpless to do anything about it. The small reduction which they might have been able to make in the assessed value would, moreover, have been of little help, and even this could not have been done without lowering the entire tax base which was already shrinking because of the decline in new construction and the fall in prices.

No local tax system, however well conceived and administered, alone can overcome difficulties of this sort; a general debility of the economic organism created by a fall in income can only be corrected by a national policy which restores income to a higher level. When, therefore, the Depression lifted and income and employment were raised, the criticism of municipal governments subsided and taxes again resumed their steady flow into the treasuries of local governments.

The experience just adverted to nevertheless raised the question: what proportion of his incomes does the taxpayer disburse as a property tax? Cursory observation disclosed that the unemployed and the aged were, in many cases, paying in property taxes more than they were receiving as cash income; whereas to many partially employed low-income groups, the property tax took more than half of their income. To the very wealthy, on the other hand, property taxes were a small item which they could bear, if not with perfect equanimity, at least without any substantial alteration in their living standards. The subsequent statistics bore out the essential truth of this observation.

PURPOSE AND SCOPE

Although the fact that the property tax takes a larger proportion of small incomes than of large incomes has long been known, we have not known just how regressive this tax was, and particularly whether it was more or less regressive than other consumption or general sales taxes. Engel's law, showing that the percentage of income spent for necessities declined whereas that spent for luxuries increased as incomes rose, gave us an early hint on this score and much additional data has been accumulated since Engel's time. These include the budgetary studies of the National Resources Committee during the 1930's, which showed the expenditures for various items of consumption at different levels. The study presented here was undertaken to find this relationship for owner-occupied homes in selected areas of Wisconsin. The data are presented in Chapter 8.

Before the burden, incidence, and effects of taxes are analyzed, it has been found necessary to give some consideration to factors affecting the cost of housing, and the supply of and demand for housing. The relation of tax costs to the total costs of owning or renting a home are shown in Chapter 2. The purpose of this chapter is not to discuss the perplexing and extensive subject of housing costs in detail, but merely to put tax costs in their proper perspective to other costs in order to grasp their quantitative significance and possible influence on the supply and demand for housing accommodations. For if tax costs increase the cost of owning a home by say 25 per cent, they will diminish the total amount of housing accommodations demanded and hence affect the volume of construction.

The relation of demand for housing to incomes is consequently considered in Chapter 3. In this chapter an attempt has been made, based on limited data, to show the relation between the value of a house built or purchased and the owner's income. The income-elasticity of demand for housing is then shown between several income groups and averaged. Income-elasticity has been presented both in terms of house value and housing space. These data further confirm the hypothesis that the proportion of income spent for housing declines as income rises.

The purpose of Chapter 4 is to explain briefly why housing is subject to the law of decreasing costs per unit of housing space. This fact is significant because it shows why low-income groups obtain less housing accommodations per dollar of housing expenditures and accordingly must also pay more taxes per unit of housing space than higher-income groups who can obtain larger and better housing amenities at decreasing costs per unit of space. Applied to the schedules showing the relative regressivity of property and of sales taxes, this fact tends to explain in part why property taxes are extremely regressive and why they appear to be even more regressive than sales taxes. A full understanding of this relationship must, however, wait consideration of these chapters.

With Chapter 5 we begin the consideration of the place of the tax on housing in our tax structure by showing the present status of the general property tax in our system of local finance. This chapter shows how all but local units of government have made substantial changes in their revenue sources in the past few decades, local government revenues from own sources being subject to smaller changes. This chapter also makes some estimates as to the division of real property into land and improvements because this distinction is necessary for purposes of understanding how a change in the tax levy would affect each form of property.

In Chapter 6 we accordingly discuss the question: who pays the property tax and what are its effects? Much as it might be desirable for purposes of simplicity, we cannot avoid facing the problem of tax incidence. A tax on residential property is a tax on this one form of ownership, use, or consumption as compared to other forms of property, to other income, or to expenditure. Because, moreover, it is levied on capital in the form of real estate, the property tax may be a tax on capital, a tax on the income from property, and thus in the short run may diminish its capitalizable value, or it may be a sales tax on shelter borne by the tenant, or the owner-occupier. We shall, therefore, need to consider which form of incidence the tax takes and whether the form varies with different circumstances.

The discussion in this chapter makes the usual separation between the incidence of a tax on land and on housing in the short and in the long run, but it adds a new feature to the discussion of incidence: the effect of fluctuations in income upon the incidence of the housing tax. If this chapter makes any contribution to the subject, it is in this attempt to combine the Keynesian-dynamic approach with the static classical theory of incidence. By doing this, we are able to explain what has often appeared to be a contradiction in the attitude of tenants and landlords. Why should landlords complain about high taxes if they shift them to the tenant? Yet they do complain and they evidently suffer from them. This chapter explains why this is so by showing the effects of high property taxes on particular incomes, on construction—and, hence, on the national income, with resulting lower rents and lower returns on investment. During periods of depression the tenant does not simply gain what the landlord loses; the whole community loses in the form of lower incomes.

The major portion of Chapter 7 is devoted to a discussion of the incidence of general sales taxes. The classical theory of tax incidence has dealt adequately with excise taxes on particular commodities but has not seemed satisfactory when dealing with a general tax on all commodities. As with the property tax, we have accordingly presented a neo-Keynesian theory of sales tax incidence which shows the effect in terms of aggregate demand, but does not neglect the varying effects on particular commodities composing the aggregate. In Chapter 8 we deal with the comparative regressivity of property taxes and sales taxes; and in Chapter 9 we present suggestions of how the property tax might be reduced.

COMPARATIVE BURDEN OF PROPERTY, SALES, AND
INCOME TAXES

The reason for introducing sales taxes into a book dealing
with the property tax is that sales taxes and income taxes
are in fact alternatives to the property tax. And if we seek
to improve the tax system, we cannot blindly substitute one
tax for another without some notion of their probable effects.
Indeed, this substitution has been taking place without any
definite philosophy of taxation during and since the Great
Depression.

As the relief burden increased during the early 1930's, the
resources of local communities became increasingly inadequate to carry this load, part of it was transferred to the
federal government, and the states and local governments
sought other sources of revenue. In Wisconsin the bulk of
relief costs was shifted to the general property tax rate.[2] In
many other states sales taxes were enacted, the proceeds of
which were used for this purpose. In effect then, sales taxes
were used as a substitute for property taxes. Since many of
those who made a virtue of opposing sales taxes were con-
senting to additional property levies, it was meet to inquire
whether the policy of putting the costs of increased expenditures on general property was as desirable as it might seem.
Granting that a sales tax was a heavy burden upon the small
man, could it be said that the property tax was much better?
Although there were some opinions about this matter, little
proof existed to show which of these two levies bore more
heavily on low incomes.

Both the property tax and the sales tax take a larger proportionate share of low incomes than they do of high incomes
and are, therefore, regressive taxes, the degree of regressivity
being a quantitative matter. In this characteristic they are to
be distinguished from income taxes and even some special
excises, which are either proportional or progressive. A proportional tax is a flat percentage rate on all incomes regardless of size; a progressive tax rises more than proportionately
as income increases. The degree of regressivity or of progression may vary within very wide limits; the income tax may

range from 1 per cent on low incomes to 6 per cent on high incomes, or it may range between 1 and 90 per cent depending upon the particular tax schedules. Whatever the slope of the tax curve may be, any tax containing any degree of progression or regression is called a progressive or regressive tax. For purposes of tax policy, however, it is paramount that the slope of the progressive tax rate be known; a tax might be technically progressive yet still very burdensome to low incomes because the rate of progression was such as to make little differentiation between the lowest and highest incomes. This is true of some state income taxes, but it is not, of course, true of the federal income tax, which is steeply progressive.

Since property taxes and sales taxes are almost without exception regressive taxes, and income taxes may be proportional or progressive, it follows that income taxes are always less burdensome on the small-income groups than either property or sales taxes would be. This fact is not, however, inherent in the taxation of income as such, for an income tax could conceivably be made regressive as well as progressive, but is a consequence of the well-nigh universal practice of making income tax schedules proportional or progressive. In this study we have accordingly thought it unnecessary to make a statistical contrast of these obvious facts, leaving them to the general conception of the reader. This omission, it should be cautioned, should not be construed to suggest that sales taxes are preferred to income taxes as a substitute for property taxes, or even that, all things considered, a general substitution of sales taxes for property taxes is a desirable objective of public policy. Indeed, in view of the general need for stimulating consumers' demand for shelter as well as for all sorts of consumers' goods, both property taxes and sales taxes appear to have a repressive effect upon the economy as compared to the taxation of incomes. This is a matter, however, which goes beyond the scope of this monograph.

DATA AND METHOD

On the specific issue of regressivity, we have used the data made available through the work of the National Resources

Committee in the United States and the study of Ursula and John R. Hicks on British rates. Major attention is given, however, to the Wisconsin data obtained through field investigation.

This investigation, the results of which are discussed in Chapter 8, was limited to homeowners. It is, of course, obvious that homeowners are not the only ones burdened by a property tax. Owners of rentable property or their tenants also pay this tax, and it would be desirable, if it were possible, to calculate these burdens as well. Estimates of rent and taxes as a proportion of income have, in fact, been made by the use of budget studies. But this method was not available to us; and even if it had been, we had no desire to repeat what had already been done on a large scale by the National Resources Committee. Furthermore, it seemed desirable to check budget data by the use of the objective data of income and taxes contained in public files.

The income data used in this study are personal income tax returns filed in the offices of the assessors of the Wisconsin income tax. These, under the law, are open for public inspection. The property tax data is found in the files of the property tax assessors. These data could not be used to show the taxes paid by tenants because they do not pay property taxes directly but merely as a part of their rents. It was, however, possible to find the income of a homeowner in the income tax file and the property tax paid by him in the property tax assessor's office, and then to compare the two.

Our study was confined to Wisconsin for two reasons: (1) the staff was located in Madison and the research grant of the WPA was made for that area; (2) Wisconsin is the only state in which this type of study could be made because only in that state is income tax data available for public inspection. The latter is, no doubt, the main reason that similar studies do not appear to have been made elsewhere. This project is, therefore, confined to taxes on owner-occupied homes and, although inferences can be made from it about the burdens on renters, they are not directly in the data themselves. The statistical study must, therefore, be considered as applicable only to homeowners in the area investigated; and although, as we shall see, there are reasons to believe that the results obtained are valid over a wider field, one would be foolhardy to apply them in specific instances without additional evidence in each case.

The objectives and limits of the study having been stated, a word may be in order regarding the method: (1) Field workers selected the names of owners from assessors' rolls and obtained among other things the data concerning (a) the value of the home and (b) the amount of tax levied. (2) The workers then obtained from the income tax returns the income of the homeowner in question. (3) The two series of data were then combined to ascertain the ratio of the property tax levy to income. (4) The consumer data of the National Resources Planning Committee were then used to calculate the percentage of income that would have been paid for taxes if the same revenue had been obtained from a general sales tax. (5) The comparative regressivity of the property tax and the sales tax could then be stated in the form of tables or curves. These methods will be explained more adequately in the proper context below.

2

Housing Costs

This chapter shows the relation of tax costs to the total cost of housing. Since the property tax is only one among the several items that determine the annual cost of living in a house, we need to evaluate all of these factors in order to put taxes in their proper perspective. The most important factor is, of course, the capital cost of the house itself and the annual carrying charges arising therefrom. Compared to these costs, taxes are less important. They are, nevertheless, a strategic factor because, unlike the others, they are not inherent in housing as such, and are therefore amenable to public policy. In this chapter we shall give considerable attention to construction costs because of their intrinsic significance and also because of the widespread belief that they are out of line with the costs of other goods and services. This will further emphasize the fact that, while we may stress the importance of taxes in this study, we are not unaware of the other considerations relating to the volume of construction and the cost of shelter. Any reduction in construction costs will lower total annual carrying charges, but it will also raise the percentage of tax costs to total costs because tax costs are determined by total revenue needs. If these remain the same, a reduction in the aggregate value of the property subject to taxation will raise the tax rate.

A house is usually conceived of as the shelter for individual persons or families used as a dwelling. It is this conception that we shall have in mind in the present consideration of housing costs. The word housing, of course, also has a broader connotation: the sheltering function performed by buildings of all kinds whether used to house livestock, persons, or things, in the city or in the country, on the farm or in the factory, for residential, commercial, or industrial

14

purposes. These various forms of real estate are traded in noncompeting markets; and though some interchangeability exists in their use and in their construction, they compete directly with one another for materials and labor. It is the use of common materials that creates such uniformity as exists between the supply prices of buildings of various kinds; the long-run supply price is a function of costs which varies with the amount of labor and materials used in construction. Once buildings have been erected, however, their value is determined by the supply and demand at the time; and hence, if supply is excessive in relation to the demand, buildings will sell even below reproduction cost, whereas during periods of scarcity they rise above this amount. Regional differences also exist because of geographical variations in the cost of labor, materials, and transportation costs.

Economically, a building is a durable capital good which gives off the service of shelter over the period of its life. If the supply of this service is scarce relative to the demand for it, it will have a price. For a tenant this price is rent; for an owner-occupier it is an imputed income; and in either case the cost of this service may be called the economic cost of housing. This comprises the original cost of creating the house plus the additional costs of providing shelter and maintaining the capital intact over its life.

ECONOMIC AND INSTITUTIONAL COSTS

Housing costs are of two basic kinds, economic and institutional. The inherent economic costs are those attributable to the existence and maintenance of a house as such, whereas the institutional costs are those, like property taxes, which exist because of law and social arrangements. Such inherent economic costs as interest, risk, depreciation, maintenance, and repairs would continue under any form of institutional arrangements, whether the property was owned by the government, the occupier, or the landlord, although the burden of the costs might be different under each of these circumstances.

The property tax is an institutional rather than an inherent cost of shelter because it is no more indigenous to housing as such than an excise tax on cigarettes or beer is implicit in the cost of cigarettes or beer. Perhaps this puts the case too strongly, for certain inherent economic costs connected with building maintenance and operation are paid for by taxes. Fire protection affords an example of the type of service given to a building as such and paid for by taxes. The cost of elementary education, on the other hand, even though paid largely by taxes on property, is clearly not an inherent cost of shelter but an institutional cost.

The purpose of the distinction between economic and institutional costs is to make it clear which of these are basic to shelter itself and which are simply the outgrowth of conventional ways of taxation and therefore amenable to public policy. Taxes, being the creature of law, can also be changed by law. The amount of property taxes levied is, moreover, a product of the mores and social values of the community that set the standard of services required of state and local governments. A community with high educational and service standards may impose greater taxes on property than one with low standards, and a government using other sources of revenue may place a smaller burden upon the property-tax payer than a government relying exclusively on this tax. There is accordingly a choice of policy regarding how these moneys shall be raised.

It shall be our purpose to seek out all of the costs of producing shelter, be they economic or institutional, in order that we may assay the significance of each element in the total. Since we are primarily concerned with the tax problem, our aim is not to ascertain minutely and exhaustively each element of cost, but to approximate its size in order to contrast it to tax costs in order that we may see the importance of taxes in the composite.

Shelter is a service with a time dimension, and its cost must therefore be expressed as a rate per unit of time. We shall accordingly express housing costs as percentages per annum of capital cost. What we seek then is economic cost plus institutional costs, not rental cost or even actual cash outlay.

Either of the latter may be greater or less than the economic cost of a given type of shelter. The cost of housing as such much accordingly include all of the costs of creating and maintaining the house, no matter whether they are actually paid and regardless by whom they are paid.[1]

Costs to the owner have sometimes been computed on a cash-outlay basis. Such a method simply lumps together all annual expenditures for repairs, maintenance, depreciation, interest, taxes, and amortization regardless of whether they are greater or less than the true economic costs for a particular year. This is valuable information, but it does not give a true cost picture. For if a house is not repaired, no cost outlay will be shown; whereas if it is kept in good repair and also improved, an excessive outlay will appear. Some houses have no mortgages, others have large or small mortgages, creating differences in the cash outlay for interest between identical houses—something related to the personal finances of the owner and not to housing as such. Amortization payments should not be included because they are not a true cost but a saving. Sometimes, however, amortization is counted as a cost because this payment is spread over the expected life of the house and is therefore just about equivalent to the annual charge for depreciation. If the mortgage happens to be paid off before the house has completely deteriorated in value, part of the mortgage payment turns out to be a net saving; whereas if the house deteriorates faster than the rate of amortization, its actual cost has been greater than the money outlay, and the difference between the two may result in a loss to the lending institution.

CAPITAL COST

The capital cost of a house to its owner is the price he pays for it or its present value, new or depreciated. If the housing market were always in equilibrium, the price of a house would be equal to its cost of production new, minus depreciation and obsolescence. In reality, houses are in oversupply at one time and in undersupply at another, and hardly ever, therefore, in precise relation to their cost of reproduction.

When they are in undersupply, rents are high and incentives
to new construction are great; when vacancies are high, new
construction is diminished, so that some sort of equilibrium
is brought about only after many oscillations over a period
of many years.

Annual costs per dollar of capital value are not the same
for houses of all materials, sizes, or ages, so that what we shall
have in mind as a model is a new house of moderate value
having a construction cost in the $5,000-$20,000 range, and
then leave it to the reader to make allowances for variations in costs with houses of a greater value.

The initial outlay for a house consists of the price of a site
and a building; the annual cost of shelter will be a function of this amount. Although land is durable physically, it
can appreciate or depreciate in value over the term of use.
Depreciation may be treated as an annual cost, though not a
money outlay, and appreciation as a gain or an addition to
net worth. The larger a building, the greater will be its initial
cost and its maintenance; and the better it is constructed, the
less will be these annual outlays. In housing it is literally true
that it is not the first cost that counts; cheap jerry-built houses
may sell for less per square foot of floor space, but the purchaser will be faced by rapid deterioration and heavy outlays
for repairs. A sturdily constructed house, on the other hand,
will have a longer life and smaller repair bills. In the former
case, the initial cost will be lower but the maintenance higher,
and in the latter, just the opposite. It is consequently impossible to give any valid figures for original costs or maintenance without regard to all of these characteristics, so that
all the estimates used will apply only to average types.

Land

The value of the land and the value of the houses built
upon it are directly related; cheap houses are built upon
cheap land and expensive houses on high-priced land. The
cost of land ready to build upon generally is estimated at
from 10 to 25 per cent of the total capital cost per dwelling
complete with land and utilities.[2] One writer says that it is

a rule of thumb in the building industry that land costs with
lot and street improvements should be about 20 per cent of
the cost of the completed single-family home, although 10
per cent is enough where land is cheap and improvements
few. In the case of farm homes, where so-called street improvements are often absent, the site cost may be an insignificant fraction of total cost.[3]

The proportion of the value of land to the total value of
the property ranges between 10 per cent and 25 per cent for
single-family homes, loans upon which were insured by the
Federal Housing Administration. In general, the cheaper
the property the lower will be the percentage invested in the
land, and the more expensive the total property the larger
will be the land proportion. Land valuations are generally the
highest in metropolitan centers and are also proportionately
more for existing homes than for new homes. The reasons
for the latter result are not given, but it seems probable that
it is the consequence of physical depreciation of older homes.
Table 1 shows the average percentage of land to total property valuation during recent years.

TABLE 1

LAND VALUE AS PERCENTAGE OF PROPERTY VALUE

Year	New Homes	Existing Homes
1937	14.7%	.....
1938	13.3	18.7%
1939	12.6	17.8
1940	12.0	17.2
1942	11.8	17.7
1946	11.6	14.0
1947	11.8	13.5
1948	12.0	12.8
1949	12.0	12.6
1950	12.5	13.0
1951	12.1	12.4

SOURCES: For 1937–40—Federal Housing Administration, *Seventh Annual Report,* 1940, Table 40, p. 76. For 1942–48—Computed from FHA, *Fifteenth Annual Report,* 1948, Table 13, p.
36; see also Colean, *Am. Housing,* p. 349, Table 3, and pp. 25-30
of Colean for further comment on relation of land to total property costs. For 1949–51—Computed from FHA, *Eighteenth
Annual Report,* 1951, Table 16, p. 50.

The rule seems to be, the larger the city the smaller the land area per home and the higher the value of land per square foot. It follows that with the small lots in large cities and larger lots in smaller communities, the percentage of the land covered by the building varies directly with the size of the city. In 1937 the average value of land per square foot of homes insured by FHA was $0.10, the highest being $0.29 for cities above 500,000 in population, and the lowest $0.07 for cities with less than 2,500 residents. The average per cent of land coverage for all cities in the United States (insured mortgages) was 18.6 per cent.[4]

In Wisconsin the cost of land (based on local assessment) is reported by the Department of Taxation to approximate 24 per cent of the total cost of residential property in 1948, more for mercantile property and less for manufacturing establishments.[5]

If the site value of land remains constant throughout the life of the building, then the current cost of land consists of interest plus taxes. If the land depreciates in value, then the annual depreciation must be added to cost; whereas, if its price rises, the annual appreciation can be treated as a cost deduction. Otherwise land is to be distinguished from the buildings upon it because it has low maintenance costs and, once land is owned, a reduction in either the interest rate or taxes reduces the monthly carrying cost.

The last conclusion is true, however, only if we take the value of land as a datum and then calculate the carrying cost to present owners. But it is by no means true that lower interest rates (and lower land taxes) will reduce the carrying costs of land to new purchasers. For the value of a site is obtained by capitalizing its expected annual income for housing purposes at the current rate of interest for investments of equal risk and liquidity. If then the economic rent of a piece of land is $100 and it is capitalized at 6 per cent, it will sell at $1,666; but if the alternative uses of money are such that it will be capitalized at 3 per cent, it will sell for $3,333. The new purchaser will be no better off, so far as annual interest charges are concerned, under the one or the other circumstance. This illustration, of course, merely represents the principle involved and is not to be taken as a dogmatic assertion that the factors affecting land values are quite so simple. It cautions us, however, against expecting that a lower rate of interest will decrease the annual dollar outlay for carrying land.[6]

And what has been said regarding interest applies also with respect to taxes. Taxes on land are a deduction from the economic rent and, if these taxes are reduced, the economic rent rises and the value of land also increases. The owner of existing land therefore gains by reductions in either interest rates or taxes, but the new purchaser is left with as large carrying charges as formerly. At least, that is the theory of the matter, and for the most part it is also the practice. We conclude then that cheap money and lower taxes would tend to inflate land prices; and if these are accompanied by a large demand for building sites, they tend to raise the cost of land very greatly to new purchasers. The seller thus capitalizes in his selling price the future annual increments of income which purportedly should have accrued to home builders.

It follows, therefore, that in the long run a reduction in interest rates or in land taxes is of doubtful value in reducing the monthly carrying cost of land. Interest policy and tax policy can, however, be differentiated. The monetary and fiscal policies affecting the money market and the rate of interest are not, of course, primarily determined by their effect upon land values but rather by their influence upon economic activity as a whole and particularly upon borrowing for new construction and general capital investment. The influence of cheap money upon land values is therefore not likely to be a ruling consideration in decisions affecting monetary policy. But taxes upon land are another matter; they can be raised or reduced independent of other taxes and their effects isolated. As a stimulus to new construction, it is wiser to reduce taxes on improvements without reducing them upon the site value of land, because the latter policy, as we have just seen, simply raises net economic rent which is capitalized into land values.

Improvements on land such as grading, planting, sewer and water connections are capital items whose value new depends upon their cost of production, and whose value old is determined by cost of reproduction less depreciation, or by their utility to the prospective purchaser, which may be less than actual reproduction costs. A reduction in the costs of producing improvements will therefore reduce the actual outlay for improved land.[7]

Building Costs

In the United States wooden frame construction is the dominating type, although in some cities like Philadelphia and Washington buildings of frame construction are only about 2 per cent of the total. Bemis estimates that, as of 1932, 68 per cent of all buildings in the United States were of frame construction.[8] The *United States Housing Census,* 1940, Vol. II, Part 1, shows construction of residential structures to be as follows: wood, 81.9 per cent; brick, 11.3 per cent; stucco, 4.2 per cent; all other, 2.6 per cent. The exteriors of new and old houses on which the FHA made loans in 1939 are shown in Table 2.

TABLE 2

EXTERIORS OF HOUSES

Exterior Material			Per Cent Distribution of Homes			
			New		Existing	
Wood				40.8%		55.5%
Brick	on masonry	11.1%	} 29.6	} 9.9%	} 20.1	
	on wood	18.5		10.2		
Stucco	on masonry	2.5	} 11.6	} 1.3	} 14.6	
	on wood	9.1		13.3		
Stucco in combination	on masonry	0.1	} 8.8	} 0.4	} 6.0	
	on wood	8.7		5.6		

SOURCE: Federal Housing Administration, *Sixth Annual Report,* 1939, pp. 59 and 60. See also, FHA, *Seventh Annual Report,* 1940, pp. 74–75.

By value, the higher-priced houses are predominantly of brick, whereas the cheaper houses have wood exteriors. If we include under frame construction all houses composed of brick on wood or stucco on wood, we find that these data closely resemble the census data for type of construction which show wood as 81.9 per cent of total construction. The main reason for the preponderance of frame construction is the cheapness of wood compared to other building materials. The larger proportion of stone, brick, and other fireproof construction is found largely in apartments and multiple-family dwellings. The cost of construction will then vary with the size, quality, durability, type of materials, and the price of labor and materials at the time of construction. The prices of various building materials are affected by general changes in the value of money and by the particular factors affecting the market for each commodity. Some of these factors are the existence of monopoly or competition among producers, cartels, price-fixing agreements, patents and trade secrets, whether the industry operates at constant, increasing, or decreasing costs as output rises, the remuneration of labor, the nearness to markets, transportation and distribution costs.

Hitherto wage rates of building trades labor have followed, with few exceptions, a steady upward trend.[9] Building costs in general rise and fall with changes in the general level of prices and the stage of the business cycle. They are also affected by secular factors, such as the exhaustion of the timber supply, which has increased the real cost of lumber, and the gradual rise in the wage level.[10] What this indicates is that over the years there is little stability in building costs and that the most important factor determining the cost of a house to an individual is the stage of the cycle when he builds or buys. While it is, of course, desirable to use discretion in what is purchased, it is much more important to buy at the right time than to buy the right house.[11]

The cost of building nevertheless appears to fluctuate less widely than other prices. It fell less during the 1929–32 depression than other commodities and rose faster in the ensuing recovery. Building costs in depression have therefore been relatively high compared to the wholesale price index, which has led some to attribute the paucity of building during the 1930's to this rigidity.[12] Construction costs, however, contain a large labor factor; and since wages are largely inflexible, the building cost index is not likely to fluctuate as widely as the wholesale commodity index, which is weighted heavily with farm products. It is, moreover, doubtful whether cost rigidity was the main reason for lack of investment in building during the 1930's and whether cost flexibility could remedy it. Worthy of note, however, is the fact that the price of lumber fell much more drastically during the Depression than the price of steel, cement, brick and tile, and other commodities made by large-scale industry with rigid wage costs.[13] It has also been found that marginal building costs rise considerably with an increase in volume, and this is attributed to the fact that this industry is not organized so as to handle a large volume at constant, decreasing, or even slowly increasing marginal costs as in the case of steel, automobiles, and other manufactures.[14]

The National Housing Administration estimates that in 1944 the national weighted average of the cost of a house and land was divided as shown in Table 3. For the building alone,

TABLE 3

HOUSING COSTS

Item	Percentage	Total Percentage
House		
Cost of materials at site	45.70	
Cost of site construction labor	29.50	
Contractor's and subcontractors' overhead and profit	12.30	
		87.50
Land		
Value of unimproved land	7.00	
Cost of land improvements	5.50	
		12.50
Total capital cost		100.00

the percentage of total construction cost would be as follows: materials, 52 per cent; labor on site, 34 per cent; and profit, 14 per cent. This comes close to the rule of thumb that the cost of building can be apportioned 60 per cent for materials and 40 per cent for labor, these amounts varying in different parts of the nation depending largely on the proximity to materials and the price of labor.[15]

Costs can also be computed by distributing them on the basis of structure, finish, and accessories, and Bemis estimates a fair distribution as follows for a representative suburban building: structure, 45 to 50 per cent; finish, 25 to 30 per cent; and accessories, 25 per cent.[16] Of the materials used, lumber is the most important, running as high as 20 per cent of the total cost, the balance of the material items—masonry, concrete and mortar, plaster, lath and wallboard, insulation, roofing, flooring, millwork, paint, finish hardware, plumbing, heating, and electrical—each ranging between 1 and 5 per cent of total costs. It follows accordingly that only a consistent price reduction over the whole range of materials can appreciably affect total costs.

The high costs of materials are in part due to the primitive methods of distribution, which make manufacturing costs less than half the final cost to the builder, the balance going for distribution, transportation, and profit[17]—a factor that can be changed only by reorganization of the industry on an integrated and mass production basis, and this has thus far not been feasible.

Labor Costs

Hourly wage rates in the building trades have been the highest paid in any important industry. From 1890 until 1930 they were consistently higher than wages paid in the metal trades, coal mining, boots and shoes, cotton goods, or in all other industries combined.[18] The wages of skilled workers were in many years double those in other industries; and although the building trades are seasonal, average annual wages were still higher in the building trades than in other work,[19] and have maintained this position until the present time, although the differential above other groups has been narrowed somewhat.

It has been argued that the high wages in the building trades make it harder for other workers to buy the products of these craftsmen and thereby restrict the demand for building. There is some truth in this contention, but it must be put in its proper setting. Of course, a high wage restricts demand in the case of building workers as it does in any other line of endeavor. In the same way the demand for the services of doctors, lawyers, executives, general managers, superintendents, and foremen is also restricted by the higher wages they receive. What also happens, however, is that these persons take a larger share of the national product than those who receive less; and so long as the total income is maintained at the same level, total product is not decreased. If the wages of any group are held up by other forces than the demand for their output and result in idleness, then only can we say that they are above their equilibrium and should come down. But there is no more substance to the argument that skilled building craftsmen should not be paid for their skill than that doctors or lawyers should receive income no higher than the unskilled. What is important is that these high rates should not be maintained by monopoly power, denial of entry into the trades by apprentices, or other restrictive practices, and in the face of high unemployment for a particular group of workers.

It has also been an old lament that building trades labor is ineffectively utilized and that it has a low productivity because of deliberate restrictions on output found in union rules and practices. This question is beyond our present scope; but it may be remarked that, although the years of full employment in building should have provided encouragement to remove these restrictions insofar as they were due to fear of job scarcity, this has not been done and does not appear in prospect. The high labor costs compared to other industries are also attributed to the fact that the construction industry and residential construction in particular is a handicraft industry and lacks mechanization.[20]

Decent housing has long been a scarce commodity. One way of looking at this scarcity is to say that it is too expensive for lower-income groups. Another is to say that the community prefers to spend its income for automobiles, radios, refrigerators, and other goods that give more satisfaction per dollar of expenditure. Many feel that they do not get the same value for their money in housing that they get for mass-produced goods; and although sentiments of this kind may be described as ill-conceived and based on inadequate knowledge, still they cannot be disregarded altogether, especially when reflected in a decided preference for other goods and by the decision to get along with small houses upon the part of those who need housing accommodations. The willingness of the public to purchase any commodity in quantity at the price offered is the ultimate test of whether it is overpriced, and this applies to housing and the materials and labor used in it, as well as to anything else.

Any measures that are taken to lower building costs, such as lower material prices, better utilization of labor, or prefabrication, will lower the initial outlay and thus decrease interest and maintenance costs.[21] It should also act as a stimulus to construction. So long, however, as the total amount of revenue raised by property taxes remains the same, a decrease in housing value due to lower building costs will not lower the annual dollar tax costs because a smaller taxable base will require a higher tax rate in order to produce the same revenue.

Depreciation and Obsolescence

A house depreciates when it diminishes in value and appreciates when it increases in value. The depreciation base is a function of costs and the rate is dependent on the solidity of physical construction, which determines its service life, and all other factors determining obsolescence. Since a house presumably has the highest value at the time of its completion, physical deterioration and obsolescence are functions of time. The useful life of houses according to some estimates is forty years, but this figure seems to be a minimum one.

Depreciation, which must vary according to the estimated life of a structure, is consequently a very uncertain factor. A house that will last forty years must allow 2.5 per cent per year for depreciation; one that will last a hundred years, only 1 per cent, etc. For maintenance of capital intact, a larger rate must be collected in earlier years and a lower rate as times goes on.

Obsolescence occurs when a structure, though physically unimpaired to perform its original functions, loses value because of a change in demand induced by changes in taste, in choice of location, or in function and design. The most common evidence of locational obsolescence is found in "old neighborhoods" where once grand houses cease to be used for residential purposes or are rented out at a low price. Accompanying such change in use is usually also a lack of maintenance and repairs that also brings about marked physical deterioration. It often happens that obsolete housing in the center of cities rests on land that has become valuable for commercial and industrial purposes and that will soon be converted to these uses.

Obsolescence may be also due to changes in the function expected of houses—the preference of small houses with modern conveniences as compared to the great establishments capable of accommodating large families, relatives, and friends, and requiring expensive maid service. Obsolescence in design is found when the exterior does not please the eye and the interior arrangements cease to satisfy modern architectural standards. Such a house, though physically adequate, is no longer desired and falls in value.

It is now held by some housing experts that locational obsolescence can be greatly minimized if the ownership of the property over a large area rests in the hands of a single person, presumably a large corporation having an interest in maintaining its desirability as a housing center. Such a corporation would keep the entire area in good repair, avoid eyesores and slums which grow up on areas having finely divided ownership where the action of one owner may hurt the property values of others in the neighborhood. Under the latter conditions, individual owners acting in isolation have little power and hence no incentive to alter the downward trend.

When we ask how long a building will last before becoming obsolete, we seek an answer to a question upon which experience differs widely, an answer which is likely to change in the future. Different rates of depreciation are allowed for brick and family dwellings and for different types of apartments. Bemis, for example, shows depreciation and obsolescence on brick single-family dwellings to be 1 per cent per annum and on frame 2 per cent.[22] This may be questioned as failing to allow for the factors of obsolescence due to location, function, and design, which can be just as great for brick as for frame buildings.

Depreciation estimates must also be used in computing the net income of any building for purposes of taxation or of private sale. An outstanding authority with long practical experience says that "the estimate of future economic life of a building is the crux of every appraisal based on net income."[23] Buildings which have been entirely written off through depreciation will be found to have another long span of life and, unless one can guess what this period is going to be, the depreciation rate used may be far wide of the mark.

It is difficult, therefore, to give a satisfactory figure for depreciation—the allowance of 2–2.5 per cent will be used here because it reflects a common judgment even though it may overstate or understate the case in specific instances.[24]

Maintenance and Repairs

Unlike depreciation, the rate of which must be guided by expected life, maintenance and repairs are annual costs due to wear and tear. Maintenance and repairs consist of the amount spent to keep a building in usable condition; when it goes beyond this amount, the expenditure is capital investment. (Major alterations that improve a building or bring it up to date fall in this category, because they are designed to maintain or increase its value. Capital improvements may increase the size, change the function, or extend the life of a structure that might otherwise become obsolete in function or design.

Annual maintenance—such as exterior and interior painting, papering, replacement of roof, furnace, or plumbing—is generally irregular; the need for this work may accumulate over a number of years and then be done at one time. It will vary furthermore from house to house in accordance with the treatment given it by the occupant and his willingness to put up with things that are not the best. Tenants will demand more in the way of improvements, painting, and repairs than owners and when housing is plentiful will succeed in their demands. Carpentry and masonry repairs will be higher if the original construction is poor, and if they are neglected to the point that extensive damage results. Homeowners seem to neglect maintenance when their income is low and to spend for this purpose when it is high. Thus the income of the particular homeowner rather than need alone affects this expenditure over the period of the business cycle.

The maintenance base is the value of a house and the rate is a percentage of this value. This rate is not constant because repairs do not come regularly and because labor and material prices may be altogether different at the time repairs are made from what they were at the time of construction. Who knows what it will cost to repair or paint a house ten or twenty years hence?

Some estimates of maintenance are made to include household operation, such as heat, light, and water. For apartment buildings, janitor service is also included. When this is done, maintenance charges may run as high as 35 per cent of total costs; whereas in the case of a home, with these charges excluded, they are only 15 to 20 per cent of total annual costs.[25] We shall include here insurance against loss by fire, wind, and hail as a cost of maintenance. This rate is about two-tenths of 1 per cent. Including this item, but omitting heat, light, and other items of household operation, we shall use a figure of about 2 per cent (of present value) per year for an owner-occupied residence.[26] This generalization must be modified in particular instances to allow for the great variability in the type of construction, use, prices, and the part of the country in which the building is located.

Interest

The simplest way to compute the interest cost of owning a home is to use the actual amount paid on the mortgage. But this is obviously an unsatisfactory measure as it depends on the size of a particular debt at a particular time, something that is infinite in its variations. These debts could, of course, be averaged to show the average amount of interest paid, but such information would be of little value for our purposes.[27] One home may carry a heavy mortgage while its owner is in possession of interest-bearing bonds; another carries no mortgage but the owner borrows elsewhere; still another may be occupied by its owner who holds it clear of debt and has no other assets or liabilities.

The interest cost of carrying a house is the putative income from an alternative investment opportunity of the homeowner in an asset of similar risk and liquidity. If he could obtain say 5 per cent on such a security, then the interest cost of real property ownership is 5 per cent of the amount invested. What then is a comparable investment opportunity? For some the actual alternative may be government bonds at 2 per cent; for others it may be a stock in a local corporation yielding 10 per cent. For large insurance companies the actual alternative to investment in a building program may be the holding of fractional interest government securities or idle cash.

We shall therefore use the rate paid on home mortgages as the opportunity cost of property ownership. Thus if the mortgage rate is 5 per cent, we shall assume that the interest cost on a $10,000 home is $500. The principal amount of a mortgage being usually merely a fraction of total value, it may appear that the use of this rate understates the true cost, which would obviously be higher with a 100 per cent mortgage because of the greater risk that it entails. This argument would be convincing except for the following considerations.

In our computations we have allowed 2 per cent to 2.5 per cent each for depreciation and for repairs, making a total cost for those items of from 4 per cent to 5 per cent. This is greater than the amount of the annual payment on the principal of a mortgage usually called for in amortization plans and would provide very ample protection to a mortgage holder.

But what is the rate paid on mortgages? This rate is related (1) to the general level of rates at a particular time and place and (2) to the amount of the mortgage. Rates change from year to year, over the secular trend and the business cycle, and are higher in some parts of the country than in others.[28] The rate on a 50 per cent mortgage in 1947 was about 3.5 per cent, on a 60 per cent mortgage a little higher, and on a 90 per cent mortgage or on second or subsequent mortgages still higher.

During the 1920's many homes were financed by a first mortgage bearing a rate of 6 to 8 per cent and a second mortgage carrying a rate as high as 10 per cent. The purchaser of the second mortgage also demanded commissions which raised the effective interest rate in some cases to 20 per cent.[29] This practice made the interest cost of carrying a home 60 to 70 per cent of the total costs. These excessive interest costs came to an end after the liquidation in the first part of the 1930's and the creation of amortized mortgage plans under the Home Owners Loan Corporation and the FHA.

Market interest rates may be reduced through reduction of risk or its absorption by government through guaranty of all or part of the mortgage. Likewise government lending agencies may deliberately charge rates lower than would have to be paid in the open market. Limited dividend building companies may go into housing with the aim of providing shelter at a profit less than they could make if they charged all that the traffic would bear. All of these schemes alter actual interest outlays.

Data on home mortgage interest rates are scarce and inadequate, but such as are available show a wide variation of rates in different communities.[30] The nominal rates, moreover, must be adjusted for special charges and even then they do not portray the true cost of financing. This is because they apply to first mortgages only, whereas total interest costs consist of the first mortgage interest plus financing charges, plus second mortgage interest and financing charges. In Massachusetts for the years 1907 to 1948 average interest rates charged by the Massachusetts co-operative banks (building and loan societies) on real estate loans ranged from about 5 per cent to 6 per cent.[31] The following is a breakdown of interest rates for these years:

1907	5.37%	1915	5.58%	1923	6.01%	1931	6.08%	1939	5.62%
1908	5.41	1916	5.59	1924	6.05	1932	6.07	1940	5.58
1909	5.42	1917	5.60	1925	6.08	1933	6.05	1941	5.52
1910	5.44	1918	5.64	1926	6.11	1934	6.03	1942	5.51
1911	5.45	1919	5.70	1927	6.10	1935	5.68	1943	5.49
1912	5.47	1920	5.78	1928	6.09	1936	5.65	1945	5.12
1913	5.50	1921	5.88	1929	6.07	1937	5.63	1946	5.10
1914	5.54	1922	5.95	1930	6.08	1938	5.63	1947	4.83
								1948	4.85

Reports of the Bureau of the Census and of other agencies similarly show the range between the years 1920 and 1940 to be between 5 per cent and 6 per cent.[32] The Home Owners' Loan Corporation has had a tendency to bring about lower and more uniform rates. At its inception in 1933, when funds were scarce, it began to charge 5 per cent and continued this rate until 1939 when the rate was reduced to 4.5 per cent, thus anticipating somewhat the general downward trend later found in other agencies. After 1940 rates all began to fall to below 5 per cent, varying inversely with the size of the mortgage.[33]

By 1940 the interest rates charged by the various lending institutions were quite similar, except for the Home Owners' Loan Corporation whose rates were almost 1 per cent below other lenders, as shown in Table 4.

TABLE 4

AVERAGE INTEREST RATE FOR FIRST MORTGAGE ON 1–4 FAMILY,
OWNER-OCCUPIED, NON-FARM HOMES IN APRIL, 1940

Lender	Average Interest Rate (Unweighted)	Percentage of Debt of Value
Building and Loan Associations	5.92	49.9
Commercial Banks	5.67	48.6
Savings Banks	5.53	51.3
Life Insurance Companies	5.42	52.6
Mortgage Companies	5.61	55.8
Home Owners' Loan Corporation	4.50	56.1
Individuals	5.79	49.9
Other	5.49	55.6
All	5.54	51.6

The Federal Home Loan Bank Board regards the changes
in methods of home financing during the 1930's as revolu-
tionary. Effective interest rates including all special charges
were reduced from a range of 6–8 per cent at the beginning
of this decade to 4.5–6 per cent at the end. Further interest
savings were obtained for the borrower by charging only
on the unpaid balance, whereas formerly they were often
made on the original principal of the loan. Interest costs
were also reduced because the first mortgage was made to
cover the entire amount of the loan, thus obviating expensive
junior mortgage financing at rates running as high as 10 to 12
per cent. The Board also reports that "discounts and charges
incidental to the making of home-mortgage loans such as
commissions, fees and bonuses, are now better fitted to services performed."[34] In 1947, building and loan companies were
lending at 4.5 per cent on 80 per cent mortgages, and banks
and other lenders had reduced rates to 3.5 per cent on 50 per
cent mortgages. The decline in interest rates since 1930 may
be attributed to the lack of demand for funds in the capital
market, the inauguration of the cheap-money policy in 1933,
and the creation of federal institutions to facilitate mortgage
lending. When compared to other money market rates such as

high-grade marketable bonds and long-term government securities, mortgage rates seem to follow the same trend but
to change less often. The decline was rather slow, showing
that it has taken almost ten years for the cheap-money policy
begun in 1933 to take something resembling full effect.

Because of the variations in rates, we shall use 3.5 per cent
to 5 per cent as the current opportunity cost of owning a
home, with the caution that each individual must use a figure
that actually represents his cost.

Interest is the largest single item in the cost of housing,
running from 40 per cent to 60 per cent of total annual cost
under ordinary circumstances. When the home purchaser is
bilked by sharpsters in the mortgage field, or when he himself engages in foolish methods of finance, the top figure may
be even larger.

But interest is of significance in another respect—it is an
item subject to large variations over time and is partly subject to control by monetary and fiscal policy, and by the direct
lending activities of governmental agencies. The large reduction in average interest rates of mortgages since 1933 has
reduced the annual cost of carrying a home by 15–20 per cent.

Amortization

Amortization payments reduce the principal of the debt
and are therefore not costs at all, but savings. They are
nevertheless included in some studies of housing costs. When
this is done, it is usually because the principal payments are
considered to be equal to depreciation, and no separate allowance is made on account of the latter. Sometimes, however,
the object of the cost computation is not to discover actual
economic costs but the necessary outlays in the purchase of
a house. Since, in fact, this is the way that many prospective homeowners figure, it gives a good index of the manner
in which monthly cost payments affect the total expenditure.

The length of the amortization period thus becomes a vital
factor in this motivation. The tendency, in recent years, to
extend the period of payments over a longer term of years has
the end result that the borrower saves at a slow rate and thus

TABLE 5

INTEREST RATES ON MORTGAGE LOANS BY TWENTY-FOUR LIFE
INSURANCE COMPANIES AND SAVINGS AND
LOAN ASSOCIATIONS

Year	Life Insurance Companies*	Savings and Loan Associations†
1920	6.1%	.....
1921	6.2	.....
1922	6.1	.....
1923	5.9	.....
1924	5.9	.....
1925	5.9	.....
1926	5.8	.....
1927	5.9	.....
1928	5.9	.....
1929	6.0	.....
1930	6.0	.....
1931	6.0	.....
1932	6.0	.....
1933	5.9	.....
1934	5.8	.....
1935	5.5	.....
1936	5.2	.....
1937	5.1	.....
1938	5.1	4.85%
1939	4.9	4.98
1940	4.6	5.44
1941	4.6	5.58
1942	4.5	5.76
1943	4.5	5.51
1944	4.5	5.43
1945	4.4	5.24
1946	4.2	5.00
1947	4.0	4.79
1948	..	4.79
1949	..	4.80
1950	..	4.82

* Average contract interest rates on a sample of straight urban mortgage
loans of 1–4 family dwellings. SOURCE: R. J. Saulnier, *Urban Mortgage Lending*

pays a greater amount of interest than he would with a faster amortization rate. Having already made allowance for depreciation, we shall accordingly omit amortization as a cost of home ownership.

Taxes

With interest, we have concluded the consideration of the inherent economic costs of housing. We have already adverted above to the fact that taxes are an institutional cost rather than an economic cost of shelter, a means of raising revenues needed by local and state governments. They pay for items entering into the cost of living but not the cost of shelter alone; they provide the decencies and amenities of life, schools, health, streets, police, and justice; only a part of them is a cost attributable to shelter, as such.

The amount of property taxes varies from community to community and from state to state depending upon the standards of expenditure and the other sources of revenue. The Detroit Bureau of Governmental Research estimates the average true rate for over 200 cities to be from 2.5 per cent to 3 per cent between 1923 and 1950. The tax rate in villages averages about the same as in cities, but the rate in towns is much lower. Urban rates run about 50 per cent higher than rural rates. (See Chapter 5.) This figure would make the tax cost from 20 per cent to 25 per cent of the total annual cost of carrying urban real property.[35]

Taxes, being a creature of law, can be altered by law and are therefore the one item in the cost of shelter that can be directly affected by public policy. After considering the burden of taxes in the following chapter, we shall suggest ways and means of reducing this hindrance to building activity.

by Life Insurance Companies (National Bureau of Economic Research; N.Y., 1950), quoted by James J. O'Leary in *Law and Contemporary Problems,* Winter, 1952, p. 31.

† Gross rates of income on mortgage loans, savings and loan associations—members of the Federal Home Loan Bank System. Compiled by Investment Research Staff of the Life Insurance Association of America and quoted *ibid.,* p. 36.

SUMMARY OF ANNUAL HOUSING COSTS

SUMMARY OF ANNUAL HOUSING COSTS

Table 6 shows the items entering into the annual cost of housing and their probable quantitative significance. These

TABLE 6

PROPORTIONS OF HOUSING COSTS

Cost	Per Cent of Capital Cost per Annum			
	Low	Total Low	High	Total High
Inherent Economic Costs				
Depreciation and obsolescence	2.0		2.5	
Maintenance and repairs and insurance	2.0		2.5	
Interest	3.5 (1946)		5.0 (1954)	
		7.5		10.0
Institutional Costs				
Property taxes		2.5		3.0
Total Cost		10.0		13.0

data do not include the expenditures for household operation—such as fuel, light, refrigeration, telephone, laundry, and similar items—because they are not costs of shelter as such, although fuel and light are closely related to the size of the building. Others are determined by the living habits and standards and would not vary appreciably regardless of the size of the house. Indeed, if anything, some other expenditures might be larger if housing costs were smaller, since an adequate house may serve to some extent as a substitute for other forms of entertainment.[36]

INDIVIDUAL AND SOCIAL COSTS

The economic costs of shelter exist regardless of ownership. If housing is owned by the state, these costs are borne by the state and paid for out of general taxes or out of the rents collected. The individual owner-occupier or landlord meets these costs out of his income or rental revenue. When

they are all paid, they represent the total social costs of
shelter. We have already noted that only that part of property taxes is really a cost of housing which represents such
items as fire and police protection to property. Since, however, these costs are distributed over the whole community
by taxes, they do not necessarily represent the actual cost
attributable to each housing unit. Indeed, it has long been
known that bad housing costs the taxpayer more than good
housing because it increases disease and delinquency. Infant
mortality, tuberculosis, and other infectious diseases thrive
in blight areas and children raised there lack the opportunity
for healthful recreation and wholesome activity.[37]

The slum area has higher costs for fire and police protection and public health services than the rest of the city. But
since these costs are spread over the entire tax base, they
increase the cost of shelter to the entire community. In this
way the social costs of bad housing become financial costs to
the individual property owner. Straus shows that in one slum
area the cost of fire protection was $18.27 per capita com-
pared to $3.12 for the rest of the city; for police protection,
$11.50, compared to $4.20; for public health work, $2.02 com-
pared to $0.64.[38] One slum area in Cleveland, Ohio, shows
total expenses of $1,356,978 and tax rate income of $225,035,
resulting in an operating loss to the City of Cleveland and
Cuyahoga County of $1,131,943 in 1932. The operating loss to
the community was $76.58 per capita or $333 per family. The
cost of fire protection in the slum section was $18.27 per
capita compared to between $2.00 and $3.00 in other sections
of the county.[39]

There is, nevertheless, another aspect of social cost not
directly reflected in tax accounting, the loss of enjoyment and
satisfaction by the residents of the slums. Physical and moral
deterioration is a real loss even if it cannot be measured in
monetary terms. The real cost of sickness and crime is found
in additional expense to the community at large and is reflected immediately in lower productivity and lower income
for the unfortunate residents of blighted areas and hence for
the nation as a whole. Modern slum clearance and public

housing projects are consequently designed to lower costs and
increase income in the nation, as well as to improve the standard of life of their direct beneficiaries.

We hope it will not be construed as an argument for the
maintenance of bad housing that we enter a word of caution
regarding the tendency to attribute to the existence of the
slum all of the human and social evils found there. We are
not even warranted in assuming that the higher crime, disease, and delinquency rates found in slum areas are due alone
to housing conditions and the circumstances attendant upon
them. Criminals may choose slum areas in which to live, and
persons of low income because of illness, mental deficiency, or
moral delinquency may drift into these areas because of economic pressure, or because they find these surroundings con-
genial. Such persons might be subject to higher crime and
disease rates wherever they resided, and better housing would
hardly be a cure for all moral, physical, and social evils. Bad
housing is undesirable in itself even if it did not lead to other
evils and even if the slum dwellers were as healthy and as
satiated with moral rectitude as those residing on the gold
coast. In that case, we should certainly argue that they deserved something better, and find it as good an argument as
the one we now use, that better housing will improve health
and moral character. Needless to say, the deleterious influence of bad housing has been sufficiently demonstrated that
it should not be necessary to overemphasize it to create en-
thusiasm for a slum clearance program. Neither does it appear necessary in these times to combat the old argument
that slum residents are so bad that they will create new slum
areas out of good housing accommodations; that is a doctrine
of original sin which is unsupported by experience.

3

The
Demand for
Housing

The demand for housing accommodations like that for other commodities and services is a function of their price, as well as the price of substitutes and the income of the purchaser. If housing costs are high, the amount demanded will be less than if they are low. This applies to the original capital cost of creating a house as well as to the amount of monthly carrying charges. If other commodities like automobiles are considered more desirable at the prevailing prices, they will compete for the consumer's dollar and thus in effect act as substitutes for housing. And other things being equal, the demand for housing will vary directly with the income of the public.

In the preceding chapter we have treated the annual cost of housing as a percentage of the value of the occupied premises. We found there that the annual cost is from 10 per cent to 12 per cent of the capital cost. This is in agreement with the working rule adopted by realtors that monthly rentals should be about 1 per cent of the value of the real estate. Whether, therefore, a family owns or rents a house, the monthly charge will vary directly with the value of the premises; some years it may be above this amount, and others below it, but over a period of time it is likely to fluctuate about this mean.

The same factors accordingly determine the demand for housing whether considered as a monthly expense paid by the owner, rental paid by a tenant, or as a capital outlay. A family able and willing to spend $50 monthly or $600 annually

for house expense could afford a capital outlay of about
$6,000. Whether, however, the premises are rented or owner-
occupied, the size of the house that any family can afford
to live in must depend on the family's income.

HOUSING EXPENDITURE AND INCOME

Housing is, of course, only one of the many items in the
family budget, and the amount that can be expended for this
purpose depends on the size of income and the importance
of this service compared to other needs. These, of course,
vary from person to person, some preferring to spend more
for one thing and less for another. In any event, if housing
absorbs a disproportionately large share of income, other
satisfactions must be foregone. Any family must therefore
apportion its expenditures according to the scale of urgency
which it adopts, and this allocation of income determines its
demand for housing. Naturally, if prices are high for such
items as food and clothing, which are high in the order of
urgency, less will be available for housing; whereas if these
prices are low, more, though probably not proportionately
more, will be devoted to this purpose.[1] On the other hand, if
items lower in this scale—such as entertainment, automobiles,
and furniture—are made relatively cheap, they will attract
expenditures to themselves and divert them from housing.
Should, perchance, the capital cost of housing, its carrying
charges, or both, be reduced, the demand for housing amenities can be increased; higher capital costs or carrying
charges, on the other hand, will have the opposite effect.

The size of a living establishment that any family can
afford depends therefore not only upon the immediate costs
of maintaining the physical structure referred to in the previous chapter, but also upon the costs of household operation
such as heating, lighting, and cleaning, all of which also bear
some relation to the size of the living quarters.

Because of the absolute necessity of shelter, housing stands
with food very high in the order of urgency; it is among the
first demands upon income, and if income is small it will take
a large share of the total. If, on the other hand, income is

large, a smaller proportion will be spent for shelter, food, and other necessities, and a larger proportion will be devoted to luxury items and to savings. Housing expenditures, accordingly, do not bear a constant but a decreasing ratio to income. Engel's law was one of the first statements of this principle, and subsequent investigations, while altering its quantities, bear out its essential truth.

The most extensive study of family expenditure in recent years was made by the National Resources Committee. This study showed the proportion that housing expenditure bore both to the size of income and to total expenditures of all kinds.[2] It was found that the outlays of a family for housing were second only to food and that low-income families apportioned about one-third of their expenditures to housing and household operation, whereas higher-income groups spent only about one-sixth. In general, housing costs rise with total expenditures, but at a slower rate; the higher-income groups accordingly spend more money but a smaller percentage of their income for this purpose. This pattern of expenditure was found to hold true for large, for middle-sized, and for small American cities.[3]

So much for the proportion spent by each income group. The average housing expenditure for all income groups combined appears over a period of many years to run between 15 per cent and 20 per cent of total expenditure.[4]

The data of the International Labour Office show that rents in Poland, Germany, and Hungary before World War I were about 18 per cent of income; in Great Britain, 16 per cent.[5] During the later 1930's, expenditures for housing accommodation (gross rents) in Great Britain varied from 12 per cent to 15 per cent of total average expenditure.[6]

The exact proportions vary somewhat between periods of high and low incomes. During periods of low incomes, rental costs tend to fall as well as incomes, but the economic cost of housing is then borne by the landlord as a financial loss. Various cost of living studies between 1874 and 1930 show that the amount expended for rent has varied for the most part around 16 per cent to 20 per cent of total expenditure.[7]

What is important for our purposes, however, is that the
amount spent for housing increases with income but at a
lower rate. And this fact necessarily establishes the conclusion, further verified below, that the demand for housing is
inelastic relative to income.

Price and Income Elasticity of Demand

The demand of any particular purchaser for housing accommodations is a function of three factors: the size of the
family, the price of housing, and the size of income. The
effect of the size of family on the size of the house needs
little elucidation. The relationship is not, however, a simple
one for the reason that large families may also have large
expenditures for food and other items of consumption and an
income insufficient to provide suitable housing accommodations. Some of them are among the third of the nation that is
ill housed. What can be said in this respect is merely that a
large family spends more for housing than a small one if
income permits.

The demand for housing both for rental and ownership
varies directly with income. The income elasticity of demand
is therefore positive but inelastic, families with larger incomes demanding better and larger housing accommodations.
When incomes fall, families double up, move into smaller
quarters, and otherwise decrease their demand for space;
when incomes rise, they seek more adequate quarters with a
resulting scarcity of housing. Inasmuch as the supply of
housing is fixed in the short poriod, this income elasticity of
demand causes rents and house prices to rise when the national income rises and to fall when total income declines.
Should, however, a high level of income persist over a considerable period of time, the total demand for living quarters
will be raised to higher levels. The resulting higher rentals
and house prices will thus provide a stimulus to new construction, and the average number of rooms occupied by each
family will be increased.

New construction may, however, be limited severely if the
increase in income is offset by a rise in house prices. If, for

example, an increase in income of 25 per cent is offset by a rise in construction costs by a similar amount, the positive increase in demand caused by the income effect will be offset by a decrease caused by the price effect. Just how much depends upon the price elasticity of demand as compared to income elasticity of demand. The total effect on construction is thus a function of both the changes in income and the changes in price. In depression, the fall in construction costs neutralizes somewhat the fall in incomes, and in the boom the rise in costs offsets to a considerable extent the rise in money incomes.

Ratio of Value of House to Annual Income

Since 1938 the National Housing Administration, which insures home mortgages, has elicited information regarding the financial status of borrowers.[8] These data give the value of the home on which the loan has been made and the income of each group of borrowers. As compiled into tables by income classes, they show the relationship between income and the value of the house. The FHA borrowers are a selective sample and may not therefore be typical of all borrowers, but they should provide a clue as to the income-housing demand relationship. These data (Table 7) show that those in the lowest-income groups must pay a disproportionately large share of their annual income for housing, the value of the home being about three times annual income. The ratio falls steadily as income rises until, for incomes above $10,000, the value of the home is equivalent to the annual income. For all groups, the average price of the house is a little less than twice the average annual income.

Income Elasticity of Demand for Housing (Value)

Another way of looking at the relationship between the value of the houses (single family, owner occupied) purchased by each income group and their income is in terms of elasticity. The income elasticity of demand for dollar's worth of housing is the percentage change in the value of the house purchased associated with a percentage change in income. We know in general that lower-income groups neces-

TABLE 7

RATIO OF VALUE OF HOME TO INCOME

For the Years 1938-47

Income Group (Annual)	1938	1939	1940		1941		1942		1946		1947	
			New	Old	New	Old	New	Old	New	Old	New	Old
Less than $1,000	2.8	3.02	3.38	3.54	3.29	3.12	...	...	...	...	...	...
$ 1,001-$1,499	2.5	2.55	2.68	2.44	2.69	2.40	2.71	2.46	...	...	...	...
Less than $1,500	...	...	...	...	...	...	...	...	‡	‡	3.34	3.37
$ 1,500-$1,999	2.3	2.33	2.44	2.13	2.44	2.16	2.57	2.26	2.64	2.39	2.85	2.60
2,000- 2,499	2.1	2.14	2.22	1.95	2.23	2.00	2.29	2.05	2.47	2.15	2.55	2.34
2,500- 2,999	2.0	1.95	2.01	1.82	2.05	1.89	2.07	1.97	2.27	2.05	2.45	2.25
3,000- 3,499	1.8	1.82	1.88	1.72	1.91	1.77	1.85	1.84	2.11	1.90	2.30	2.09
3,500- 3,999	1.7	1.70	1.74	1.67	1.77	1.69	1.67	1.71	1.85	1.74	2.13	1.91
4,000- 4,999	1.6	1.57	1.61	1.53	1.62	1.61	1.52	1.58	1.63	1.57	1.92	1.76
5,000- 6,999	1.5	1.43	1.42	1.43	1.48	1.48	1.31	1.45	1.31	1.43	1.66	1.56
7,000- 9,999	1.3	1.24	1.19	1.26	1.12	1.30	1.11	1.23	1.02	1.17	1.32	1.36
10,000 and over	0.9	0.85	0.77	0.92	0.82	0.98	0.68	0.84	0.49	0.97	0.84	0.98
Average	1.8	1.87	1.94	1.85	1.95	1.85	1.98	1.73	1.81	1.71	1.97	1.83

TABLE 7 (Continued)

For the Years 1948–51

Income Group (Monthly)	1948 New	1948 Old	1949 New	1949 Old	1950 New	1950 Old	1951 New	1951 Old
Less than $150	3.4	3.3	‡	3.3	‡	‡	…	…
$ 150–$199.99	2.9	2.7	3.0	2.6	3.0	2.6	…	…
Less than $200	…	…	…	…	…	…	3.3	3.1
$ 200–$249.99	2.6	2.4	2.6	2.5	2.6	2.6	2.8	2.8
250– 299.99	2.4	2.2	2.4	2.3	2.4	2.4	2.5	2.6
300– 349.99	2.3	2.1	2.2	2.2	2.2	2.2	2.3	2.4
350– 399.99	2.1	1.9	2.1	2.1	2.0	2.1	2.1	2.2
400– 449.99	2.0 }	1.8 }	1.9	1.9	1.9	1.9	2.0	2.1
450– 499.99	}	}	1.8	1.8	1.7	1.8	1.8	1.9
500– 599.99	1.7	1.6	1.7	1.7	1.6	1.7	1.7	1.8
600– 799.99	1.5	1.5	1.5	1.6	1.4	1.6	1.4	1.5
800– 999.99	1.3	1.3	1.3	1.4	1.2	1.4	1.2	1.3
1,000 and over	1.0	1.0	0.9	1.0	0.8	1.0	0.8	0.9
Average	2.0	1.9	2.0	1.9	2.0	1.9	2.0	2.0

* "New" means new construction. † "Old" means old or existing houses. ‡ Data not significant.

sarily purchase houses of lower value than higher-income
groups. By use of the data furnished by the Federal Housing
Administration, we can show in a rough way the percentage
relationships between income and the value of the house.

Because of the smallness of the sample, the brief period of
years, the changes in tastes, changes in prices of other commodities, changes in price of houses, and other variables, this
computation is merely intended to show approximate percentage relations. Not too much importance should be at-
tached to the elasticity coefficient here used because in deriv-
ing it no effort was made to eliminate all of the influences
other than income affecting the value of houses purchased.
The coefficients should therefore be taken merely to illustrate
a principle and a trend rather than to provide a precise quantitative measurement.

Before the war, families in the lowest-income group, $1,000
per year, had to pay about $3,000 for a suitable house. Since
the war, the income levels have risen and the cost of construction has also been raised, but it is still true that the
lower-income groups spend proportionately more for their
housing than the higher-income groups. The coefficient of the
elasticity of demand for housing is shown in Table 8. The
Average elasticity for the range of incomes up to about
$10,000 per year shown in the table is about .5 to .6. This
means that for each 1 per cent rise in incomes we may expect
the value of the house purchased to rise about .5 to .6 per
cent. Although these data have been derived for single-
family, owner-occupied homes, it may be presumed that somewhat similar behavior would probably apply to rental properties as well. This bears out the general principle that the
higher the income group, the smaller tends to be the proportion spent for housing. And as we move up the scale from one
group to another, we find that at the lowest and medium levels
the amount spent for housing increases much faster as income
rises than at the higher levels. The reason seems to be that
low-income groups have inadequate housing and are anxious
to increase these amenities when they can afford to do so.
After a certain level of income is reached, say about $7,000–

TABLE 8

INCOME ELASTICITY OF DEMAND FOR HOUSING (VALUE)

| 1938–47 Annual Income | | 1948–51 Monthly Income | |
Income Group	Av. Elasticity	Income Group	Av. Elasticity
$1,000 and less		Less than $150	
	.769		.805
1,000–$1,499		$150–$199.99	
	.757		.635
1,500– 1,999		200– 249.99	
	.595		.597
2,000– 2,499		250– 299.99	
	.713		.577
2,500– 2,999		300– 349.99	
	.556		.469
3,000– 3,499		350– 399.99	
	.467		.444
3,500– 3,999		400– 499.99	
	.509		.536
4,000– 4,999		500– 599.99	
	.615		.505
5,000– 6,999		600– 799.99	
	.351		.430
7,000– 9,999		800– 999.99	
Average of Arc *Elasticities*	.622	*Average of Arc* *Elasticities*	.555

SOURCE: Data from Annual Reports of the Federal Housing Administration and of the National Housing Administration. Computations our own.

$9,999 per year, the desire for better housing does not grow apace with the rise in income. Hence income groups getting about $10,000 spend less and less for housing in proportion to their income because they have satisfied their demand for these accommodations as for many other necessities of life. Even though, we repeat, the precise percentage relationships are not known, all available data show the general truth of this observation which, as we shall later see, explains why a tax levied on housing takes proportionately more of the income of low-income groups than of high-income groups.

Those data also help to explain the greatly increased demand for housing when the national income rises. As already mentioned, however, a rise in income may be offset by a rise in price; and if, as it appears to be, the housing industry is subject to increasing costs during the cycle as the volume of building rises, it may very well be that the rise in construction costs operates as a powerful factor in offsetting the demand for housing created by a rise in incomes. The demand for housing, we may then conclude, varies directly but not proportionately with incomes and inversely with the cost of housing construction.

Relation of Income to Demand for Housing Amenities (Housing Space)

We have just described income elasticity in terms of dollar value; we now need to examine it in terms of physical factors which we may call the size of the house, housing space, or as is more usual, housing amenities or housing accommodations. How many additional housing accommodations will buyers bargain for as their income rises? If housing were subject to constant costs per unit of area, then the dollar amount of housing purchased would vary exactly with the physical amount of housing purchased—that is, the value coefficient would be exactly equal to the physical coefficient. A 1 per cent increase in dollar expenditure would result in 1 per cent more house.

When, however, we allow for the fact that housing is subject to the law of decreasing costs (see Chapter 4), it follows that each per cent of additional expenditure as income rises gives more than a per cent of additional housing, in the physical sense. Let us assume that the lowest-income groups obtain a house of 600 square feet at an index cost of 100, and a higher-income group spends twice as much for their housing. If housing were subject to constant costs, the higher-income group would pay twice as much and get twice as much house, or 1,200 square feet. But since the larger house would cost only, say, 80 per cent of the base figure per square foot, its builders would get not 1,200 square feet of housing but 1,500 square feet, or two and a half times as much. The income-amenities elasticity of demand is accordingly greater than the income-value elasticity of demand. We may accordingly translate income-elasticity for housing amenities by applying the correction for decreasing costs shown by the decreasing cost curve.

The income-amenities elasticity of demand is equal to the income-value elasticity of demand divided by one, minus the cost coefficient for the size of house. Since the cost curve declines at a decreasing rate, it follows that the ammenities elasticity of demand is greater by from 33 per cent (at low-income levels) to 15 per cent (at high-income levels) than the value elasticity of demand for housing.[9]

To illustrate this point: Let us suppose that at the $3,000 income level the income elasticity of demand for dollar's worth of housing was .6; and that the type of house built at this level was a small house whose costs per unit of space were measured by an index number of 100. Then the amenities elasticity of demand would be $\dfrac{.6}{1 + (1 - 1)}$. This means that at this income, for each 1 per cent increase in income, there will be .6 per cent increase in the amount spent for housing space acquired by the same percentage.

Let us now suppose that at the $6,000 income level the income elasticity of demand for dollar's worth of housing was still .6; and that the type of house built at this level of income as a larger house whose costs per unit of space were measured by an index number of 80. Then the amenities elasticity of demand would be

$$\frac{.6}{1 - (1 - .8)} \text{ or } \frac{.6}{1 - .2} \text{ or } \frac{.6}{.8} = .75$$

This shows that the income elasticity of demand for dollars' worth of housing is less than the elasticity of demand for housing amenities.

To summarize:

1. Income-Housing Value Elasticity of Demand is equal to $\dfrac{\% \, \Delta \, \text{Value}}{\% \, \Delta \, \text{Income}}$ which we found to be from .5 to .6 on the average.

2. Income-Housing Amenities Elasticity of Demand is equal to the above divided by 1 minus the cost coefficient. This elasticity we found to be from 15 to 33 per cent greater than the value coefficient.

3. (A) If housing were subject to constant costs, the value elasticity would be equal to the amenities elasticity. (B) If housing were subject to increasing costs, amenities elasticity would be less than value elasticity. (C) But since housing is subject to decreasing costs, amenities elasticity is always greater than value elasticity.

The actual relationships (based upon the elasticities found in this study) between income-value elasticity, income-amenities elasticity, and the level of income under three conditions of construction costs—constant, increasing, and decreasing—are shown in Figure 1, prepared by Mr. Pao Lun Cheng. Along the constant cost line, any point on the line will give same value for both elasticities. The 80 per cent decreasing cost index line, when income-value elasticity is 0.6, gives an income-amenities elasticity of 0.75, as shown above.

Causal Relations

The fact that the income elasticity of demand for housing amenities is greater than the elasticity of demand for housing value raises the issue of causal relationship. How are these two facts related? Do individuals determine to spend a given amount of money for housing and then take the resulting physical accommodations? Or do they determine upon their physical accommodations and then make the necessary expenditure?

Let us deal with these questions by relating them to the law of decreasing costs in housing. In the above paragraphs the income elasticity of demand for housing value was first derived. It was then shown that the amenities elasticity was

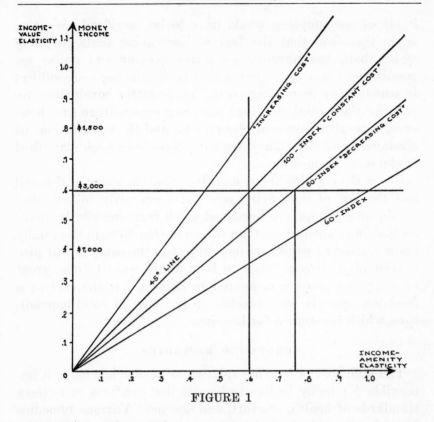

FIGURE 1

necessarily greater because of decreasing costs. These data could not, however, by themselves show what the value elasticity would have been if housing were subject to constant or increasing costs. If housing were subject to constant costs, it follows that all income groups would have to choose between larger expenditures or smaller accommodations, and if subject to increasing costs the same choice would be even more severe. What would that choice be? It seems likely that under these conditions the size of the house would be reduced somewhat and the total expenditure increased somewhat. This is because the demand for housing is for the amenities and not for a given amount of money value; but the necessity of distributing a given income over all items of consumption would necessarily reduce the demand for physical accommodations below what it is at present in order that less of other

items of consumption would have to be sacrificed. We conclude therefore that the fact of decreasing costs probably
makes both the physical amenities greater and dollar expenditures lower than they would be if housing were subject
to constant or increasing costs. These latter conclusions regarding the causal relations affecting expenditure are, however, a result of general observation and the assumptions of
diminishing utility. They are not provable by such statistical
evidence as we now have.

Given the existing facts, namely, value elasticity of demand
and the law of decreasing costs, it necessarily follows that
low-income groups are burdened much more heavily by taxes
on housing expenditure than for any other item in the family
budget, most of which are not subject to the same law of proportionality. Heavy taxes on food might constitute as great
or a greater burden measured in dollars, but the cost of a
food tax scarcely ever reaches 25 per cent of total expenditure, which is common for housing.

PROPOSED REMEDIES

The high cost of housing relative to income has made it impossible for many to live in houses that conform to modern
standards of health, comfort, and decency. Various remedies
for this situation have been proposed, but they come eventually to four: (1) lower housing costs; (2) subsidies to private builders; (3) government construction or operation; (4)
higher mass incomes.

Lower Housing Costs

Hitherto attempts to reduce the original cost of building
have not been very successful; and although many predic-
tions have been made regarding the economies of prefabrication and factory building methods, these want to be demonstrated in the future. What is true of original costs remains
valid for maintenance and repairs, the cost of which is determined by the same factors. Obsolescence may, however, be
reduced to a minimum by better architecture and city planning. The main factor reducing housing costs since the 1930's

is low interest rates, the continuance of which depends on
the future demand for real capital and upon monetary policy.
There remains the item, taxes, which is our main concern in
this volume. It provides a clear case of an institutional cost
diminishable by new methods of government financing. This
item constitutes about 25 per cent of housing costs and is
worthy of great consideration even if nothing can be done to
reduce costs on other fronts.

Subsidies to Private Builders

Subsidies have many different forms: grants to the builders of homes, subsidies to manufacturers of building materials, loans below market rates, tax exemption for a given
period of years, government construction, and sale or rental
below cost. None of these methods changes the economic cost
of housing; it simply shifts that cost to some other source.
The ultimate burden of any subsidy is then determined by its
incidence and the nature of the tax system: federal subsidies
—insofar as they are paid out of income, corporation, and
excise taxes—will shift part of this cost to the income-tax
payer, to corporations, and to the purchaser of other commodities; state government subsidies are uncommon, but local
subsidies through tax exemption simply diminish the burden
on one set of properties and increase it on those that are not
tax exempt. The beneficiary of a subsidy may be the specu-
lator, the permanent landlord, the homeowner, or the tenant,
the precise incidence depending on the nature of the subsidy,
the time of levy, and the supply of and demand for housing.

Housing subsidies, to be generally effective, must be paid
out of funds collected out of income from whatever source
derived. When this is done, a part of the economic cost of
housing is paid by someone other than him who receives the
shelter. It is coming to be recognized that minimum housing
standards, like standards of education and health, are the
responsibility of the community, to be met regardless of the
income of the beneficiaries. Whether, however, the objective
of subsidies can best be achieved by grants to private build-

ers or to owners or in the form of low-rent government housing projects goes beyond the scope of this study.

In order, however, to put subsidies in their proper perspective, it should be realized that insofar as the property
tax now pays for items of government not attributable to
shelter as such, it is an institutional cost that can be construed as a subsidy paid by housing to other forms of economic activity. And it may therefore be well to consider
whether a diminution of this burden on housing may not itself
be a great incentive toward better housing for lower-income
groups which would make other subsidies unnecessary.

Subsidies to low-income groups are furthermore a con-
fession that the relation between mass incomes and housing
costs are out of line. Although in recent years mass incomes
have been raised to a new high level making it possible for
the great bulk of the population to furnish their own shelter
without the aid of subsidies, higher building costs are already
impairing realization of this possibility. The inflation of
housing costs raises the ratio of building costs to incomes
and thus offsets by so much the effect of higher incomes. It
accordingly re-creates the demand for government subsidies
to offset their higher costs. With the exception of slum clearance and similar projects, it seems absurd to resort to housing subsidy when what is needed is a reduction in the cost of
owning a house.

Government Construction or Operation

Federal housing programs came to be advocated during
the 1930's on four grounds: as a part of city planning and
slum clearance; to improve available housing for low-income
groups; to subsidize these groups; and as a part of a program to increase employment and the national income through
useful expenditure.[10]

Public housing is needed where the nature and the scope
of the project is such that it cannot be undertaken profitably
by private enterprise, or when private enterprise breaks
down. City planning, zoning, and slum clearance, on the other
hand, are socially supervised activities that create the frame-

work within which both public and private activity must function. They are not a substitute for private activity but guides designed to channel such activity into socially desirable forms. Conversely, the free play of competition cannot be considered a substitute for zoning or planning, for competition without socially imposed rules need not work for the public good. It may even cause a degeneration of standards and result in the creation of new slums and residential areas falling far short of a practical ideal. The existence of city planning need not, therefore, inhibit private building at all and is not inconsistent with it, but can be carried out in conjunction with private and public construction agencies.

A crying need for low-income family housing was found during the years of the Great Depression when building activity was at low ebb, millions were unemployed and without incomes sufficient to pay for housing suited to their needs. During this period, low-cost housing provided useful public works, although, foolish as it may now seem, fears existed at the time that cities would be overbuilt to such an extent as to destroy the return to private owners. The purpose of government building at the time was twofold: to provide employment and to improve housing standards. To the limited extent that the program was carried out, it succeeded in both aims.

Higher Mass Incomes

Higher incomes, especially for the lowest third of our population, will enable them to improve living standards in general. That a portion of this increase will go toward better housing is well illustrated by the demand for shelter following the war. Unfortunately, however, the cost of housing construction appears to rise as the national income rises, and this reduces the incentive to spend for housing as against other commodities.

It is suggested that the expenditure for the capital cost of a home should not exceed twice the annual income. For very low incomes this amount must even be lower because of the higher amount spent for food. When incomes rise say from

$1,500 to $2,500 per year, expenditure for the home can be expanded from $3,000 to $5,000. But if, with the expansion of income, housing costs also rise so that the higher-priced house is now no better than could have been formerly bought at the lower price, nothing is gained, building is not undertaken, and housing standards are not improved. Only, therefore, insofar as housing costs can be kept down to a reasonable relation to incomes will low-income groups be able to afford better shelter.

The great increase in the cost of residential construction after the war operated to diminish the demand for new construction among the lower-income groups, while that for the higher incomes appears to have held up somewhat better. Under these circumstances some proposed vast government expenditures to bid away materials and labor in the open market for construction of small homes, subsidized by government, for occupancy by those unable to build at existing prices. Such a program, if carried into effect while demand for new construction remains strong, would be quite likely to lead to a further rise in building costs and to bring a further diminution of private demand and a new demand for additional government expenditures. Proposals to deal with housing during a period of scarcity of labor and materials in the same manner as during the depression overlook the essential difference between policies desirable during inflation and deflation. A fall in housing construction due to an inflation of housing costs should be met by policies designed to lower those costs, not by policies to subsidize further cost inflation whose only effect can be to create a clamor for still more inflation.

A better relationship between living costs and income is also desirable from the viewpoint of full employment. When incomes are unduly concentrated, savings are high at the same time that markets for the products of new investment are relatively low. Under these circumstances investors hoard their savings because they find inadequate profitable investment outlets. A wide distribution of income and reasonable housing costs, on the other hand, provide an incentive to investment because the demand for shelter is provided at the same time as the outlet for investment by those who build their own homes. Home building for own use, moreover, is not beset by the uncertainties of other private investment which must always look to an uncertain future and a doubtful market.

Some have advocated overcoming this hesitancy by reducing income taxes drastically on the high-income groups and even conferring special exemptions upon income derived from capital investment in the form of interest and dividends. Others propose tax exemptions for new capital formation. There are, however, millions of Americans anxious and willing to invest their savings in new homes who would need no special incentives. They need not face the uncertainties of future markets because they provide their own markets, and they need not save without investing because the purchase of a home provides an outlet for all the savings they can make for years to come. A family without a home can readily find an investment outlet for any amount up to $10,000, and it will take a long time for most small-income groups to save even this amount. Unlike the landlord, the homeowner also escapes the costs of vacancies because he will occupy his home in good times and in bad. It follows then that a wide distribution of income and low housing costs, including low tax costs, will provide a field for housing activity and provide personal security for millions of American citizens.

Instead of emphasizing public construction, we should therefore provide further incentives to private housing.

4

The Law of
Decreasing Costs
in Housing

In Chapter 3 we showed that the expenditure for housing accommodations rises with incomes but at a slower rate. The ratio of property values to annual incomes is as high as 3.5 to 1 for the lowest-income groups, and as low as 1 to 1 for the highest, the average being around 2 and thus confirming the familiar rule of thumb that a family should not buy a home worth much more than twice its annual income. It was also shown that the income elasticity of demand for housing fell as income rose, the average for all incomes being about .5 to .6. We would accordingly expect that a uniform property tax on homes would be regressive to income, a fact which we will find confirmed in Chapter 8.

The data in Chapters 3 and 8 thus show that families live in bigger and better homes as their incomes rise, but that property taxes are a larger part of low incomes than of high incomes; a wealthy man eats better food and wears better clothes than a poor man, but he does not increase his expenditures on these items indefinitely. It is the same with housing; more is spent for a home as income rises, but this expenditure reaches a limit in each income class which satisfied the standards of that group. Regardless then of whether housing units were subject to constant, increasing, or decreasing costs per unit of space, the ratio of housing expenditure to income, like the ratio of other forms of consumption to income, would be expected to vary inversely with income.

The slope of the housing-income curve would, however, be most in the direction of proportionality if housing were subject to increasing costs, and least so if it were subject to decreasing costs. This follows because at increasing costs housing expenditure would rise faster than the size of the house; at constant costs, in the same proportion; and at decreasing costs, in a descending ratio. What increases the regressivity of the property tax is that housing is in fact subject to the law of decreasing costs per unit of space. And it is this fact and the reasons therefor which shall occupy us in this chapter. We shall show that the housing tax is regressive to income primarily because housing expenditure increases less than proportionally with the size of income. This regressivity is further aggravated by the fact that housing costs per unit of space vary inversely with the size of the house. Thus a man in the higher brackets pays relatively less housing tax than the one in the lower because he spends a smaller percentage of his income for housing and he also gets more housing for his money.

INCREASING COSTS IN THE HOUSING INDUSTRY

The housing industry seems to be subject to increasing costs over the business cycle because the costs of all types of construction tend to rise as the scale of output approaches full employment proportions. Thus all housing costs, regardless of the structure, tend to move upwards during periods of high employment and to recede somewhat when the volume of building is at a low ebb. This fact is to be distinguished from the next characteristic of the industry, the relative costs per unit of floor space for large and for small buildings at all times.

The individual house is subject to decreasing costs per unit of usable space. After a given size is reached, say 600 square feet of floor space, the unit cost of additional space decreases as the size of the house increases. An eight-room house of the same quality does not cost a third more than a six-room house; its cost rises, but at a decreasing rate. It is this tendency to which we refer when we state that housing is subject to the law of decreasing costs per unit of usable space. With reference to property taxation, this is an additional reason that the property tax is especially regressive on the owner of the small home.

We shall first show that the housing industry is subject to increasing costs as building activity rises and then present the reasons that the cost per unit of space varies inversely with the size of the house.

The usual conception of an industry is an aggregate of many firms engaged in the production of similar products. It is not easy to visualize the construction industry in these terms because it does not consist of firms engaged in the production of houses in the same way that a firm builds automobiles or makes steel, woolen, or cotton goods. True, there are a few firms engaged in building prefabricated houses, and their costs are probably subject to the same type of cost analysis as firms engaged in other lines of endeavor. By and large, however, the housing industry is a heterogeneous aggregation of a large number of more or less related industries which manufacture a house.[1] The division of work follows no clear lines, but ordinarily excavation, foundations, bricklaying, stone masonry, carpentry, and wood finish are done by the general contractor. Other contractors, either directly for the owner or under subcontract, take care of structural iron work, ornamental iron work, roofing, plumbing, steamfitting and heating, lathing, plastering, tiling, electrical work, painting, metal sash and glazing, shades and screens.[2]

Past experience appears to show that the housing industry is subject to the law of increasing costs per unit as the level of construction rises. Because this industry has wide cyclical fluctuations, it is hard to discover a normal output or a normal cost under average conditions, except as this may be done by aggregating quantities over time in a purely mathematical way and defining them as normal. Small output is found in depression and high output in prosperity accompanied by high and low costs per unit of output respectively. Whenever output rises to a high level, costs rise rapidly. This is in part caused by the rising prices of materials and of labor, but it is also probably caused by the entrance of less efficient operators into the field. (See Chapter 2.) In this sense, increasing costs are not the simple result of physical or of economic factors that are inherent in the nature of housing as such but rather in the structure, organization, and history of the industry. Great cyclical fluctuations tend to drive labor and capital into and out of construction work. The depression of the 1930's bankrupted many contractors and delayed the training of apprentices in the building trades, which made for a scarcity of skilled labor when it was needed after 1940. It seems reasonable to suppose that, if the scale of the industry were enlarged to produce a larger and steadier output with more and steadier employment, increasing costs to scale would not be found until output reached a much higher level than has hitherto prevailed. It is probably true that most other industries are faced with increasing costs at high levels of output so that the difference between them and housing is not wholly one of kind but merely one of degree.

The total production of housing units from 1919 to 1944 was 12,600,000, or an average of 485,000 units per year. In 1925, production reached a peak of 937,000 units for the year, and in 1933 fell to a low of 100,000 units. Years of high production were years of high building costs, and years of low production of low building costs. In 1945 it was said that the industry was geared to produce about 500,000 units a year without greatly increasing costs, whereas 1,000,000 units per year were needed.[3] Unless, therefore, the industry was expanded to produce more of the lumber, steel, cast iron, plumbing supplies, glass, copper, and other materials used in housing construction and to train new artisans in the building trades, it was predicted that the large production would have to be carried on at high unit costs.[4]

PRICES OF LARGE AND SMALL HOUSES

It was a matter of common observation during the 1930's that large houses sold much further below their reproduction cost than small houses. The higher-income groups were accordingly able to get more for their money in the purchase of existing real estate than those with lower incomes. If, then, we combine the fact that a large house costs relatively less to produce per cubic foot than a small house with the observation that during depression it also sells at a smaller proportion of its initial cost, we see why the depression buyer is able to obtain exceptional bargains in large houses.

During any short period, particularly during depression, the supply of houses is fixed, and price is determined by the offers of buyers and the reservation prices of sellers. Incomes being at a low level, the demand for small houses is relatively greater to the supply than the demand for larger establishments. While small houses sold fairly close to their cost of reproduction, large houses sold far below such costs. Thus the widespread impression that a person with a large income could obtain more in the way of housing accommodations for his expenditure was probably close to the truth. This is, however, a short-run or temporary situation during which the price of houses remains out of line with the cost of reproduction. Insofar as it does exist, the owners of large homes which are valued either temporarily or permanently far below reproduction costs will pay a much smaller proportion of their income as property taxes than those occupying more modest dwellings.

The point we wish to emphasize, however, is that the advantage possessed by large-income receivers is not merely a more or less transitory result of a cyclical price pattern but the result of long-run equilibrium conditions. For in the long run, houses, regardless of size, will sell close to their reproduction costs; since the large house is cheaper per room than the small house, it must be because housing is subject to the law of decreasing costs of production per unit of usable space, a fact which we may now consider.

Decreasing Costs of Construction to Size of House

The experience of house builders as reflected in appraisers' manuals clearly shows that housing is subject to decreasing costs per unit of space. These manuals are based upon engineering estimates for the types of houses actually built and take into account variations in conformation and type of construction. In general, these data show that for single- or multi-family residences of the same quality, the cost per room falls as the size increases until the building reaches a height of about five or six stories. When this point is reached, additional space for stairways and elevators must be provided and these installations are themselves quite expensive and space devouring. The strength of foundations and of the structure must be increased, so that as a general rule buildings above five stories are subject to increasing costs and are erected only to utilize expensive building sites. We shall, therefore, confine our discussion to single-family residences, although much of what is true regarding these is applicable as well to larger structures.

Appraisal engineers have compiled construction data on various types of single-family residences. These are classified as bungalows, cottages, and residences: one story, one and one-half stories, and two stories. For each of these types, estimates are made for cheap, average, good, and expensive construction.

The dollar cost per square foot of space changes over time with fluctuation in the prices of labor and materials; but since these prices are likely to change proportionately for buildings of all sizes, the relative costs of construction per square foot probably retain the same proportions. We have therefore reduced the absolute dollar figures to relatives which show the relative costs of constructing buildings of various sizes and grades, using 600 feet of floor space as a base. The relative costs of each type of building with cheap, average, good, and expensive construction were computed, these relatives were then averaged for each type of building, and all of the relatives were averaged into a total.

These construction cost indexes show that the cost of construction per square foot falls all the way from 400 square feet to 2,200 square feet of floor space and that this decrease continues throughout the whole range for all types of buildings and for all types of construction. A house with 2,200 square feet would cost only about half as much per unit of space as one with 400 square feet. This indicates without much question that dwellings are subject to the law of de-

creasing costs per unit of floor space. We must now seek out
the reasons for this law.

TABLE 9

RELATIVE COSTS OF CONSTRUCTION
(COST OF 600 SQUARE FEET = 100. AVERAGE RELATIVES FOR ALL GRADES.)

Square Feet	Cottages			Bungalows		Residence 2-Story	All Types Combined*
	1-Story	1½-Story	2-Story	1-Story	1½-Story		
400	113.95	115.65	114.25	.....	.....	116.85	115.18
500	106.40	107.65	107.80	107.90	107.67	108.30	107.62
600	100.00	100.00	100.00	100.00	100.00	100.00	100.00
700	93.60	93.75	93.90	93.96	93.82	94.00	93.84
800	88.50	89.50	88.15	89.45	89.50	88.05	88.86
900	84.30	85.55	83.25	84.98	85.62	83.78	84.58
1,000	81.15	82.60	79.75	82.20	83.08	79.92	81.45
1,100	78.50	80.25	77.20	79.55	80.72	.....	79.24
1,200	75.85	77.60	75.55	77.00	78.58	75.92	76.75
1,300	67.65	.....	.....	74.90	76.52	.....	75.71
1,400	.....	.....	.....	72.88	74.85	72.38	73.37
1,500	.....	.....	.....	70.35	73.32	.....	71.84
1,600	.....	69.95	68.95	69.60	71.97	69.32	69.57
1,700	.....	.....	.....	68.60	.....	.....	68.60
1,800	.....	.....	.....	.....	.....	68.25	68.25
2,000	.....	.....	.....	.....	.....	65.02	65.02
2,200	.....	.....	.....	.....	.....	63.10	63.10

* Average of average relatives.

Source data from E. H. Boeckh, *Boeckh's Manual of Appraisals* (3rd ed.; Indianapolis, Ind., 1937).

The Law of the Cube

The basic reason for the fall in the cost of housing per
square foot of floor space lies in the law of the cube. The
volume of a cubic area varies as x^3, whereas the area of the
outside walls varies as $6x^2$. The contents of any cube increase
at a faster rate than the area of the six sides, and the larger
the cube, the larger will be the cubical content in proportion
to the area of the outside walls. Since it is the six outside
walls (floor, roof, and four walls) which constitute the cost of

the building, it follows that the cost of producing cubical content decreases as the size of the house increases.[5]

The purpose of a house, however, is not simply cubage but floor space with head room divided into rooms so that its cost does not follow the law of the perfect cube. What is wanted is square feet of floor area with a height of seven or eight feet above each floor and partitions within this area. The house, though differing in shape, accordingly resembles a rectangular box whose cubical content increases not as fast as that of a perfect cube but still at a faster rate than the area of the outside walls.[6]

We conclude then that the house viewed as a geometric form is subject to the law of decreasing costs per unit of cubic feet of usable space. It is now necessary to analyze the construction of a house in more detail in order to see how the law of the cube applies.

Distributing the cost of a house over three fields according to structure, finish, and accessories, we find that the benefits of the law of the cube accrue to structure and finish. Accessories, however, must be considered separately for each item to ascertain whether it is subject to constant, increasing, or decreasing costs.

Structure and Finish

Structure includes excavation, stone masonry, brick masonry, rough carpentry, cement work, stair work, structural steel, roofing, general labor, sheet metal work, hardware, and glazing.

Finish includes finish carpentry and mill work, lathing and plastering, painting, tile work, cabinet work, finished hardware, and paper hanging. All of these are a function of the amount of wall, floor, and roof space and are consequently subject to decreasing costs.[7] Of the total cost of a house, Bemis estimates 45 to 50 per cent to be assigned to structure, 30 to 25 per cent to finish, and 25 per cent to accessories.[8] It follows, then, that from 70 to 75 per cent of the cost of a frame house is subject to the law of decreasing costs as it applies to structure and finish.

Accessories

Accessories include plumbing, heating, electric wiring, lighting fixtures, range, gas water heater, refrigerator, radio and telephone, and screens and shades. Most of these are now subject to mass production methods and should be produced at decreasing costs as the total volume of output increases. But this does not necessarily mean that the cost of any of these accessories varies with the size of the individual house, which is the subject now under consideration. Besides manufacturers' costs, there is installation made by skilled labor on the ground. We shall consider briefly the three most important accessories—electric wiring, heating, and plumbing—with a view to their variation in cost with the size of the house.

Electric Wiring and Fixtures.—The cost of wiring a house of six to eight rooms is made up of a large fixed cost for basic installations plus a small charge for additional outlets. The modern house is wired for 60 amperes with one-inch pipe for the entrance service and three No. 6 wires. This is true for six as well as for eight rooms. Regardless of the size of the house, it has the same service, the same meter, the same meter-test block, the same distributor cabinet, the same ground, and the same pipe in the basement. The cost of these will not vary much more than about $10 per house. In practice, considerable difference in cost may arise because of superior equipment; but to make a usable comparison, the same quality of equipment must be considered.

Automatic heat, whether oil burner or stoker, requires practically the same electrical hookup regardless of capacity. The same holds true for hot-water heaters, refrigerators, and other outlets.

The increased costs then come in for the additional room outlets in the larger house, but at most these would not increase the cost of wiring of an eight-room house over a six-room house by much more than 5 per cent.[9] We conclude, therefore, that the dollar cost of wiring and fixtures changes only slightly with the size of the house. Strictly speaking, wiring is subject to the law of decreasing costs; the marginal costs per additional cubage are of a small order of magnitude. Thus house space may be increased from 25 to 75 per cent with an increase in electric wiring costs of as little as 10 per cent or 15 per cent.

Heating.—A central heating system consists of the warm-air furnace or a hot-water or steam boiler and the system of pipes and radiators. It may come with or without the automatic oil burner, gas burner, or stoker.

Although both warm-air furnaces and hot-water boilers are produced by mass production techniques, the furnaces usually cost less and are subject to different costing than boilers. The chief difference between the cost of manufacturing a larger furnace and a smaller one is the amount of material the furnace contains and the additional cost of handling. The price of furnaces consequently does not increase proportionately with the size and is therefore subject to decreasing costs per unit of heating capacity. Inasmuch as heating systems for a six-room house are in greatest demand, they are usually the cheapest per unit of heating capacity because of large quantity production. In general, warm-air heating systems increase in cost about .5 per cent for each additional per cent of heating capacity.[10]

The cost of hot-water and steam systems is only slightly decreasing with size compared to hot-air systems.[11] The advantage of size is gained only with multi-dwelling units. In 1953 a boiler with burner for a six-apartment dwelling unit cost about $950; for eight units, $1,250; and for fifty dwelling units, $3,600.

It appears then that hot-water and steam installations for small dwellings run some 20 per cent higher than warm-air installations and are not subject to appreciably decreasing costs with increasing size, tending rather toward proportionality.

We conclude then that warm-air systems are definitely subject to decreasing costs, that hot-water and steam systems tend toward constant costs for house sizes and toward sharply decreasing costs for apartments.

Plumbing.—Plumbing is clearly subject to decreasing costs. Water and gas pipe and meter connections from the city service line vary in cost only with the size of pipe, labor cost being about the same regardless of the size of service. Sewage connections likewise vary little if at all for a four-, six-, or eight-room house. The cost of kitchen, laundry room, and bathroom fixtures is about the same for all houses for the same quality goods. The main item increasing the cost for larger houses is the installation of the bathroom on the second floor, or the installation of two bathrooms rather than one. Plumbing in larger houses, however, usually does cost more because the quality of fixtures is better in houses designed to sell at a higher price. On the whole, however, plumbing installations approach constant costs for the small-house range and are therefore subject to the law of decreasing costs per unit of space.

SIZE OF FAMILY AND SIZE OF HOUSE

The significance of the above decreasing-cost data for the regressivity of property taxes becomes apparent as soon as we notice that the bulk of the American people live in single homes of six rooms or less. Our dwellings are therefore predominantly of a size subject to high costs per unit of usable space. The mass of our population accordingly get little for their money and also pay relatively high taxes for the space they occupy.

The shrinking size of the American family, attributable to the fall in the birth rate, has been the most potent cause affecting the size of dwelling units. Better medical care and a longer life span have increased the number of older people in the population, and the tendency for parents to maintain separate households when economic circumstances permit has increased the number of independent living units.

In 1850, the average number of persons per family, and accordingly the number of persons per dwelling unit, was 5.6. From then on the number has steadily fallen, reaching 4.1 persons in 1930, 3.8 persons in 1940, and 3.3 in 1950, according to the census.

The great majority of our people live in single-family homes. According to the 1930 census, 76.3 per cent of the population of the United States lived in single-family dwellings, 11.6 per cent in two-family dwellings, and 12.1 per cent in multi-family dwellings.

With the shrinking size of the family and the urbanization of the population, apartment building has increased relative to the total in recent years. Of the total of 25,204,976 dwellings in the United States in 1930, 90.6 per cent were one-family residences; 6.9 per cent, two-family residences; and 2.6 per cent, multi-family residences. By value, the single-family residences were 77.9 per cent of the total; two-family, 8.4 per cent; and multi-family, 13.7 per cent. By 1940, the number of dwelling units had increased to 29,313,708, of which only 85 per cent were for single families, 8.7 per cent for two families, and 6.3 per cent for a multiple number. The increase in multiple-dwelling units has been largely in the metropolitan centers.[12]

That the bulk of our people live in small houses is also shown by Table 10, showing the number of rooms per dwelling in the years 1940 and 1950. This table indicates that in 1950, 47.2 per cent of the population lived in units of four rooms or less, 68.6 per cent in five rooms or less, and 85.5 per cent in six rooms or less. And since the bulk of these dwellings are single-family residences, it follows that the mass of our people live in houses of a size that has not been able to take advantage of the law of decreasing costs. It is notable that the tendency to live in small units has increased between the years 1940 and 1950. Insofar as the property tax is a factor making for small housing units, it is detrimental to economic efficiency and community welfare because it results in smaller satisfactions per dollar of housing expenditure.

The small man is accordingly penalized in two ways by the law of decreasing costs of housing: first, he must pay relatively more for the housing that he obtains; second, he must pay higher taxes in proportion to the space he occupies. In many jurisdictions where assessment is unfair, he is also assessed at a higher proportion of market value because he lacks political and economic power.

A reduction in real estate taxes would encourage larger dwelling units for those who could use them, thus providing more convenience and comfort per dollar of capital expenditure and of operating costs, and would also reduce the inequities in the taxation of low-income groups.

TABLE 10

NUMBER OF ROOMS FOR ALL DWELLING UNITS FOR THE UNITED STATES, 1940 AND 1950*

No. of Rooms	Number of Dwellings		Percentage Distribution		Percentage Cumulated	
	1940	1950	1940	1950	1940	1950
1	1,307,344	1,239,000	3.5	2.8	3.5	2.8
2	3,215,423	3,443,000	8.7	7.7	12.2	10.5
3	5,331,572	6,635,000	14.5	14.8	26.7	25.3
4	6,891,990	9,783,000	18.7	21.9	45.4	47.2
5	7,302,053	9,573,000	19.8	21.4	65.2	68.6
6	6,321,630	7,550,000	17.2	16.9	82.4	85.5
7	2,868,719	3,126,000	7.8	7.0	90.2	92.5
8	1,886,121	1,863,000	5.1	4.2	95.3	96.7
9	737,986 ⎫		2.0 ⎫		97.3 ⎫	
10	481,339 ⎬	1,499,000	1.3 ⎬	3.4	98.6 ⎬	100.0
11 or more	488,009 ⎭		1.3 ⎭		99.9 ⎭	

* Calculations were made on the following basis:

	1940	1950
Number reporting	36,882,106	44,711,000
No report	493,284	1,164,000
Total:	37,325,470	45,875,000
Median:	4.73	4.60

SOURCE: *U.S. Census, 1940. Housing*, Vol. II: *General Characteristics*, Part 1: *U.S. Summary*, pp. 26, 27; and *U. S. Census, 1950. Housing, Preliminary Reports*, Series HC-5, No. 1, p. 10.

CONCLUSIONS

Housing is subject to the law of decreasing costs per unit of space.

This can be explained by physical factors, the law of the cube which governs structure and finish, and the decreasing costs of some of the accessories.

High-income groups consequently obtain more housing per dollar of capital expenditure and also have lower operating costs per unit of space.

The property tax accordingly is more regressive to income than it would be if housing were subject either to constant or to increasing costs.

The property tax is not merely undesirable because of its regressivity, but it also has bad welfare effects. The house tax creates the additional loss of real income to all members of the community that exists whenever a tax is placed on a product subject to decreasing costs. Such a tax decreases the volume of output and hence raises price by an amount greater than the tax. The cost to the community is accordingly greater than the amount of the tax. On the probability that the house tax decreases the size of houses, it raises the unit cost of living space and thus increases the real burden of the tax and decreases community welfare.

We must add also to the disabilities of this tax the fact that decreased housing expenditure during periods of low total demand for capital expansion creates unemployment and lowers the national income.

5

The
General Property
Tax

Our primary concern in this monograph is with the burden of the property tax on incomes and its repressive effect on housing. If, however, these facts are to lead to fruitful policies, we must look at the tax in its broader aspect as a means of providing the revenues to support needed community services. We would be remiss unless we pointed out that the burden of the tax is offset by many benefits to the community necessary and desirable to enhance the well-being of its citizens. To consider a tax merely as a cost without regard to the good that it provides is so partial and prejudicial that it might bring harmful results, such as the oft-recurring demand for tax reduction heedless of its consequences to municipal finances. Tax reduction is not, after all, an ultimate goal of fiscal policy, and it would be foolish to pursue this end utterly oblivious to substitute sources of revenue and the great harm that might be done by the impairment of local government functions. We must accordingly consider the historical development of the property tax, the reasons for its existence, its functions in the fiscal life of local and state governments, the types of property on which it is levied, tax rates and assessments. After that, we will be prepared to study its burden relative to other forms of taxation, and in the final chapter to consider various tax policies.

HISTORICAL ORIGINS

The present tax on real estate is the result of a long history and only in part is it the direct product of a consciously con-

74

trived theory of taxation. Historically considered, taxes were
first levied by the strong against the poor and the weak in any
manner that would yield revenue. Later as the taxing power
became more conscious of itself and subject as well to social
criticism, principles of taxation satisfying the demands of
equity and practicability came to be recognized. These principles vary with the times and the stage of economic and political development.

Early societies were supported by gifts, special levies, fees,
customs duties, excises, tolls, and other imposts. In Great
Britain the king "lived off his own" until the revenues from
his landed estates became insufficient to support widening
governmental activity. The property tax came into being
when feudal dues consisting of services and payments in kind
which had been assessed against the land were transmuted
into money obligations. Later, as other forms of wealth became more abundant, the land tax became a general property
tax. And finally with the failure to tax intangible personalty,
the property tax again reverted to its original form as a levy
on tangible personal and real property, which is its primary
status today.[1]

Although Continental European and British tax systems
influenced the early American practice, the general property
tax as developed in the United States was to a large extent
indigenous.[2] In colonial times taxes on property were supplementary to poll taxes, fines, fees, forfeitures, excises, and im-
post duties.[3] When rationalized, however, the property tax
was conceived as a part of a general tax system based upon
the "faculty" principle. By "faculty" was meant taxable
capacity, or what is now called "ability to pay." In 1634 this
view was expressed by the General Court of Massachusetts:
"In all rates and public charges the towns shall have respect
to levy every man according to his estate, and with consideration all other his abilities, whatsoever, and not according to
the number of his persons." Ability to pay was measured by
real and personal property, by the person himself, and by his
income. This conception of "faculty" embodied the principle
that taxes were levied against persons not against things and

that the amount paid should vary with productive power as
distinguished from actual income. According to this view,
a diligent and industrious man might have a larger income
than one of equal ability and less industry, but both would
pay the same tax. As late as 1888, President Walker concluded that "faculty" constituted the only theoretically just
basis of taxation; but recognizing the impossibility of administering such a tax, he concluded that in practice it had to be
an income tax.[4] The latter then came to be widely advocated
by many economists before the end of the last century as a
substitute for the property tax.

Throughout the nineteenth century the growing revenues
of state and local governments were obtained from property
taxes, even though it had been recognized at an early date
that, as this tax was administered, it did not conform to the
"faculty" principle. The levies grew steadily but at a slow
rate until about the time of the Civil War, when the general
increase in federal expenses and the rising expenditures of
state and local government brought about much heavier taxation. Population, wealth, and government services on state
and local levels were on the increase, and the growing importance of taxation promoted official inquires by the various
states into the sufficiency of the tax system and means of improving its form and administration. These inquiries turned
into criticisms of the general property tax and of the futile
attempts to tax mortgages and other intangibles.

An example of the problem faced by the various states is
given in the report of a New York commission headed by
David A. Wells, which reported in 1871.[5] The commission
commented upon the threefold increase in aggregate taxation
in New York, from 1850 to 1860, from $6 million to $18 million annually; by 1870 this figure had reached $50 million.
Similar experiences were had throughout the union. The
commission found many anomalies and inconsistencies in the
taxation of real property but added that "great as may be the
inequalities in the valuation and assessment of real property, those which obtain in respect to personal are so much
greater as to almost preclude the idea of comparison."[6] In-

tangibles had already been escaping taxation and other personal property was not contributing its share, thus increasing the proportion paid on real estate.[7] The actual experience of the various states in this era confirmed historical inquiry that, under a general property tax, personal property gradually escaped from the duty of contributing. This was the fate of the property tax wherever it was tried, in Ancient Rome, in England, as also with the French Taille and the later Dixièmes and Vingtièmes of the eighteenth century.[8]

In 1888 Ely, making a survey of American taxation, found that, in spite of a demand on the part of farmers that personal property be taxed, it almost everywhere had escaped its share of contribution to the state. This evasion furthermore burdened the poor for the benefit of the rich because intangible personal property was held largely by the wealthy. It was Ely's conviction that a uniform tax on all property "never has worked well in any modern community or state in the entire civilized world";[9] but recognizing that the real estate tax was needed for local purposes, he added that "it ought not in any American city to exceed one per cent of the true selling value of the property." For state purposes he advocated the income tax as the main source of revenue.[10]

Seligman also emphasized that the property tax was in reality a real estate tax and defective as a main source of public revenue. Although property taxes had represented a rough sort of equity when real property was the predominant source of income, this condition no longer existed because large incomes could now be derived from other sources. Because of his insistence upon income taxes as a substitute for property taxes in the several states, Seligman came to be known as a leader among American tax theorists espousing the principle of ability to pay.[11]

There was indeed little dispute among tax administrators and economists in this country as elsewhere that taxation should conform to the ability principle; and though property was recognized as one of several criteria of ability, if used alone it was conceded to be a very inadequate, and in practice a very unfair, one. After the turn of the century, state gov-

ernments did in fact rely to a lesser extent upon property
and more upon income taxes and other sources of revenue,
whereas the property tax has remained as the mainstay of
local government but has raised a continually smaller percentage of total local revenues. Meanwhile what has also happened as a result of the two world wars and the Great Depression is that federal expenses have increased greatly and
income taxes have now reached hitherto undreamed of
heights, so that the question today is no longer, as it was in
the nineteenth century, whether income taxes should be used at
all, but whether the relative proportion of these taxes which
are already heavy should be increased and property taxes decreased. As a consequence of new views concerning the relation of fiscal policy to prosperity and depression, it is also
held that tax policy should be designed to perform a dual
purpose: to promote both equity and full employment. To
this end we must ask among other things whether in fact the
tax on realty is a burden upon the owner or the occupier of
real estate, how the burden is distributed by income groups,
who bears the tax, and how it affects the volume of construction and hence national income and employment.

REAL ESTATE TAXES

Real estate taxes are levied upon land and improvements.
Sometimes the land and the buildings are assessed separately,
although under many state constitutions both must be taxed
at the same rate. Land comprises the bulk of ratable value
in rural areas, whereas the buildings constitute a larger proportion of the total value of urban real estate. The value of
farm land is a function both of its productivity and its close-
ness to markets, whereas the price of urban land depends
upon its site. In the cities, high-priced land is generally used
for retail trade and other commercial purposes, residential
areas being confined to land of lesser value. Economic forces
are thus combined with social forces to divide residential from
commercial areas, though the result is far from what might
be achieved by better zoning.

For purposes of public policy, the main ground of distinction between land and the buildings upon it is that land as a site exists independent of human effort, whereas buildings are capital created by working, saving, investing, and risk taking. We now know that the fertility of land and, to a lesser extent, its site value are not indestructible but may be lost through wrong methods of cropping and by leaching and erosion. But urban sites, except for filled-in areas here and there, are not created by man and cannot be augmented or diminished by social policy. Quite the contrary is true of building, which has hitherto been affected by social policies that influence income, prices, rents, interest, and taxes, and hence the volume of construction.

PERSONALTY AND REALTY

The general property tax is a tax on all property, personal and real, tangible and intangible, at uniform valuations and rates in each taxing jurisdiction. This form of taxation is typically American and has no counterpart in other parts of

TABLE 11

PROPORTIONS BETWEEN ASSESSED VALUE OF REAL AND PERSONAL PROPERTY IN THE UNITED STATES

| | U.S. Census Data* | | Doan's Data† | |
Year	Personal Property	Real Property	All Movable Equipment	All Real Property and Improvements
1850‡	35.0%	65.0%	...	...
1860‡	42.5	57.5	...	...
1880	24.0	76.0	...	...
1902	25.0	75.0	...	...
1912	25.0	75.0	...	...
1922	26.0	74.0	37.3%	62.7%
1930	...	...	33.9	66.1
1938	...	...	33.4	66.6

* U.S. Bureau of Census, *Wealth, Public Debt and Taxation: 1922, Estimated National Wealth* (Wash., 1924), pp. 14 and 15. Figures for 1850 are from the Seventh Census.

† Robert R. Doan, *The Anatomy of American Wealth* (N.Y. and London, 1940), pp. 192, 220, and 248.

‡ Includes value of slaves.

the world. In the United States it was originally used by the
states and local governments, but it is now used predominantly only by the latter. In practice, however, it remains
a general property tax in name only; in almost all jurisdictions, intangible personal property has ceased to be assessed
or taxed at the same rate as tangible property and in some
jurisdictions tangible personal property is sometimes partially exempted from application of the law. In Wisconsin,
for example, the tax on tangible personal property is confined
to income-producing assets and is not assessed against the
ordinary household.

Intangible property consists of titles to property and evidence of debt: stocks and bonds, notes, mortgages, and ac-
counts receivable. These are not social wealth but merely
individual property, an evidence of ownership or a chose in
action against another person. Taxation of intangibles is consequently viewed as the multiple taxation of wealth. This becomes clear if we visualize the taxation of a farm and of the
deed to the farm, the physical property of a corporation and
the shares of stock of that corporation. It is still true but
less clear if we tax a $10,000 home at $10,000 and the mortgage on it, say, at $8,000. The multiple character of such
taxation is obscured in practice because the physical property
and the mortgage upon it may lie in two different taxing
jurisdictions. If, however, the intangible evidence of ownership and the physical asset were both taxed in the same jurisdiction, the tax base would be doubled and the net burden
would remain unaltered. In the same way if the physical
property and the mortgage on it both be taxed, the total
tax base would be enlarged and the rate paid on tangible property would be lowered. But such an enlargement of the base
would be at the expense of mortgaged property and accrue
to the benefit of debt-free property.[12]

The taxation of incorporeal property at the same rate as
other property has been inequitable, erratic, and confiscatory;
and the statutory provisions for these taxes have become a
dead letter. Attempts to tax intangibles have also been de-
feated by concealment and by transfer of the property into

jurisdictions where the law was not enforced.[13] Assessors, faced with an impossible tax, have ignored intangibles or compromised on the valuations. Again and again the demand has been made by owners of real property to assess intangibles in order to lower the rate on realty, but it has always failed.[14]

These considerations would lead us to the conclusion that the general property tax is in fact predominantly a tax on real estate, and the data bear out this view. For all taxing bodies, tax levies on real estate were 86.5 per cent of all property taxes levied in 1940.[15]

THE TAX BASE

Estimates of the property subject to taxation have their source in the United States Census. The Bureau of the Census began to collect data of this sort in 1850. The most exhaustive report was made in 1922. This report was modified by the work of the Federal Trade Commission, published in 1926, which broke down the figures for real estate into land and improvements, made revised estimates for railroads and utilities, and added the value of streets and roads.

The census shows an increase of the assessed value of property from $6 billion (including value of slaves) in 1850 to $124.6 billion in 1922. On a per capita basis, this increase is from $308 to $2,731.[16] Doan estimates total physical assets in the United States to be $428.3 billion in 1930 and $388 billion in 1938.[17] A census figure gives the assessed valuation of property subject to property taxes for state or local purposes as $124 billion in 1922, $165 billion in 1929, and $144 billion in 1940, the last being $1,098 per capita.[18]

LAND AND IMPROVEMENTS

Estimates of the division of the value of real estate between land and improvements, though differing in detail, show a great deal of similarity. Table 12 gives the views of four different statisticians. They find that realty comprises about two-thirds of the total wealth, and personality about one-third. Land and improvements are each about one-third of total wealth. A later estimate by Goldsmith shows that in

TABLE 12

VARIOUS ESTIMATES OF THE VALUE OF LAND AND BUILDINGS IN THE UNITED STATES, 1922, 1930, AND 1938

(IN BILLIONS OF DOLLARS)

Year	Source*	All Land	All Bldgs.	All Land & Bldgs.	Land as % of All Land & Bldgs.	Non-Farm Land	Non-Farm Bldgs.	Non-Farm Land & Bldgs.	Residential Land as % of All Land & Bldgs.	Farm Dwellings†	Total Farm & Non-Farm Residential Property†
1922	Bemis	101.4	75.0	176.4‡	57.5%	…	48.0§	…	20.0%–25.0%	…	…
"	FTC	122.2	108.2	230.4	53.0	…	…	…	…	…	…
"	Doane	111.9	89.3	201.2¶	55.6	34.9	30.1	65.0	53.8	6.1	71.1
"	Keller	104.4	97.7	202.1¶	51.7	35.8	32.1	67.9	52.7	6.4	74.3
1930	Bemis	125.0	115.0	204.0	52.1	19.0	63.0	82.0	23.2	7.0	89.0
"	Doane	138.5	144.7	283.2	48.9	56.1	51.6	107.7	52.1	7.1	114.8
"	Keller	125.2	143.4	268.6	46.6	52.2	46.8	99.0	52.7	6.5	105.5
"	Wickens	…	…	314.2	…	…	…	122.6	…	…	…
1938	Doane	117.1	141.6	258.7	45.3	48.3	44.0	92.3	52.3	5.3	97.6

* SOURCES: Albert Farwell Bemis, *The Evolving House*, Vol. II: *The Economics of Shelter* (Cambridge, Mass., 1934), pp. 11, 14, and 518. Federal Trade Commission, *National Wealth and Income* (Wash., 1926), p. 34. Robert R. Doane, *The Anatomy of American Wealth* (N.Y. and London, 1940), tables facing pp. 192 (for 1922), 220 (for 1930) and 248 (for 1938). Edward A. Keller, *A Study of the Physical Assets, Sometimes Called Wealth, of the United States, 1922–1933* (Notre Dame, Ind., 1939), p. 38. David L. Wickens, *Residential Real Estate* (N.Y., 1941), p. 2.

† No allowance made for the value of the land occupied by the farm dwellings.

‡ Does not include value of streets, public roads, railroads, and utilities.

§ Includes both farm and non-farm buildings.

¶ Includes railroads and utilities but not streets and public roads.

1946 land was about 20 per cent of total wealth, structures about 45 per cent.[19]

In Wisconsin the proportions between land and improvements differ between city and country, and according to the type of property. The real estate in towns is chiefly agricultural; in villages and cities it is commercial, industrial, and residential (Table 13). Land is in the neighborhood of 20 per cent of the total value of residential property. The value of land to total, however, varies with the value of the residence; high-priced residences have more land value in proportion to the total than low-priced houses.

TABLE 13

WISCONSIN REAL ESTATE, 1951

| | Per Cent | | Per Cent of |
	Land	Improvements	Total Real Estate
Type by Use			
Residential	18	82	51.0
Mercantile	26	74	15.0
Manufacturing	5	95	13.0
Agricultural	60	40	20.2
Swamp, cutover, and waste	100	0	.3
Timber	100	0	.4
Total			100.0
Average	51	49	
Type by Assessing Body			
Towns	45	55	32.0
Villages	15	85	8.0
Cities	18	82	60.0
Total			100.0
Average	26	74	

SOURCES Wisconsin Department of Taxation, *Property Taxes, 1951* (Bull. No. 163; July, 1952).

The division between land and improvements also varies with assessing districts. Agricultural districts are in the towns. Here land is a high proportion of total value. Hence any change in the tax structure made by adding to the land burden and subtracting from the tax on improvements would not greatly alter the proportions paid by various owners. They would pay about the same amount of tax as formerly. If, however, a taxing district was composed of both agricultural land and city property, a heavier tax on land would burden the farmers more than the city folk.

The data indicate that in states having a property structure similar to Wisconsin a reduction in taxes on real estate would affect different taxing districts unequally, but in general it would affect buildings more than land. In cities and villages a reduction in the levy would affect buildings more than land because this property is primarily residential, mercantile, and manufacturing. In the country it would affect land much more. The property tax in the cities is therefore partly a tax on site value of land and predominantly a tax on improvements; in agricultural areas it is predominantly a tax on land used for productive purposes.

Changes in the value of land do not affect the total wealth of the nation. The land area was just as great a hundred years ago as it is today and land was more fertile as well. True, it has been improved by clearing, draining, and other preparation for use, but its value as land to the nation rises and falls with the economic rent. Hence higher land values mean that land has become relatively more scarce compared to population and use—not that more of it is available.[20]

The value of farm buildings once erected is affected by the same factors as land; a farm is bought with the buildings, and both values tend to rise and fall together. Farm dwellings being reproducible goods, their price is, however, related in the long run to cost of reproduction. Changes in the valuation of farm buildings is accordingly composed of changes in value and in physical quantity, increases in physical quantity being the only additions to real wealth.

ASSESSMENTS AND TAX RATES

A wide variation exists in the practices of the several states with regard to uniformity of valuation and assessments; the various jurisdictions assess real property at different percentages of full value. Most states specify that assessments shall be at "full," "true," "cash," "market," or "fair" value; a few provide for an assessment at a designated percentage of full value. The practice, however, diverges widely from the prescription, and in order to compute the actual values it is necessary to correct for the usual undervaluation. In seven states—Connecticut, Illinois, Oregon, New York, Virginia, Washington, and Wisconsin—the state tax commissions make an attempt to estimate the percentage of estimates to "true" value.[21]

Ratios for real property assessments range from 20 per cent of full value for unplatted real estate used as a homestead to 40 per cent not so used, 10 per cent on agricultural products, 50 per cent for iron ore, etc. Of twenty-three states reporting, Minnesota, under a classified property tax, has the lowest assessment of real estate, 34.2 per cent of true value; Wisconsin has 90.81 per cent for cities and 88.91 per cent for villages; and three states claim 100 per cent valuations.[22]

The assessed value of taxable property changes with the growth of the country and fluctuates with the business cycle.[23] Table 14 shows the changes in the property tax in Wisconsin from 1872 to 1951. There is a tendency, however, for assessments to be more stable than actual market prices.[24] Speculative types of urban land values were drastically deflated in the Depression, when apartment buildings were refinanced at less than replacement cost of the structures alone, and vacant lots were sold for less than the cost of streets and utilities that served them.

During the low point of the Great Depression, it is estimated that the volume of new construction was hardly equivalent to annual depreciation. The value of existing real estate was being greatly impaired, and pressure for reduction in assessments came from property owners who were finding it

TABLE 14

ASSESSED VALUE OF GENERAL PROPERTY, TOTAL PROPERTY
TAXES, AND AVERAGE STATE (FULL VALUE) TAX RATE
IN WISCONSIN FOR SELECTED YEARS

Year	State Assessments (Millions)	Total Tax Levies (Millions)	Average State Rate
1872	$ 390	$ 7	....
1880	445	9	....
1891	623	14	....
1900	630	19	....
1910	2,743	30	$0.01125
1920	4,570	96	0.01895
1930	5,896	120	0.02044
1937	4,340	106	0.02321
1944	5,015	112	0.02234
1945	5,328	126	0.02373
1946	5,827	146	0.02510
1947	6,540	171	0.02618
1948	7,928	194	0.02455
1949	8,490	209	0.02466
1950	9,201	226	0.02452
1951	10,419	246	0.02364

SOURCES: For 1872–1937—Wisconsin Tax Commission, *Taxes of the State of Wisconsin and Its Political Subdivisions, 1901–1936* (Bull. No. 76; Aug., 1936), Table 8, p. 32; and *Wisconsin's Property Tax* (Bull No. 86; Des., 1938), pp. 2 and 3. The large increase in assessment after 1901 is partially due to the fact that supervision over local assessments was established in 1901, in which year state assessments jumped 128 per cent over the previous year. For 1944–51—Wisconsin Department of Taxation, *Property Tax Bulletin* for each year.

hard to meet their obligations. Owners of large properties with low rentals and high vacancies had their net income turned into a deficit.[25] They contended that the value of the property was its capitalized earning power, and the tax assessor was then asked to value the property by capitalizing the loss! While it is not theoretically correct or sound assessment practice to value a building by earning power alone and particularly not by the earning power of a single year, a continuation of the depression did have a tendency to reduce assessments. Even so, they were not reduced as far as general property values had fallen because such reductions prove to be fairly permanent, because cities needed revenues, and, finally, because they were so heavily bonded that a reduction in assessments might put them over their debt limit.[26]

The rate of taxation is derived by dividing the total levy by the tax base. If real estate is valued at full value, the base will be higher and the tax rate lower than if rated at only a percentage of its value. From the year 1923 to the present time, the rate on real property in cities has fluctuated around $25 per thousand of true valuation.[27] This is a rather noteworthy stability in view of the general upward trend in the rates for the entire period of our history up to about 1920.

The Detroit Bureau of Governmental Research has compiled data on the tax rates of about 250 cities since 1922. This data shows the actual rate and the full value rate but does not cover the same cities each year. The following list shows the adjusted full value rate for the large number of cities, using dollars per thousand of assessed valuation:[28]

1925	$24.14	1932	$26.25	1939	$27.57	1946	$28.09
1926	23.66	1933	25.53	1940	27.49	1947	28.04
1927	24.02	1934	26.03	1941	27.26	1948	29.57
1928	24.07	1935	25.70	1942	27.49	1949	28.09
1929	23.95	1936	25.43	1943	27.14	1950	24.93
1930	24.71	1937	25.84	1944	27.04	1951	23.65
1931	25.03	1938	27.12	1945	27.25		

While it is ordinarily the custom to assess below true value, a rapid fall in values as during the 1930's may bring the two assessments together, and a rapid rise in values such as has come about from 1942 to 1953 will bring market values above assessed values. Table 15 shows the assessed rate and the true rate for a group of the largest cities for the year 1951.

GOVERNMENTAL UNITS

Property taxes are not levied by the federal government because of the constitutional provision that direct taxes shall be apportioned among the several states according to popula-

TABLE 15

TAX RATES IN LARGEST CITIES
(PER $1,000 OF VALUATION)

Cities	Assessed	100% Rate
New York	$30.80	$30.80
Chicago	32.88	32.88
Philadelphia	29.75	18.45
Detroit	39.14	.....
Los Angeles	61.84	30.92
Cleveland	35.40	24.78
Baltimore	26.80	26.80
St. Louis	28.50	28.50
Boston	62.80	62.80
Pittsburgh	40.92	22.51
Washington	21.50	15.05
San Francisco	61.90	30.95
Milwaukee	44.94	31.01
Buffalo	43.61	41.43

SOURCE: *National Municipal Review,* January, 1952.

tion. Although this rule does not prohibit levy of property taxes by the federal government, it makes this levy rather impractical; property taxes were levied for short periods only three times in our history. The federal government also has income taxes, inheritance taxes, estate taxes, excise taxes, and customs that make other sources of revenue unnecessary. The property tax has therefore been left to the use of state and local governments.[29]

So long as the smaller governmental units raise their own revenues, they are obliged to rely on real estate taxes, supplementary sums from other sources of revenue, and grants from the state and the federal governments.

State Sources of Revenue

Prior to 1900 the property tax was the main source of revenue for state governments, but since then the states have gradually withdrawn from this field in favor of other sources. In 1922, 40 per cent of state revenues was obtained by property taxation. This percentage has declined steadily since then, until in the year 1952 it reached 3.8 per cent.[30] This reduction was in spite of a fourfold increase in state expenditures over the same period, and was made possible by substitution of new sources of revenue such as gasoline taxes, sales and income taxes, and federal aids.

The sources of revenue for the states ranked as follows in order of importance in 1951: general sales, motor fuels, motor vehicle licenses, individual income, corporation net income, alcoholic beverages, tobacco products, property, public utilities, severance, corporation in general, death and gift and others.[31] Table 16 shows the declining importance of the property tax as a proportion of total taxes in Wisconsin.

Local Sources of Revenue

The property tax has remained the chief source of revenue for local governments which, since 1902, have continued to take in the neighborhood of 90 per cent of all property taxes levied.[32] The percentage of property tax revenues to total revenues, however, has declined slightly because of new sources of total revenue, because of aids received from the state and federal governments, and because of income, sales, and other taxes collected by the state and shared with the local community.[33] These aids moved drastically upward after the beginning of the Depression.[34] While, therefore, the property tax has not diminished as a source of total revenue, local expenditures have increased and the gap has been made up by the state and federal governments.

Sources of local revenue ranked by relative size in 1950 were as follows: property; charges and miscellaneous; gross receipts and sales; licenses, permit, and others; individual income; corporation income.[35]

Out of a total of $16,941 million state and local tax revenue (excluding interflow of revenues), $7,366 million or 43.48 per cent was yielded by the property tax.[36] In per capita terms, in 1950 out of a total revenue for the states of $60.62 per capita, $2.10 was from the property tax; whereas of a total revenue of $54.17 per capita for the localities, $44.77 was yielded by

TABLE 16

REAL ESTATE, PROPERTY, AND TOTAL STATE AND LOCAL TAXES LEVIED OR
COLLECTED IN WISCONSIN, 1918–52

Year Ended June 30	Total State & Local Taxes	Total General Property Taxes*	Total Taxes on Real Estate*	% General Property of Total	% Real Estate of Total
1918	$ 66,917,012	$ 50,134,004	$ 40,825,387	74.92%	61.01%
1919	74,686,241	56,271,297	43,766,025	75.34	58.60
1920	105,742,960	77,128,835	60,419,803	72.94	57.14
1921	117,931,638	96,268,625	75,405,260	81.63	63.94
1922	124,122,826	97,142,844	74,366,585	78.26	59.91
1923	121,676,060	97,003,652	77,897,819	79.72	64.02
1924	132,162,093	100,120,302	79,886,319	75.76	60.45
1925	138,150,304	104,119,726	82,180,815	75.37	59.49
1926	142,799,752	99,948,768	80,451,895	69.99	56.34
1927	154,971,433	105,584,287	85,359,338	68.13	55.08
1928	148,916,906	111,094,527	92,220,786	74.60	61.93
1929	172,686,315	117,520,468	98,383,998	68.05	56.97
1930	184,120,797	122,253,862	103,635,996	66.40	56.29
1931	183,683,744	120,855,119	102,912,368	65.80	56.03
1932	173,700,069	106,756,277	95,863,460	61.46	55.19
1933	157,250,068	94,304,494	86,091,444	59.97	54.75
1934	150,917,589	90,269,379	82,988,429	59.81	54.99
1935	156,777,819	91,538,981	83,643,095	58.39	53.35
1936	170,333,325	93,956,021	85,144,540	55.16	49.99
1937	188,192,311	98,991,277	89,055,201	52.60	47.32
1938	202,273,206	106,261,011	94,444,267	52.53	46.69
1939	216,944,772	110,834,995	98,896,557	51.09	45.59
1940	204,677,479	109,719,277	98,264,097	53.61	48.01
1941	214,853,783	110,009,328	98,325,026	51.20	45.76
1942	235,651,035	113,241,772	100,069,591	48.05	42.47
1943	247,679,446	110,138,082	95,000,423	44.47	38.36
1944	269,784,408	107,345,430	90,977,926	39.79	33.72
1945	269,060,440	112,060,333	93,889,484	41.65	34.90
1946	269,774,538	126,461,295	105,401,261	46.88	39.07
1947	298,874,451	146,289,568	121,048,378	48.95	40.50
1948	360,229,440	171,233,651	137,130,009	47.53	38.07
1949	392,229,440	194,621,342	153,249,595	49.59	39.07
1950	419,350,385	209,355,996	165,621,255	49.92	39.49
1951	469,643,891	225,610,044	180,701,414	48.04	38.48
1952	500,947,226	246,310,477	192,574,370	49.17	38.44

this tax.[37] These figures show rather conclusively, therefore, that if there is to be any substantial change in the levy on real estate it must be on the level of local government.

FISCAL IMPORTANCE OF PROPERTY TAXES

The total revenues from property taxes derived by all units of government followed a rather steady upward trend until the Great Depression. Then, like all other revenues, they declined slightly but made a recovery after 1940 and are at present reaching new high levels. While, however, the total amount of property taxes has been rising, these taxes have been a smaller proportion of total taxes collected because of the practical abandonment of the property tax by state governments, the growing importance of income and corporation taxes by the federal government, and the growing use of federal and state aids to local government. Total property tax collections by state and local governments for selected years are as follows:[38]

1922	$3,321,484	1945	$4,802,000	1948	$6,128,000
1932	4,684,784	1946	4,990,000	1949	6,842,000
1941	4,473,545	1947	5,507,000	1950	7,366,000

Since the beginning of this century the total revenues of state governments have increased thirty fold, property taxes collected only threefold; local government total revenues have multiplied about eight times, and property taxes have increased proportionately.[39]

Breaking down the local government figure, we find that in 1902 counties received 20.3 per cent of all property taxes, in 1941, 20.7 per cent; municipalities 44.7 per cent and 49.5 per cent; school and other districts 23.4 per cent and 24.2 per cent.[40] The disparity in the practices of the state and local governments might appear at first glance to indicate a rather drastic change in state taxation policy. What happened, how-

---

* General property and real estate figures are preceding year's levy collected in current year.

SOURCE: Basic data from Wisconsin Department of Taxation. Taxes on real estate, 1918 through 1923, are estimates based on Department of Taxation figures.

ever, is that local government continued for the most part in the old groove, while the new revenues of state government were obtained from other readily accessible sources such as sales taxes, gasoline taxes, motor vehicle taxes, income and corporation taxes, which were feasible for state but not for local government. It is of some significance that the recent (1950) data (except as regards the federal government) show substantially the same trends noticed by students of this matter before the Great Depression.[41]

Before the 1930's, writers on taxation, in referring to the nation as a whole, could truthfully say that the property tax yielded more revenue than any other tax. This is no longer true because individual and corporate incomes taxes now occupy first place as sources of revenue, property taxes taking second place. In 1945, income taxes comprised 69.81 per cent of all federal, state, and local taxes combined: property taxes, 8.85 per cent; alcoholic beverages, 5.24 per cent; gasoline 2.34 per cent, etc.[42]

The proportions of total taxes taken by federal, state, and local governments has undergone a radical transformation since 1911. In that year the federal government took 23.89 per cent of the total, states took 11.12 per cent, and local governments took 54.99 per cent. World War I brought a radical increase in the federal proportion, which reached 65.33 per cent in 1920 and then declined steadily to a low of 22.36 per cent in 1932. World War II and its aftermath again increased the federal proportion, which reached a high of 82.44 per cent in 1945. In 1951 the proportions were as follows: federal, 73.14 per cent; state, 13.67 per cent; local, 13.19 per cent.[43]

DELINQUENCY

Property taxes are a lien against the property assessed until they are paid; and when they are unpaid at the date set by law, they become delinquent and subject to penalty. Delinquency may be the result of a deliberate decision by the property owner that he would rather lose the property than pay the annual tax bill. Cutover timber lands, marginal farm

land, and vacant lots in overextended city real estate develop-
ments often come under this classification. If the tax lien
remains unsatisfied, it may be bought by the county. Later
the property is sold for taxes to a private bidder or is bought
by the county. This deliberate delinquency stands in contrast
to the experience during the Great Depression when much
city and farm real estate became delinquent because its owners either preferred to use what little money they had for
other purposes or because they simply could not raise the
tax money at all.

Homeowners permitted their taxes to go unpaid when they
became jobless, and landlords did the same when their net
income from rents fell to a low level. This is a temporary
or cyclical delinquency caused by a fall in national income
rather than permanent delinquency created by a judgment
that the current income from a property or even its future
value does not make it worthwhile for the owner to keep his
title clear by making all tax payments.

Annual reports of tax delinquency based on census data
have been made available by Dun and Bradstreet, Inc., since
1930.[44] These reports use the following criteria of delinquency: (1) the delinquency on each year's current tax levy;
(2) the ratio of total collections (which includes arrears) to
the year's levy; (3) the percentage of taxes still delinquent
at the end of a year on the levies of the previous four years;
(4) the total accumulated delinquency as a ratio of the levy
of the current year.[45]

Year-End Delinquency

The following list shows the median percentages of year-
end tax delinquency for 150 cities over 50,000 in population:[46]

1930	10.15%	1934	23.05%	1938	10.70%	1942	6.00%
1931	14.60	1935	18.00	1939	9.25	1943	4.70
1932	19.95	1936	13.90	1940	8.70	1944	3.90
1933	26.35	1937	11.30	1941	6.80		

This list shows that in 1930 the cities tabulated failed to collect 10.15 per cent of the taxes levied that year—a figure that

reached a high in 1933 of 26.35 per cent and then declined to
3.90 per cent in 1944. The effect of depression, recovery, and
war prosperity on tax payments is obvious. The average collection figure is made up of cities having a wide variation—
some cities have notably low and others exceptionally high
delinquencies.

Ratio of Collections to Total Levy

Ordinarily total tax collections may be expected to approximate the year's levy. That is, the collection of arrears will
offset current delinquency provided total levies remain stable
and all taxes are ultimately collectible. During the five years
following 1929, collections were abnormally low and large
amounts of uncollected taxes had accumulated. Hence the
heavy delinquencies in 1932, 1933, and 1934 when paid in
subsequent years made the annual collections in these years
exceed the current levy.[47] The rise in current collections
varied from city to city with the size of the accumulation, the
degree of recovery, and the vigor of tax administration.
Cities with stable collections experienced a lesser change
than those with unstable collection records. The latter had
total collections in some of the years between 1935 and 1942
ranging from 110 per cent to 120 per cent of current levies.

The contrasting effects of stable and unstable tax collections is shown by comparing the records of San Francisco
and Atlantic City. The former had a peak current delinquency of 5.4 per cent in 1933, while the latter closed that
year with 63.6 per cent of the year's levy uncollected. In the
years 1935, 1936, and 1937, Atlantic City's annual collection
ran 122.4 per cent, 117.3 per cent, and 112.4 per cent of the
annual levy, while San Francisco's collections remained close
to 100 per cent.[48] For one hundred cities the median percentage of collection was, however, remarkably stable around
100 per cent, the high point being 102.8 per cent in 1937 and
the low 99.8 per cent in 1938. This average, however, con-
ceals a wide range of variation, the lowest city collecting only
74.6 per cent in 1935 and the highest 141.7 per cent in 1937.
Roughly a third of the cities had collections above 105 per

cent in 1935–37, but by 1942 the number making collections
of this size was only 10 per cent.[49]

Accumulation of Delinquent Taxes

When taxes remain unpaid for a period of years, the county
government may obtain a tax deed on the assessed property.
The number of years that must elapse between the non-pay-
ment of a tax levy and the acquisition of title by the county
varies in different jurisdictions, being a little more or less
than four years. Hence when any property becomes tax delinquent, it is to the interest of the owner to pay those taxes
that have been delinquent for the longest period. If an owner
did not pay taxes in 1931, 1932, and 1933 and in 1934 finds
he is able to meet a single year's levy, he will protect his
interest by allowing the latest levy to become delinquent and
will pay the 1931 levy.

The current year's unpaid taxes consequently always exceed
that of any of the preceding years, which diminish with time.
This is true even in depression. Thus while 22.25 per cent of
the current levy was unpaid in 1934, there remained uncollected 11.70 per cent of the 1933 levy, 5.90 per cent of the
1932 levy, and 2.95 per cent of the 1931 levy.[50] By 1937 the
unpaid portion of the current levy was only 10.2 per cent,
other unpaid taxes less proportionately, following the same
pattern.[51] At the end of the 1942 fiscal year only 1.9 per cent
of the taxes levied in 1939 remained unpaid. It seems, therefore, that delinquent taxes are gradually reduced year by year
at a slow or faster rate depending on business conditions, but
that they tend to reach a minimum before the passage of four
years.

It follows that accumulated delinquencies will be small or
large at any time, depending upon the rate of payment on
new and old levies. After several years of depression the
ratio of accumulated delinquent taxes to the current year's
levy will be high and in recovery will tend to be reduced to
lower levels. In 1934 Pontiac, Michigan, had an accumulated
delinquency of 208.9 per cent; Saginaw, Michigan, 130.5 per
cent; whereas Binghamton, New York, had only 9.5 per cent—

the median figure for a group of one hundred cities being
57.45 per cent,[52] indicating that the average municipality was
at that time short of one-half year's revenue due at that time.

The accumulated delinquency ratios in subsequent years is
shown in the following list:[53]

1934	57.45%	1937	41.60%	1940	33.60%	1943	21.50%
1935	48.40	1938	43.10	1941	32.20	1944	18.70
1936	43.60	1939	45.90	1942	25.50		

The data for delinquency show the unpaid levies still carried on the books of a city at the end of a year and not the
actual amount of taxes levied and unpaid. Some cities write
old taxes off their books and eliminate them from current
records. A city has the legal power to collect its property
taxes in full by the use of penalties, sale of tax levies, and
ultimate foreclosure of the property; but this power is not
always exercised at once. Except when the owner of a property is unable or unwilling to retain title to it, it must be
assumed that a lien of about 2.5 per cent of its value will
generally be paid. Unpaid taxes consequently constitute a
valid expectation of future revenue for a municipality which
it gauges in making expenditures.

Cities basing their budgets on full collections increase their
floating debt when delinquency increases. Collections of arrears, on the other hand, raise the ratio above 100 per cent
and make possible a reduction of outstanding notes and warrants which were issued in anticipation of tax collections or
of the redemption of bonds issued to meet current deficits
in years of low revenues. Because of this behavior of the
floating debt, actual funds available for expenditure vary,
somewhat less than might be expected from the flow of tax
payments.

Reasons for Delinquency

Delinquency is cyclical and chronic. The former condition
is brought about by a general deflation in incomes, rents, and
property values, and tends to disappear with general economic recovery. Chronic delinquency exists when the owners

of property fail to pay taxes because the accumulated taxes and assessments on the property exceed its value. This usually happens only with vacant land: marginal farm land or cutover areas in the country and vacant platted lots in urban areas. A small amount of chronic delinquency is occasioned by procrastination of some taxpayers and by the deliberate choice of others to permit taxes to accumulate while they make other uses of their funds. There is no remedy for cyclical delinquency except to minimize economic fluctuations. Meliorative action was taken during the last depression by various state legislatures which enacted legislation providing for moratoria on the payment of delinquent taxes, postponement of tax sales, and the waiving of penalties, interest, and collection charges on such properties. Although many communities were greatly alarmed about delinquencies during the Depression, it proved to be a temporary phenomenon for improved real estate, few owners being willing to lose their titles through failure to pay taxes equivalent to only a small part of their value.

The Bureau of the Census reported that in 1934 the average delinquency in 57 cities measured by assessed value was divided as follows: vacant lots, 31 per cent; apartments and other multi-family structures, 38 per cent; single-family houses, 23 per cent. By number of parcels, delinquency was greatest on vacant lots, 45 per cent; on single-family and multi-family dwellings, 29 per cent each.[54] Delinquency predominated in speculative subdivisions and speculative building for rental purposes. Homeowners paid up their taxes quite well, whereas slum and blighted areas contributed heavily to delinquency, presumably because those properties were occupied by those least able to pay rentals during depression.[55]

Chronically delinquent properties in rural areas consist of submarginal farm land or cutover timber lands which have declined in value. This decline may be caused by a change in agricultural prices or by the removal of timber.[56]

Improved real estate in urban areas is delinquent only temporarily; chronically delinquent property generally consists

of vacant subdivided lots which real estate developers have
provided far beyond existing needs. These lots, being un-
salable, are also subjected to heavy assessments for street
and sewer improvements which may make it inadvisable to
hold them indefinitely. In the Detroit area, Professor Ernest
M. Fisher estimated that in the period 1920 to 1930 population
increased 70 per cent and subdivided lots 100 per cent, or for
every 100 newcomers to Detroit 74 lots were prepared. Professor Herbert D. Simpson estimated that in the Chicago area
it would be 1960 before 90 per cent of vacant lots could be
used.[57]

Even as the Depression waned, a hard core of delinquent
property remained on the tax duplicate. Cuyahoga County
(Cleveland), Ohio, had so much delinquent real estate that by
1940 it had become the biggest real estate agency in Ohio.
It was in a position to dump onto the market over a quarter
of the area of Cuyahoga County at low prices because of its
command over tax-delinquent properties subject to forfeiture
or foreclosure and tax sale.[58] Taxes on this property remained unpaid because owners did not believe the land worth
the amounts of taxes and special assessments against it. By
now many realize they were mistaken.

In 1940 there were 159,704 delinquent parcels, representing
42 per cent of the total parcels in the county. One hundred
thousand, two hundred forty-six or 26 per cent of the total
had been delinquent more than four years and under existing
laws were subject to foreclosure or forfeiture. That these consisted of the parcels of lesser value is shown by the fact that
this 42 per cent of the total parcels had a taxable value of
$64,836,270 which was, however, only 4.6 per cent of the value
of all the land and buildings in the county. Accumulated
delinquent taxes against these properties amounted to $50,-
545,243 or 80 per cent of the assessed value, and for 35,399
parcels accumulated taxes exceeded assessed value. Of the
100,246 delinquent parcels, 96.4 per cent were vacant, 97.2
per cent were subdivided lots, and just short of 3 per cent
were acreage parcels.[59]

The basic reason for this delinquency lies in a lack of urban planning, in overdevelopment and speculation. In Cuyahoga County, as elsewhere, the available building lots provided for a population increase of 50 per cent. Some of the heaviest charges against the property were for special assessments to pay for improvements. This form of delinquency is then the penalty for wrong business judgment and should not be attributed to tax policy. Public policies providing for best use of land areas were, however, needed and suggested.[60]

The burden of the property tax is particularly onerous during depression because it continues regardless of the income of the taxpayer, whereas the income tax and even the general sales tax become smaller in amount as income and expenditure fall. A lower rate of property taxation, though it will alleviate somewhat the burden on income and bring about a smaller volume of default, is not likely, however, to prevent the cyclical pattern. For if income falls, property taxes are one item that can be deferred. The federal government finances a deficit by borrowing during depression, and state and local governments might possibly do the same. Unfortunately, however, at the advent of the last depression local governments were generally in bad financial straits and additional indebtedness was not welcomed by the municipal bond market or by the citizenry, who cried for reduction in expenditures.[61] In retrospect, the panic regarding the delinquency in the 1930's appears to have been unwarranted as was also the fear that many cities would have to retrench permanently on current expenditure. These were symptoms not so much of unsound city government, but of the low level of national income that had to wait upon national policy for a remedy.

6

Incidence
and Effects of
Property Taxes

The immediate impact of a tax is upon the person who pays it; its incidence is where it ultimately rests.[1] Impact is a matter of law; incidence depends upon economic power. The property tax is assessed against the property and paid by the property owner who must bear it himself unless he shifts it to others. We shall distinguish between the incidence of a tax on land and a tax on buildings because, as we shall see, they may be quite different.

Since the homeowner is also the occupier, the problem of incidence is purely academic in his case. Where, however, the property is occupied by a tenant, he may pay all or any part of a higher house tax through higher rents, and he may benefit by the reduction through lower rents, both of these processes taking place only after the passage of enough time to permit supply and demand factors to be adjusted to the new conditions. A tax burdening the owner will reduce the profits on his capital; whereas, if it is shifted to the tenant, profits will remain unaffected. The immediate effect of higher rents may be to reduce the amount of space demanded, so that the burden of a new house tax may be wholly on the owner, or, as is more likely, it may be temporarily divided between the owner and the tenant.

When this happens, profits after taxes may be reduced below the level which encourages new construction. Available housing will remain constant or even diminish until demand catches up and raises rentals to a profitable level. At this point, the tenant begins to bear the house tax, and the capitalized value of old houses less depreciation becomes equal to the cost of producing similar housing space. Thus, in the short run, any increase in taxes on improvements rests on the owner and in the long run on the tenant, subject to the various qualifications stated hereafter.

When the house tax rests on the owner, it temporarily reduces the capitalized value of the building. When the tax rests on the occupier, as it does in the long run, the value of the building is unaffected. As we shall see, tax capitalization, though applicable with numerous qualifications to land and sometimes temporarily to housing, is generally inapplicable to housing in the long run.

The word "incidence" in tax theory has generally been confined to mean the effect on prices, whereas the term "effect" includes all other economic consequences. We shall not adhere strictly to this practice because there is, in fact, no exact line of demarcation between immediate price effects and other more remote consequences. For example, a tax diminishing real estate profits may cause a drop in new construction which reduces employment, wages, the prices of building materials, and national income. Lower incomes in turn impair the demand for housing and tend to reduce rentals and profits still further. All of the price and income effects result from the tax whether we call them incidence or effects. An economic event is like a stone cast into a lake; it creates waves which diminish as they recede from the source. We cannot trace all of these events, but we can follow those of vital consequence and of larger magnitude.

INCIDENCE ON CAPITAL, INCOME, OR EXPENDITURE

If the general property tax were a nonrepetitive, unanticipated capital levy for a single year, it would diminish the capital by the amount of the tax and constitute a true capital levy. Since, however, it is usually an annual tax equivalent to only a part of the year's revenues, it is a tax on the income of property graded by the amount of property. Should, perchance, such a tax continually exceed present and expected total revenues from the property, it would make the property

worthless. A tax levied on a percentage of property value
which would destroy that value is, however, quite unlikely if
not theoretically impossible—theoretically impossible because
a tax levied on a value that has ceased to be would yield no
revenues.[2]

Since the realty tax is not a capital levy, it must be paid
out of the annual output of the real estate. The output of
any capital good is the marginal value of the service that it
gives off. The service of residential real estate is shelter.
Now, shelter itself is a form of consumption, and consumption
is one type of income. Hence, we commonly treat the shelter
value of an owner-occupied home as an imputed income of the
owner. A tax on shelter is, therefore, a tax on a consumption
good and is accordingly an expenditure tax similar to any
other sales tax. A sales tax on shelter, like any other sales
tax, may be borne by either the buyer or seller of shelter:
if it is borne by the former, it raises rents; if borne by the
latter, it decreases profits.

A Sales Tax on Shelter

The characterization of the property tax as a sales tax on
shelter is not, however, true under all circumstances. Some
buildings may be unoccupied and still subject to the tax levy,
in which case the tax payment is an operating loss paid out
of capital. The rent on others may be so low that the yield is
insufficient to pay expenses, and the taxes become a burden
to be paid out of other income of the owner or, eventually,
out of the capital itself. The homeowner without other income may borrow or mortgage to pay the tax levy, or the
house may become delinquent and eventually be sold for taxes,
in which case the owner pays the taxes out of capital.

The designation of the realty tax as a sales tax on shelter
may accordingly be misleading during a period of depression
or in stagnant or shrinking communities when rents are low
and, perhaps, even uncollectible, or during a period of high
vacancies when real estate taxes must be paid on unoccupied buildings that are not in fact performing the sheltering

service. The tax thus becomes in fact a tax on capital or on the income of the owner from other sources.

The characterization of the tax on dwellings as a sales tax on shelter must be taken, therefore, to hold only in general and in the long run; but it is still the most significant single generalization that can be made.

A Universal Property Tax

A genuine general property tax would consist of a uniform levy on all capital goods of every kind. (Because of the special problems of taxes on intangibles and their duplicative character, we omit these taxes from consideration at this point and confine the discussion to real capital goods.) The immediate effect of such a tax would be to reduce the income derived from capital goods; the ultimate effect would be determined by the effect of the tax on the present and future supply of capital. When the supply of capital is diminished by the lower return resulting from the tax, all or part of the tax may be shifted by the owner of the capital to other factors of production. To the extent that the supply is inelastic, the tax must be borne by the capitalist as a reduction in profit. We must, therefore, distinguish between reproducible goods and fixed-supply goods, of which land is the most important case, and also consider how a fall in the rate of profit may affect the volume of saving and investment and hence the supply of capital goods.

THE CAPITALIZATION PROCESS

The owner of fixed-supply goods is sometimes said to escape a tax by the capitalization process.[3] The value of a fixed-supply capital good is determined solely by the demand for its products or services. If a piece of land were expected to yield $100 per year gross income, and taxes and expenses were zero, it would yield the same net income, which capitalized at 10 per cent would make its market value $1,000. If, now, a tax of $25 reduces the annual income to $75, the value will fall to $750; and the present owner, if he sells, will lose $250 of his capital. He thus bears the present tax levy and all

future levies. The new owner actually pays the annual taxes
out of the $250 that he saved in the purchase price when he
capitalized the property at income minus taxes. If, however,
taxes are now increased to $50 per annum, the value of the
property drops to $500 and the second owner bears the future
increments of $25 per year in taxes. A third owner who buys
at $500 buys tax free and gains by any tax reduction, which
raises net income and, hence, the capitalizable value of the
land. What is true of land holds as well within limits for any
form of capital which is (temporarily) fixed in supply. Its
value is temporarily determined by capitalizing expected annual increments of income and is not immediately determined
by cost of reproduction.

In practice the market values of land are not found quite
so simply. What is the anticipated future gross and net
income? What are the probable future tax rates and future
interest rates? Buyers and sellers speculate on these matters,
sometimes bidding higher for land because they anticipate
future increases in value or future reductions in taxes. Real
estate values, like stock market prices, fluctuate with the business cycle for the hundred and one reasons that cause individuals to change their ideas about the future. Whether,
therefore, any purchaser actually capitalizes future income
correctly or anticipates tax changes and, therefore, in fact
buys free of existing taxes is not a matter that can be predicted with much certainty. Some buyers pay a higher
present price because of an expected rise in future rental
values. All that can be said with certainty is that the existing
tax rates are a factor that probably influence present prices.
Economic rent, even the future unearned increment, cannot,
therefore, be easily taxed away without working hardship on
someone.

There seems to be little doubt, however, that the existing
taxes and the creation of additional levies during depression
tend to depress real estate values. Consider the outcry made
everywhere for tax reduction as incomes and rental revenues
diminished, and consider also the low prices at which real
estate could be purchased! The State of Wisconsin made it

a policy to shift many relief and welfare costs of the Depression to local government, thereby causing local levies of taxes to be increased by about 25 per cent above what would have been necessary if all of these revenues had been raised from other sources.[4] If we capitalize this additional expense, the loss to property owners who had to sell their properties during this period would run into a large figure for the whole state.

Limitations of the Tax Capitalization Theory

The tax capitalization theory usually assumes that although the income from property is reduced the rate at which that income is capitalized remains the same. Hence the value of the property falls and the present owners bear the tax. This assumption that the rate of capitalization is not affected by a general fall in earnings from property has, however, been called into question. Instead, it is sometimes claimed that a general property tax or a corporation income tax may depress the rate of earnings of all business enterprise. This reduces the marginal productivity of capital and reduces the rate of interest which determines the rate of capitalization. If then it be true that a general tax reduces both the income from property and the rate of interest at which all property is capitalized, it will have no effect on nominal capital values. If the income from a given property was $100 and the rate at which it was capitalized was 10 per cent, its capital value would be $1,000. Now if the income is reduced by a tax to $80 and the capitalization rate also falls to 8 per cent because of a general fall in the marginal productivity of capital, the capital value would still be $1,000. No capital loss would appear as a result of the tax capitalization process. But can we say that the owner has suffered no loss? He has the same piece of land with the same physical characteristics and valued at the same number of dollars, but in terms of net value of output he suffers a loss of $20 per year in income. This is a real loss and no theory that losses are escaped by capitalization can gainsay it.

Three questions are crucial in dealing with the capitalization of taxes: (1) Is the tax shifted in the price of the product? (2) If not, is the tax capitalized? Or (3) does the tax lower earnings and the capitalization rate, and if so to what extent? Thus far no data or analysis has provided a satisfactory answer to these questions, though they have long been debated and are still receiving considerable attention.

Is the Land Tax Burdenless?—It is commonly asserted, as a corollary of the tax capitalization theory, that the land tax is burdenless tax and that any remission of property taxes constitutes a gift or windfall to all landowners. Strictly speaking, we have seen that the burden is escaped only by the person who acquired landed property after the tax was imposed. But the first statement is made because it is impossible in practice to distinguish in tax legislation between old and new owners of property. Hence any change in the tax affects them all. It follows from this view that if we seek to compare the relative burden of property and sales taxes we ought to exclude the taxes paid on land in computing the ratio of property taxes to income. We discuss this matter further in Chapter 8, showing that only a minor difference in relative regressivity would exist if the property tax on land were eliminated from our calculations. At this point, however, we shall examine a little more closely the accuracy and implications of the view that the land tax is burdenless.

A new land tax diminishes the owner's income and the value of the land. It is discriminatory because it cannot be shifted and because it does not affect the person whose assets are in other forms. A farmer with practically all of his assets in the form of land is discriminated against by a land tax compared to a merchant who owns no land but holds all his assets in cash and goods. Whether the redistribution of wealth resulting from the land tax is equitable depends upon the wealth and income of the persons affected.

Once the tax is imposed, the landowner, when he wishes to sell, takes a capital loss and the new owner buys "free of the tax." To the latter, the tax is burdenless because in the absence of the tax he would have paid in interest what he now pays as taxes. Capitalization does not remove the burden of the land tax. It merely shifts the burden from the new to the old owner. This is not, however, the end of the story. Landowners may buy one piece of property and sell another. When they do this, they gain on the purchase what they lose on the sale. Annual income is, however, decreased by the amount of the tax, and this constitutes a real burden. The only one to whom a new land tax can be said to be "burdenless" is the person who did not own any land at the time of the original levy. It is always a tax on existing owners, never on new owners.

It follows that the tax is *not* burdenless to any owner who keeps his farm and continues to pay the tax. By the same reasoning, it is not burdenless to his heirs and assigns who continue to pay a part of their income to the state. If the land is never sold, the burden of the tax is borne annually by the landowner to eternity.

The tax, however, *is* burdenless to the new owner and his heirs and assigns because they are presumed to have saved enough in the original purchase price to pay the tax in perpetuity.

In this sense, the annual tax burdens a farmer today if he inherited his land from his forebears who bought before the tax or who homesteaded it. It does not burden a farmer today if he inherited his land from his forebears who purchased it after the tax was levied.

The contention that a tax which may take up to 25 per cent of a man's income is burdenless if he purchased his farm and paid for it by his own labor, but that it is a burden to another farmer who obtained his land by continuous inheritance, strikes most persons as absurd. Tax legislation which, following the logic of the tax capitalization theory, would continue a tax on the purchased land and lift it from inherited land would also seem patently unfair. It would be unfair, not because of any basic flaw in the tax capitalization theory as such. The injustice would arise from the manner in which taxes are actually capitalized, the mistakes in estimates of the future, and the pure speculation about future yields and interest rates. (For fluctuations in farm land prices, see Chapter 5, note 20.) But even if this were not so, application of this theory in legislation would still work injustice because of the changes in the fortunes of sellers and buyers and their heirs and assigns over generations in their property ownership and in their incomes.

To tax a poor farmer 25 per cent of his income (while those of much higher income and wealth were paying a much smaller tax) on the theory that tax capitalization had given that farmer capital out of which he pays the tax and which, therefore, makes the tax burdenless becomes a ridiculous if, in fact, the taxpayer does not actually have this putative capital fund. Such a tax would be burdening the children with the sins of their fathers. It seems therefore more just to relate present taxes to existing income and wealth. And this, in fact, is what our tax system as a whole aims to do.

From the social viewpoint, it is, of course, fallacious to say that the land tax is burdenless to the people as a whole. The property tax has existed in Wisconsin, the situs of our statistical data, for more than a century. During that period it has been increased from time to time. The logic of the tax capitalization theory is that each person who bought land at any time since 1850 bought free of the tax that existed at the time of purchase. For example, farmers who bought their land in 1910 capitalized all of the taxes imposed at that time and have not been and are not now bearing the burden of the land tax. It was borne by the owner who sold before 1910. Was the annual tax imposed, say in 1850, capitalized by the purchaser in 1851 and have all subsequent owners been free of the tax? Did the owner in 1850 bear the tax for all time to come? The answer of the tax capitalization doctrine is clearly in the affirmative. All land taxes now levied in Wisconsin are and have been burdenless, according to this view, to all those who bought after the levy or who acquired land by inheritance from someone who had capitalized the tax.

Even though it is logically coherent, without further elucidation, this view does not seem realistic. How could the people living in 1850 or in 1910 bear all of the taxes for all subsequent time? It is established that today's taxes are paid out of today's production. But how then could a tax paid out of today's production have burdened great-grandfather in 1850? The implication of the tax capitalization theory is that the tax is being paid today out of the production imputed to a capital sum which was lost by great-grandfather in 1850 (and gained by the purchaser) when he sold the property after the imposition of the tax. The interest on this fund will then make the 1850 increment of the tax perpetually burden-less to the present owners. And what can be said for the 1850 increment applies to all subsequent increments.

Another way to look at the matter is that in 1850 the state took some of the wealth of the original owner by imposition of an annual tax. Then tax capitalization enabled the new owner to escape the burden for all time to come; it also en-abled his heirs and assigns to escape it in perpetuity. The heirs of the original owner, on the other hand, are now less well off by the amount which the state took from their great-grandfather in 1850.

The tax is not, however, socially burdenless. For the real burden of any tax and its accompanying public expenditure rests on the generation which pays it. Some exception to this rule can be made where the present generation wastes the substance inherited from the past. The social burden of the public expenditure paid for out of taxes consists of the re-sources diverted from the use of individuals to the use of the state. (Of course, this burden on individuals may be offset by the benefits they receive in the form of services furnished by government.)

The correct conclusion regarding the land tax therefore seems to be that like all other taxes it is a burden on present production and is not borne by past generations. The fairness of a tax is therefore best measured (among other things) by its relation to present incomes. Nothing that has been said in this reference, however, denies that the tax on pure eco-nomic rent is likely to be less deterrent to work, saving, and investment than one on income derived from these sources. That is another matter. This analysis shows, however, why it would be foolish to propose a tax policy or to measure burdens on the theory that the land tax is burdenless.

INCIDENCE OF A TAX ON REPRODUCIBLE GOODS

If the capitalized value of reproducible goods exceeds reproduction costs, the output of new goods will increase; and
if capitalized value falls below reproduction costs, the creation of new goods will cease until the two are brought back
into equilibrium. A housing shortage generally raises the
value of existing real estate, as it has in the period 1941–53;
but it also stimulates the creation of new houses which, when
brought to the market, will tend to bring the whole market
closer to current production costs. For that reason the tax
capitalization process can be applied only temporarily to reproducible goods.

The forces ultimately affecting the volume of reproducible
capital goods are saving and investment, and dissaving and
disinvestment. Saving diverts resources from consumption to
make possible the creation of new assets; dissaving results
from insufficient maintenance repairs and depreciation or out-
right consumption of capital. The only manner in which a
general tax on all capital can be shifted is by curtailment of
either or both saving and investment in all forms of capital,
which creates a capital scarcity and raises its marginal value.

In the pre-Keynesian era, it was held that the volume of
capital goods was dependent upon the volume of saving which
was a function of the rate of interest. A reduction in interest
rates would cause savings to fall and consumption to increase,
thus curtailing the supply of investible funds and again raising the rate of interest. It has been doubted, however,
whether small changes in the interest rate had much effect on
the volume of savings; and for that reason, some economists
concluded that a tax on capital had to be absorbed by the
capitalist.[5]

When we separate saving and investment into two independent acts governed by different motives, we see that the
total supply of capital can be increased only by additional
net investment. It is decreased by depreciation not offset
by maintenance and repairs. Even if a fall in the rate of
interest did not induce savers to save less, it might induce

them to hoard cash rather than to invest and thus lower the
income of the community. With lower incomes, savings would
then decline at a faster rate than consumption. But the mo-
tivating force in bringing about lower savings would not be
changes in time preference, but changes in liquidity preference which were caused in turn by the estimates of a decline
in the rate of profit. Before deciding, therefore, whether a
tax on all capital could be shifted, we must determine how it
would affect (1) time preference, (2) liquidity preference,
and (3) the marginal efficiency of capital (expected rate of
profit).

Time preference determines the allocation of income between consumption and saving; if a lower yield on invested
capital reduces savings and increases consumption by an
appreciable amount, the lower yield will tend to restrict the
supply of capital and raise the demand for it, thus again raising the rate of profit. Just how much influence the expected
rate of interest has on the volume of saving is now a much
mooted question, with the view tending to be accepted that
the total effect is likely to be small.

It is, however, generally admitted that a lowering of the
expected rate of profit (below surplus profit levels) will increase liquidity preference and reduce the willingness to invest in the production of new assets. Such a consequence
would, undoubtedly, diminish the total quantity of physical
assets and raise their marginal value, although, as we shall
presently see, it might also decrease total national income
and aggregate demand.

But leaving this secondary effect for consideration later,
we can see that a general tax on capital can be shifted only
by increasing either or both time preference and liquidity
preference—that is, either by increasing consumption and decreasing savings or by curtailing the amount of new investment. If this is done, then the tax can be passed on to the consumer of the products of capital goods in whole or in part.
An apparent exception to this analysis is found in the case
of monopoly, where the tax merely reduces monopoly profits
to a competitive level and, hence, has no effect on either time

preference or liquidity preference. Just as with land rent, quasi-rents on improvements can be taxed out of existence without affecting the supply of products coming from the monopolists or quasi-monopolists.

We conclude then that a tax on reproducible goods, such as houses, might be a capital levy if, like heavy inheritance or estate taxes, it exceeded the income from the house. It might be a tax on the income from the invested capital (interest or profit) if it diminished its net yield. Finally, if the tax resulted in a diminished supply of houses, if would raise rents and thereby constitute a tax on housing expenditure.

The Tax on Housing[6]

The principles affecting the incidence of a tax on houses are essentially the same as those of a general tax on reproducible capital goods, subject to the following qualification. Insofar as the property tax raises the cost of housing about 20 to 25 per cent, it reduces the amount of space demanded and diminishes new investment for this purpose. Consumer demand, including the expenditure of the tax receipts, will be diverted to other consumer goods, and investment funds will also shift to supply these products. A lifting of the tax should have the opposite results. Although it is not easy to prove it by measurement, it seems that monthly housing expenditure and hence also investment are diverted from housing into other products such as automobiles, appliances, and other competitors for the consumer's dollar. Houses become smaller and cars larger. But discomfort from inadequate housing sets a limit to this substitution. There is another possibility: at times the high cost of housing space may inhibit new construction without diverting the expenditure into other channels. Thus a slump in house building might cause a fall in national income and employment. In that event, a reduction in housing costs including labor, materials, contractor's profits, mortgage loan rates, and taxes might be desirable.

Because of the durability of housing and the small effect that the new building of any year can have on total supply in a short period, the incidence of a new housing tax in the short run may resemble that of a land tax or a tax on any fixed-supply durable good. The price of buildings may fall below or exceed cost of reproduction for a time and rentals also may rise above or stay below the equilibrium amount. In this sense, the tax enters into the capitalized value of the building.

Buildings of all types are, however, not absolutely fixed in supply. They are subject to wear and tear, depreciation, obsolescence, fire, and other hazards. Housing accommodations, consequently, would be constantly diminishing were it not for expenditures for repairs, improvements, and new structures. These outlays will be made when owners believe them to be useful and profitable and can, therefore, be affected by the incidence of taxes upon the profitability of investment in real estate. If yields are diminished, construction will cease until existing assets have a higher marginal value. In the long run a tax on real estate improvements is a sales tax on shelter and an indirect sales tax on consumption goods produced and sold by industries paying the tax.

The possible effects of a house tax are these: it could rest on property (a capital levy) or on the owner's income from property (an income tax) or on the goods or services produced by the property (an expenditure or consumption tax). It would also affect to greater or lesser extent the supply of savings, the volume of investment, the volume of consumption, and the prices of goods and services, depending on the response of each of these elements in the economic system to the tax. Technically this response may be described in terms of the elasticities of time preference, of liquidity preference, of investment, and of the supply of and the demand for consumption goods—factors that can all be enumerated but hardly ever measured satisfactorily in a given case.

Land and Improvements.—In the long run houses will sell at their present cost of reproduction—allowing for depreciation and obsolescence. In cities with diminishing or stagnant population, a tax may be borne entirely by the property owners because, for a time at least, existing property is in a fixed supply greater than demand. On the other hand, if a city has a rapidly increasing population with incomes adequate to pay for housing, a tax on housing can be passed on in large part to tenants in higher rents.

During years in which housing accommodations lag behind the national income, as during and after the last two wars, except for rent controls which keep rentals down below the market price, excessive profits that might be taxed away without affecting supply may exist for a considerable period of time. The same situation holds true where cities are constantly growing at a faster pace than the supply of housing. Similar results also obtain as between prosperity and depression. During a period of rising incomes and heavy demand for rental space, a tax on housing can be readily passed on to the renter; during depression, it may be absorbed by the landlord in reduced profits.

During and after World War I up to about 1927 the scarcity of housing accommodations made it possible to raise rentals to a profitable level. But after 1930 the decline in rentals and the large number of vacancies probably caused the tax to be absorbed by owners in a lower rate of return. Rents rose again with the outbreak of the last war; and had it not been for rent controls, it probably would have been possible to shift all taxes to the tenant.

The same principle of incidence seems to hold for business as for residential property. Residential property provides a dwelling place which is a consumption good. Business property provides shelter to produce other goods or services. The tax on business improvements is then a tax on the cost of producing goods and in the long run will enter into the price of the product in the same manner as a sales tax or an excise tax. It follows that the tax on business improvements is similar to a general tax on the products of the business establishment. Just as the sales tax on residential real estate, if not absorbed by the owner, is paid by the consumer of shelter, so the tax on business real estate, if not absorbed by the producer, is paid by the purchaser of his commodities. It is therefore similar to a sales tax on consumption goods. This is, of course, only the general rule and is subject to the qualifications that must be made for monopoly products and those sold in competition with commodities produced in areas where products are not subject to the tax.

DYNAMIC FACTORS AFFECTING INCIDENCE

In static tax theory we usually make one or more of these four assumptions: (1) full employment; (2) constant income and employment; (3) that the level of income and employment is not affected by the incidence of the tax; and (4) that in turn the incidence of the tax is not affected by the level of income and employment. Each of these four is in essence the same thing in an operational sense so far as this analysis is concerned because it makes the incidence of the tax independent of the level of income.

We shall now consciously discard these assumptions and proceed with the view that the tax affects the level of income and employment and that the latter then affects the incidence of the tax. A complete static-dynamic theory of tax incidence must then include: (1) the immediate incidence and effects under the static assumptions (which analysis we have just concluded); (2) the effects upon the income of the economic system as a whole; and (3) the effects of the latter upon the final incidence during prosperity and depression. The theory of price usually deals exhaustively with the first problem, and the aggregate demand theory (Keynesian and neo-Keynesian) with the second; but the third problem in this as in many other fields has been neglected. This neglect arises from the fact that those who use static analysis generally ignore the aggregate demand functions, while those who deal with aggregates neglect their effects on relative prices. We shall therefore try to combine the theory of relative prices with the theory of income to obtain a theory of individual prices (and, hence, incidence) under fluctuating total incomes.

In concluding that the realty tax diminishes profits and that lower profits restrict the supply of shelter until rents rise sufficiently to enable part or all of the tax to be passed on to the occupier in the form of higher rents, we neglected both the dynamic effects upon the national income and the subsequent effects of changes in the national income upon rents and profits. A fall in construction without a substitute outlet for savings reduces national income and this in turn decreases demand for all goods and services, including shelter. This income effect was overlooked in analyses of the incidence of taxation made prior to the Great Depression because these analyses postulated the existence of full employment. The low rentals during the 1930's were not caused by an oversupply of shelter compared to the demand that would exist at full employment levels; housing was merely in oversupply for the demand at depression levels and the remedy for this condition lay not in further restriction of building construction but in an increase in all forms of consumption and investment that would raise the national income.

Under full employment, if a tax made investment unprofitable in one field or another, the investor would divert his funds to greener pastures. By so doing, he would tend to equalize the profits throughout the investments area, allowing for differences in safety and liquidity. A tax on one commodity, say housing, left open other fields for investment and merely diverted the flow of funds from one type of activity to another without altering the total. If, however, all fields of investment were made less profitable because of the tax, it was argued that the rate of profit (gross interest) would fall and thus provide less incentive to save. Just how a fall in the rate of either or both interest and profit will affect the willingness to save and invest is, however, a matter concerning which little concrete evidence can be adduced. Hence, it is in dispute whether property taxes on business or income taxes on corporations are borne by business units or shifted to the consumers.

Not much was said, in this connection, about the effect of the tax upon the national income because it was implicitly assumed that all resources would be fully utilized in any event. It is this assumption that we must now question. For we now know that a reduction of profitable investment opportunities without an equal diminution in the desire to save must result in part of the money otherwise allocated for investment being held idle. While this process would reduce the volume of capital investment and tend to raise the expected rate of profit if demand remained constant, demand does not remain constant. Aggregate demand falls as income falls, thus countering a shrinkage in supply with a shrinkage in demand. The immediate effect of a lower volume of construction is, therefore, to lower the national income and thus reduce the demand for all types of goods. With a declining volume of consumption comes a further shrinkage of investment opportunities and a further fall in the national income, as we have seen over the course of the business cycle.

Applying this analysis to housing, we find that when national income falls rents also tend to fall, thus making new investment in housing less profitable. Although the shrinkage in new construction considered by itself as a single item affecting the supply of houses would tend to raise rents if full employment were maintained, this fall in building activity may actually lower rents because in the absence of substitute investment it brings about the fall in employment and in national income and in the aggregate demand. During World War I, rents rose and housing provided profitable investment outlets which continued up to about 1927. Then, during the 1930's the volume of new construction reached low levels, and with it the national income and rental values. Because of unemployment, the rate of profit in housing also remained unattractive at the very time that housing construction was almost at a standstill.

We cannot know exactly how real estate taxes affect the volume of construction, but the effect of an item that raises the annual cost of shelter by about 25 per cent cannot be a negligible influence upon the willingness to spend for this purpose. The homeowner is induced to keep down his monthly costs by building a smaller house, and the renter has to be satisfied with accommodations smaller than he would like. It seems reasonable therefore to conclude that during periods of inadequate investment the heavy property taxes now levied tend to reduce the volume of new building and at the same time the demand for housing by lowering the national income and diminishing alike the share of landlord, tenant, and homeowner.

It should, however, be cautioned that local government expenditure of the revenues raised by the property tax is a sustaining factor in the national economy because it continues relatively steady over the course of the business cycle.[7] Such expenditures are not a net addition to total expenditure, because the taxpayer is obliged to reduce his possible outlays by the amount he pays to the state. But the tax and the expenditure combined also do not diminish total expenditure. The funds for city expenditures might, however, be raised in some other manner and when spent would still have the effect of maintaining the national income without the present deleterious effects on new construction. The objections to the property tax as a source of revenue are not arguments against city governmental services or a denial of their stabilizing effect on the economy. They are merely intended to show the desirability of raising revenue by means other than by a realty tax.

During depression, rents fall or are uncollectible, and the landlord's profits are diminished. In such a period he bears part or all of the tax. But the tenant is not happy about escaping the tax because he escapes it only because his income has been greatly diminished and he cannot pay it. If we take into account these dynamic effects of the tax, we can more readily understand why landlords believe they are paying it, and renters complain that it is being passed on to them. The correct view is probably that in normal or boom times the property tax is being paid by the tenant; in periods of depression, all or part of it is being absorbed by the owner. For the owner-occupier these distinctions have little significance. During normal times he pays the tax as an occupier; during depression he pays the tax as an owner. So far as he is concerned, it is an invariable burden. To the country as a whole, such a tax levied during depression probably further depresses construction activity, and through the multiplier effect creates further unemployment.

PROPORTIONATE AND PROGRESSIVE RATES

In form the general property tax is a tax proportioned to ownership of real property. We may examine briefly whether it would be possible under this tax to subject property to progressive rates.

A progressive property tax would have to be one of two types: (1) a tax made progressive according to the value of individual parcels, or (2) a tax made progressive according to the amount of property owned by an individual. The first type would levy a higher rate as the value of the parcel increased; the larger the farm or building, the higher the tax rate. But this would clearly be undesirable because it would merely put a tax upon size. A large building, even though equal in value to several small units, would pay a heavier tax. If it were carried very far, such a tax might cause a splitting up of land parcels and might create artificial restrictions upon the size of buildings. This type of progression has not been seriously contemplated, except in the form of homestead exemption which has somewhat similar effects.

It has been complained, on the contrary, that the existing property tax is regressive because of a tendency on the part of assessors to overvalue small parcels and undervalue large ones. Sometimes this indicates the existence of political influences that make for favoritism in tax administration and is therefore a matter for review boards. What is, however, sometimes overlooked in this criticism is that large properties are not always valuable in proportion to their size; large homes may sell at a discount from reproduction costs because they are no longer being reproduced or because they have high operating costs and are purchased by the owners only because of their low price and consequent low taxes. In this sense, the apparent undervaluation of large dwellings is illusory in the light of market values. However, it is also claimed that large houses are even underassessed on the basis of market values, which, if true, is a clear injustice and increases regressivity of the property tax.

Another objection to the property tax is that it is levied

against the owner of real estate regardless of his equity and hence makes no allowance for mortgage debt. If the owner of a $10,000 house were assessed only on his equity of, say, $5,000, the owner of the mortgage would have to be assessed for the other $5,000. A tax on the mortgage would, however, probably be recouped by the lender in higher rates. Mortgage money has been had as low as 3.5 per cent. If the principal amount were subject to a 2.5 per cent ad valorem tax, the net interest would be 1 per cent. Under these circumstances, it seems quite likely that either mortgage money would not be forthcoming or that the interest rate would be raised sufficiently to include the tax and the final incidence would be on the legal owner.

The agitation for the income tax in the period preceding its adoption was an explicit recognition of the failure of the property tax alone to assess the citizen according to his taxpaying ability. Two facts seemed apparent: income was derived from other sources than real property, and all income from property was not taxed equally by means of the property tax. The question is whether it could be so taxed. The earning power of business organizations is not proportionate to their assets. Valued on a cost of reproduction basis, the rate of earnings of different concerns may vary all the way from 1 per cent to 100 per cent per annum. Two property owners with the same amount of property but with widely varying income would pay the same tax under the real estate tax. If, of course, all property were assessed according to earning power, then an ad valorem property tax would also be a tax proportionate to the earning power of property alone, though not proportionate to total earning power which would include that derived from wages and salaries. The continuing demand for the taxation of intangibles during the latter half of the nineteenth century was a recognition of the disparity of earning power of corporate as compared to farm assets. Farmers saw that they were being discriminated against by the property tax because their income from property was low compared to corporate income. And in this judgment they were correct. The remedy lay, however, not in trying to tax intangibles but in enacting income and corporate taxes. A tax on property assessed according to its earning power is in reality a tax on earnings and can better be assessed directly.

We still need to consider whether the general property tax could be made a progressive tax on the property of individuals, every person being rated as to his total property and taxed at progressively higher rates as this total rises. Such a tax would be different from the present tax because it would be assessed against persons rather than against property. If the tax were levied by local authorities, each person would enroll all of his property regardless of the jurisdiction in which it existed and pay a progressive rate. Such a tax has never been attempted; and if it were, it would lead to evasion, dispersion of holdings, removal of the owner to other tax jurisdictions, and the creation of tax evasion colonies where rates would be low. Much the same has been done when attempts were made to tax intangibles. Such a tax could, however, conceivably be levied on a national basis as a tax on net worth. A tax of this sort would levy on the net worth of individuals at progressive rates. Each person would list his assets and his liabilities and arrive at his taxable net worth. Intangible earning assets would be valued by their earning power, money at face value, and physical assets by their cost of reproduction. Exemptions and progressive rates applied to this sum would come close to the original ideal of the property tax. Such a tax would, however, be difficult to administer because of the problem of valuation of assets and the inquisitorial powers needed to execute it fairly. It might have some advantage because it would tax idle as well as active wealth, whereas the income tax is levied only on fruitful activity and effort.[8] It is, however, probably unconstitutional as a source of revenue to the federal government.

In what we have just been saying, we have ignored for the moment our finding that the property tax on land is paid by the landlord or capitalized by the present purchaser and that the tax on houses may be shifted to the tenant. Our basic view then of the burden of this tax rests upon our concept of its incidence. Even though the land tax may have been capitalized by present landowners, it still does not necessarily conform to the ability canon. If a retired farmer gets an annual rental of $1,000 a year from his farm and that is his total income, a tax of $250 on that farm is equivalent to a 25 per cent tax on his income and must, therefore, be justified on other grounds than ability to pay. Even a tax on future unearned increments of value, though it merely takes for society what society has contributed, would still not be a tax according to ability to pay.

Insofar as the house tax is shifted to the tenant and the tax on commercial property enters into the sales prices of the goods sold, most of the discussion about the property tax as a faculty tax is misleading. For it is a sales tax on shelter borne by the occupier of shelter or the consumer of goods and does not burden the owner regardless of the amount of property he may possess. The house tax then becomes a tax on income in proportion to the amount spent for shelter. A uniform tax on consumption or a sales tax is a regressive tax on income because the percentage of income spent for consumption varies inversely with the amount of income. The extent of repressiveness of the property tax and its comparative regressivity to general sales tax is a matter that we will consider in detail in the following chapters.

7

Property Taxes
versus
Sales Taxes

alternative

The widespread use of sales taxes for the financing of state government is a product of the 1930's. Property taxes were heavily delinquent during the Depression and agitation was rife for reductions in these rates at the very time that state and local governments needed additional revenues. These were required to make up for the loss of property taxes, to pay for additional expenses created by the Depression, and to match federal grants-in-aid for social security and relief. It is primarily because of the dire financial straits of state governments and the particular use made of sales tax proceeds that the enactment of these taxes met with so little resistance.

It was known, of course, that they bore most heavily on low incomes and that as compared to income taxes they tended to restrict consumption at a time when it should have met with encouragement. Despite these objections, they were welcomed as a stable source of revenue with a wide base, and once enacted, presumably as an emergency measure, were continued for the most part through the war period when they raised huge sums and filled state treasuries to the brim. The effects of sales and income taxes during the war was to create surpluses in state treasuries and thus to damp down some of the inflationary pressure on prices. For that reason they were not harmful to the economy as they very well might be if so used during depression.[1]

The federal government uses excises to raise more total revenue than all of the state general sales taxes combined but has not resorted to the latter device either in peace or war.[2] During peacetime general sales taxes are unnecessary because the federal government can use the income tax; they are also politically unpalatable, and objectionable because they depress consumption as compared to progressive taxes. Although advocated during the war period when the latter objection was immaterial, they were still unacceptable to the Treasury in view of their regressive character and their probable influence upon the cost of living and the wage level.

Local governments, with few exceptions, have avoided sales taxes because of administrative difficulties and the tendency of such taxes to drive business away from local retailers. Municipalities have nevertheless benefited indirectly from state sales taxes through return by state treasuries of part of the proceeds, their further distribution as state aids, and their direct use by the state to pay for highways, schools, and other services that might otherwise have been left on the local budget. Sales taxes so used have accordingly decreased the burden that probably would have fallen upon general property and have also made possible some expenditures, especially for relief and social security, that might otherwise not have been made at all, to the detriment of those who were unfortunate enough to need them.

State general sales taxes, which raised only $7 million in the United States during 1932, grew to $632 million in 1941 and to $2,001 million in 1951.[3] Despite this increase in sales taxes, property taxes still raised about four times as much revenue as general sales taxes in 1951. Total property taxes this year were $7,926 million or 12.47 per cent of total federal, state, and local tax collections; whereas general sales taxes were $2,001 million or 3.15 per cent of total collections.[4]

Special excises are similar to general sales taxes in that they bear most heavily on lower incomes. Since, however, the consumption of alcohol and tobacco by income classification is not definitely known, it is impossible to say accurately what portion taxes on these commodities take of various incomes, except that it is probably a large amount and that these rates are regressive in character.[5] They bear, moreover, unequally upon different citizens in the same income bracket, penalizing the smoker and the drinker directly on that part of his consumption which he maintains by depriving him of funds that might be used for other purposes. In this sense these taxes are discriminatory and more unfair than a general sales tax.

A word may be in order regarding the justification of excises as sumptuary legislation, designed to root out bad habits and immoral consumption. There are some who hold that those who use alcohol and tobacco ought to be penalized for their tastes in order to reduce their use of the taxed commodities. The more virtuous citizens would not pay these levies and would thus be rewarded by the state for their excellent character. This argument may be convincing to casuists of a puritanical bent, but it can find no support from a fiscal viewpoint. For if the purchasers of these commodities adopted the tastes and habits of their critics, taxes on liquor and tobacco would raise no revenue. Such taxes may have some justification, however, on the ground that these commodities are often produced under monopolistic conditions, and a part of the taxes upon them may come out of monopoly profits and to that extent are not borne by the ultimate consumer. Selective excises levied on luxuries consumed primarily by the rich are not regressive to income, but they also raise little revenue. Because excises are used predominantly by the federal government and already raise large revenues for the states, they are not likely to serve as large additions to future local revenues.

SALES TAXES AS A SUBSTITUTE FOR PROPERTY TAXES

Any tax may be considered as an alternative to any other that might be levied. The revenue raised by sales taxes might have been collected through income, estate, inheritance, or property taxes. In any given situation the alternatives are generally limited to one or two, so that in effect the actual choice may be between sales taxes and lower expenditures, or between sales taxes and property taxes. What happens to be the feasible alternative is a matter of time and place, the tradition of the community, the complexion of the legislature,

and the influence of various classes among the electorate.
Thus in one state the possibility of enacting an income tax
or increasing the rate may be negligible, whereas in another
it may be very good.

We have already observed that local consumption taxes constitute only 1 or 2 per cent of direct local revenues and have
hitherto been insignificant as a direct substitute for local
rates. State consumption taxes are, however, assuming
increasing importance. Of total state revenues amounting to
$9,838 million in 1952, general sales and use taxes raised
$2,229 million or about 22.7 per cent, and all consumption
taxes combined, including sales, gasoline, liquor, and tobacco,
raised $5,729 million or 58.2 per cent as compared to 26.99
per cent in 1931.[6] This is the national average, which includes
thirty-one states having sales taxes and seventeen without
them; for particular sales-tax states, these revenues constitutes upwards of 50 per cent of the total.

Judging from the experience of recent years, two things
appear to be true: First, the sales tax, although used during the Depression and after to reduce property taxes in some
localities, did not generally result in any appreciable lowering of total property tax levies. Second, the proceeds of these
taxes were, however, used for new expenditures required by
state and local governments; and if they had not been levied,
either the expenditures would not have been incurred, or they
would have been financed by property taxes.

Whether, however, sales taxes are used to reduce actual
property tax levies or to make levies unnecessary, they raise
the same issue: how do sales taxes compare in their effects
to property taxes? Would a substitution of sales taxes for
property taxes be beneficial to the community, and what would
their incidence be upon the incomes of various income groups?
This question is particularly relevant at the present time as
cities are threatened with higher tax rates because of rising
wage and material costs. Numerous bodies have been study-
ing new sources of municipal revenue and many of these have
entertained the possibility of levying sales taxes of one kind
or another.[7]

The Board of Directors of the League of California Municipalities, after examining possible sources of revenue for more
than three years, came to the conclusion that sales taxes offer
the only practical solution as a revenue source which can
bring in sufficient funds to ease the increasing burden of property taxes and to support the municipal services required by
increasing population. Being reluctant to rely on state legis-
lative bodies, the investigators urged cities to levy their own
sales taxes, but stated that an effort be made to have such
taxes collected with state sales taxes so as to keep administrative expense to a minimum and to reduce the burden of
reporting on business men.[8]

In New York City, five hundred representatives of trade
unions, fraternal organizations, and veterans' groups urged
in February of 1946 the levying of a 1 per cent sales tax to
clear slum areas and to provide 250,000 dwelling units for
low-income families within the next ten years. This program
was adopted at a meeting on housing sponsored by the New
York State Liberal Party. Although there was strong opposition to the program, the Liberal Party said it would abide by
the decision. Proponents of the plan favored the sales tax
only as a last resort. They pointed out, however, that it would
yield about $33,000,000 annually to cover the cost of a $1,675,-
000,000 slum clearance program.[9]

These two examples do not and, of course, cannot prove
that the policies advocated are wise. They are merely intended to show that sales taxes are being considered as a substitute for property taxes and as a means of carrying on desired governmental functions that would otherwise have to
be abandoned. There may be those who can decide the merits
of a tax program without facing the alternative consequences. Such are the dogmatic opponents of any increase in
property taxes or in sales taxes, even if it means that the
poor starve or that schools shut down and city activities cease.
The votaries of such a view may put on a good face by advo-
cating the substitution of income taxes for these levies under
all circumstances. Indeed, if they were actually able to carry
out their plans, they would improve the tax system. But in

practice legislators do not have these alternatives. In the 1930's many state legislatures had to enact sales taxes or go without additional moneys. Faced by the choice of a sales tax and adequate relief or no sales tax and no relief, who would doubt the response of those governed by a humane impulse? When it comes to the use of sales taxes to begin slum clearance programs, the policy seems very questionable, but one would have to know all the alternatives before passing judgment on its merits. Many states have improved welfare institutions and educational opportunities in a way that could not have been done without the revenues obtained from the sales tax. The continuance of the tax thus is at least a popular value judgment in favor of the choice. In considering the advisability of any tax, we must compare it to an alternative form of taxation with the same expenditure, and also to the existing form and volume of taxation with the existing expenditure of the funds. Theoretically any number of alternative taxes could be used in a model and any number of alternative expenditures; in practice, however, it is necessary to work with fewer alternatives.

INCIDENCE AND EFFECTS OF THE SALES TAX

As with the property tax, a consideration of the burden of a sales tax by income classes requires some knowledge of its incidence. Such a tax may be levied upon the producer, distributor, or the consumer, and it is possible for any one of these three to bear all or part of it. Before it is possible, therefore, to consider the burden of the sales tax, we must make some assumption regarding its final incidence. We shall follow the usual practice by defining "incidence" as the effect of a tax on price, and use the term "effect" to cover all other repercussions. The chief effect with which we shall be concerned is the effect on economic activity: Does the tax stimulate or repress income and employment? But we shall deviate from the customary practice by considering both the tax and the public expenditure of taxed moneys in arriving at our conclusion regarding both incidence and effects.[10]

The tax we shall consider here is a uniform tax levied on practically all consumption goods at their retail value. For most purposes, it makes little difference where the original impact of such a tax is—on the gross revenue of the seller or on the pocketbook of the purchaser. A federal tax could be levied on manufacturers or retailers with about the same effect. A state tax, however, would have to be on the retail level; otherwise it would burden commodities sold outside of the state and leave free from the tax goods imported from other states.

Single-Commodity Tax

First let us distinguish between the effects of a tax on a single consumable and a general sales tax on all consumption goods. A tax on a single commodity will tend to raise its price by all or part of the tax. If the quantity purchased remains the same, total outlay will be increased and the consumer will bear the entire tax. If, however, a smaller quantity is purchased, the consumer will bear a variable part of the tax. How much depends on whether the commodity is produced under conditions of constant, increasing, or decreasing costs. Under conditions of constant cost, price will rise by the amount of the tax and the consumer will bear the total tax; under conditions of increasing costs, price will rise by an amount less than the tax and the consumer will be burdened by an amount less than the full amount of the tax; and under conditions of decreasing costs, price will rise by an amount greater than the tax and the consumer burden will be greater than the amount of the tax.[11]

A tax on any commodity generally reduces the amount purchased, the degree of reduction depending upon the type of commodity and upon the income group that buys it. Consumers who buy less of one commodity may, however, increase their purchases of another in an effort to maintain their standard of living. If, however, the tax is great enough, as say a 50 per cent excise on scarce commodities during wartime, the amount purchased may fall drastically without inducing the purchase of substitutes. In that case, the reduced sales leave the consumer with savings which he may hold as an idle cash balance or which he may invest.

The reduction in the amount bought because of the tax on any commodity may be (1) so little as to increase the total expenditure for that commodity, (2) just enough so that total outlay remains the same, or (3) great enough to reduce total outlay.

In the first event, it will decrease savings or decrease purchases of other commodities. In the second event, the tax will have no effect on purchases of substitutes or on savings, or it may cause the consumer to buy more of other consumables in order to maintain the same physical standard of consumption and thus reduce savings. In the third event, it will probably shift consumption to other goods in order to maintain living standards, or it may simply increase the amount saved.

A tax which reduces demand for a single taxed commodity may divert purchases to other commodities so that the total volume of physical consumption is not appreciably affected. It is in respect to substitution that an excise tax on a single good is radically different from a general sales tax on all commodities. For no one can escape a general sales tax by shifting his purchases to nontaxed commodities. The tax is ubiquitous; the consumer can only escape it by ceasing to consume at all; and since that is impossible, he can escape paying a portion of the tax only by reducing his total consumption and increasing his savings. For that reason we must give a general sales tax special consideration in order to see how it affects prices, total consumption, and total savings.

General Sales Tax on Consumption Goods

Let us assume that before a tax is levied "taxpayers" are spending 90 per cent ($90) of their income for consumption and saving 10 per cent ($10). The outlay before the tax will then be $90 for 90 units of goods at $1 each (Table 17, Line 1). Now a 2 per cent tax is levied on all consumption goods and these rise in price by 2 per cent.

TABLE 17

EFFECT OF GENERAL SALES TAX ON CONSUMPTION GOODS (CONSTANT COSTS)

UNIT PRICE BEFORE TAX, $1.00; TAX, 2%; UNIT PRICE AFTER TAX ON TAXPAYER'S EXPENDITURE, $1.02
GOVERNMENT EXPENDITURE OF ALL TAX RECEIPTS AT PRICE OF $1.00 PER UNIT

	Quantity Sold (Units)		Taxpayer's		Gov't Purchases		Aggregate Purchases		Transfer Payments	Income Payments
	Before Tax A	After Tax B	Outlay C	Savings D	Units E	Value F	Units (B+E) G	Value (C+F) H		
1)	90	90.00	$90.00	$10.00	0.000	$0.000	90.00	$90.00	$0.00	$90.00
2)	90	90.00	91.80	8.20	1.800	1.800	91.80	93.60	1.80	91.80
3)	90	89.00	90.78	9.22	1.780	1.780	90.78	92.56	1.78	90.78
4)	90	88.23	90.00	10.00	1.766	1.766	90.00	91.76	1.76	90.00
5)	90	85.00	86.70	13.30	1.700	1.700	86.70	88.40	1.70	86.70

Aggregate physical consumption (Col. G) is maintained at the same level, or higher, than that prevailing before tax in Lines 2, 3, and 4. It falls in Line 5.

Aggregate demand in dollars (H) is maintained at the same level, or higher, than that prevailing before tax in Lines 2, 3, and 4. It falls in Line 5.

Line 5 is the only one in which aggregate demand both in physical and value terms is reduced.

If the amount purchased by the "taxpayers" remains unaltered, 90 units will be sold at $1.02, totaling $91.80, leaving savings of only $8.20 (Table 17, Line 2). The government now has $1.80 in taxes to dispose of. Let us assume for simplicity that it spends these taxes for consumption goods. This will increase total consumption from 90 units of goods to 91.8 units. Thus the total effect of the sales tax would be to increase total consumption and to decrease savings. The incidence of the tax plus the expenditure of the taxed funds in the manner indicated would be on the consumer in varying amounts, depending on whether the various commodities purchased were produced at constant, increasing, or decreasing costs, as already discussed.

If the tax were imposed during conditions of full employment with the result mentioned in the last paragraph, it would shift part of the output from capital goods to consumption goods. Should it, however, be inaugurated during depression, to be spent, say, for relief, its net effect might be to raise total output of consumption goods with some additional stimulation to the demand for capital. We conclude then that the incidence of a general retail sales tax, under the assumption that the same quantity of goods is purchased, would be on the consumer and that its effect on output and employment would be stimulating during depression and, monetary conditions permitting, inflationary during full employment.

Reduction in Quantity Sold

The objection to consumption taxes is, however, that they tend to reduce the amount purchased. Let us therefore consider these effects under the assumptions that the tax tends to reduce the amount purchased by varying amounts. (1) The amount purchased would fall but only by an amount which would still raise total receipts, as shown in Table 17, Line 3. (2) The fall would be just enough to maintain total receipts constant, as in Table 17, Line 4. (3) Purchases would fall so as to decrease total receipts, as in Table 17, Line 5.

(1) If, at a price of $1.02, total purchases fall from 90 to

89 units, total expenditures and receipts would rise to $90.78 and savings would be $9.22 (Table 17, Line 3). The tax collected would be $1.78 which, after disbursement, would buy 1.78 units of goods, thus increasing total quantity purchased to 90.78 units, a net increase in consumption of .78 units. No repressive effect is found here in the tax accompanied by its expenditure. The effect on price after the tax would depend upon the considerations of constant, increasing, and decreasing costs already adverted to.

(2) If, however, total outlay of taxpayers remained constant, the amount taken would fall to approximately 88.23 units at $1.02 for $90 (Table 17, Line 4). As the tax proceeds were spent for consumption, total demand would be increased by 1.76 units to a total of 90 units and the net effect on total consumption would be just the same as if the tax had not been levied. Consumption has been diverted from one group of the population to another, not changed in total quantity.

(3) If, as a result of the tax, consumers reduced the amount purchased drastically as in wartime and outlay fell to, say, 85 units at $1.02 for a total of $86.70, savings would increase to $13.30 (Table 17, Line 5). Even if the whole tax proceeds of $1.70 were spent for consumption, total consumption would still be only 86.7 units, which would be 3.7 units less than before the tax was levied. Decreased consumption would be accompanied by increased saving if income remained constant. But to keep income constant would require larger investment with falling consumption, something unlikely in any except a period such as war or one of heavy desire for capital expansion. In expansionary periods the tax would reduce output of consumption goods and prices, and raise prices and output of capital goods. This is simply the diversionary effect. If, however, such a tax were inaugurated during depression and it reduced total consumption, this decrease, assuming operation of the deceleration principle, would tend to depress capital formation and thus to lower income and employment. It is this latter effect that is usually contemplated by those who contend that the sales tax is repressive to national income and employment. There are, how-

ever, other ways in which this same result would ensue even if total spending of taxpayers did not fall: if the proceeds of taxes were hoarded, used to pay principal or interest on debts, or otherwise distributed so that they would go to the higher-income groups who would save a higher percentage of them than would the individuals from whom they were collected.

Probable Effects

Having mentioned the three possible effects of the sales tax on prices, we must now ask which of these effects is the most likely. We might treat such a question by analyzing the possible effects of the tax on every commodity in the price index, each of which would have a different elasticity of demand. Thus a uniform tax might very well increase the consumption of some commodities, particularly those produced at decreasing costs, and decrease the purchase of those produced at increasing costs, thus altering somewhat the structure of the commodity market. But we must still face the question whether a sales tax would appreciably decrease the volume of consumption as a whole. Here we must distinguish between a large tax, say 20 per cent or so, imposed during a period of temporary scarcity such as war, and a continuous small tax of 2 or 3 per cent imposed during normal times.

A heavy wartime consumption tax would be expected to decrease the volume for consumption goods sold, because purchasers could contemplate the postwar period when the tax would cease to exist; they could also bear in mind the alternative of paying the tax and saving a similar amount. It must be admitted, however, that it would be hard to support this conclusion by a simple inspection of wartime consumption of commodities that were heavily burdened with excises.

A reduction in consumption expenditures as a whole will increase savings. What effect it will have on total income and employment depends on whether these savings are invested or hoarded. If a reduction in consumption automatically creates greater capital investment, as was sometimes implicitly assumed in classical theory, then the effect of the sales tax would be to reduce consumption, increase capital formation, and lower interest rates. If, however, it merely results in hoarding, then it will decrease economic activity as a whole, incomes and prices will fall, and the incidence may be on profits until firms are able to adjust their output to a lower level of expenditure. In wartime, of course, decreased consumption does not result in unemployment but releases resources for employment in war industries. Abstinence from consumption is not depressing to activity but simply anti-inflationary.

In considering the probable effects of the tax on consumption on aggregate demand, a line must be drawn between the effects on high- and low-income groups. Before the war about half of the national income went to 80 per cent of the families receiving less than $2,000 per year, and the other half to the other 20 per cent. Now let us assume that the high-income groups continue to buy the same quantity of goods after the tax as before it. This portion of consumption then remains constant and is supplemented by the expenditures of government or of the tax receivers. The other 80 per cent might restrict their demand; certainly those who are now consuming all of their income would be forced to reduce consumption, whereas the rest of them might split the difference between consumption and saving. The total effect of a moderate sales tax on taxpayers would therefore be only a small reduction in the amount sold, which, offset by expenditure of the taxes, might actually raise consumption above its previous level. In this way, a balanced budget would be stimulating because it reduced idle balances and increased aggregate demand. The incidence of the tax would still be on the consumer and it would be regressive, but its effects would not be repressive as would appear from neglecting expenditures. The important fact is, however, that a sales tax would be more repressive than expenditure of funds derived from income taxes which would come from the upper 20 per cent of the income group or from borrowed money. The main difference between this analysis and that made according to classical postulates is that we allow for the possibility of a sales tax hampering or stimulating total output and employment, whereas the effect of reduced consumption according to the classical theory, which assumed full employment at all times, would be to promote capital formation and lower the rate of interest without altering the total volume of employment.

It is, therefore, not simply a matter of taste or definition whether expenditure is considered with reference to the incidence and effects of any kind of tax, sales tax or income tax, because the results achieved by taking into account both the tax and the expenditure show any tax to be less repressive to economic activity than if the tax alone were considered without the expenditure. In the latter case, our analysis would stop simply with the elasticity of demand and the effect of constant, increasing, or decreasing costs on price. Such analysis does not lead to a large error in result when considering a single excise tax because, at best, only a very small part of the tax proceeds obtained from such tax would be spent on the taxed commodity, and this has a negligible effect on its incidence. This method is, however, altogether unsatisfactory in the case of a tax on all commodities where the proceeds are spent by different persons on all commodities in general. For such a tax may change the total amount sold and also the cost of the quantities supplied.

It should be noted that, by including in aggregate demand both the demand of the taxpayers and the demand of the recipients of government disbursements, we show the total demand for commodities need not be decreased by a sales tax. This result accords with classical theory which looked upon taxes as diversionary rather than repressive. It should not, however, be confused with incidence. It does not prove that the shifting or the incidence of the tax has been changed greatly from what it would have been if we had not included public expenditures. Unless business is depressed because of the tax, the incidence of the tax is still on the consumer, or on individuals in proportion to their consumption, and the tax is therefore still regressive. The only difference is, as we have said, that by including the total demand of taxpayers plus "tax-eaters" the effect on the total amount purchased and the costs per unit of producing this amount are likely to be different. In industries subject to increasing costs, the total cost of the tax to consumers is greater than it would be if the taxed money were not spent for these commodities; in industries with constant costs, it is the same; and with commodities subject to decreasing costs, it is lower. These modifications are not, however, important except where the tax itself is of a large order of magnitude.

The major change in the conclusions arrived at by consideration of expenditures is therefore not so much with regard to shifting and incidence but with regard to the effect on total income and employment. Should we consider, however, a sales tax of 20 per cent or 30 per cent which would raise forty or fifty billion dollars per year to be spent for war, armament, or other government expenses, or to be hoarded, used to reduce a deficit, or pay off debt, our analysis of incidence and effects would also have to be altered greatly. And what holds for a sales tax of this kind would hold to even a greater extent for the effects of progressive income and estate taxation. We are therefore justified in making our calculations on the assumption that a retail sales tax is a regressive tax.

Backward versus Forward Shifting

It has, however, been contended that the sales tax is not regressive but that it is proportional because it is shifted backward to producers and hence rests ultimately on the factors of production.[12] Professor Brown contends that, if prices remain constant after the imposition of a tax, total receipts after taxes will fall; hence the prices of factors of production must fall. Should, on the contrary (as is usually assumed), prices rise as a result of the tax, factor prices remain unchanged and the tax is shifted forward to the consumer. It is assumed that backward shifting makes the tax proportional, forward shifting makes it regressive. As we shall see, however, its incidence is independent of which way it is shifted. Consumers and producers are of course the same

persons, so that instead of saying that a tax rests on producers or on consumers, perhaps we should say that it rests
on individuals in their capacity as producers, as a reduction in money incomes received in the form of wages, interest,
profits, and rent, or in their capacity as consumers in proportion to their consumption expenditures. It is an error,
however, to assume that the direction of shifting alters the
incidence of a tax. It is a regressive tax in either case.

The ground on which it is asserted that the prices of all
goods are not raised by a sales tax is that it does not increase
the volume of money.[13] And since it is assumed that all prices
cannot rise unless the volume of money rises also, it follows
that factor costs must fall. There is, however, under most
circumstances enough flexibility in the monetary circulation
to permit the slight increase in the velocity of money necessary to make possible the higher prices.

But supposing it were true, as Professor Brown contends,
that factor incomes measured in dollars fell by the amount of
the tax.[14] Marginal costs also would fall by 2 per cent and
this would bring about an equivalent fall in the prices of
goods before the tax. The only goods that would be higher in
price to the purchaser would be those subject to the tax,
namely consumer goods, $0.98 plus $0.02 tax. Capital goods
would be tax free. Everyone's money income would be reduced to 98 per cent of its previous amount. Capital goods
would be priced at 98 per cent of the former amount; but
consumption goods, including tax, at 100 per cent. Thus the
tax paid by each income receiver would vary directly with
the portion of his income spent for consumer goods. A person with a 100 per cent consumption function would suffer
a 2 per cent reduction in real income; a person with a 50 per
cent consumption function would suffer a 1 per cent reduction in real income, because the other 50 per cent of his income that he spent for capital goods would go untaxed. Hence,
it follows that even if the sales tax reduces factor prices it is
still regressive to income because it taxes all personal incomes
in proportion to the amount spent for consumption, and this
amount is greater for low-income groups than for higher-in-

come groups. It is irrelevant whether the tax is shifted forward or backward, or whether the price level changes. The burden is always on that portion of income spent for consumption because it is the consumption function that is taxed. These results follow regardless of monetary policy which made possible either a constant, rising, or falling price level and constant, rising, or falling factor costs, because price levels, cost levels, and income levels are in fact irrelevant to this problem.

The tax does not alter the supply of the factors or the demand for them, and hence does not change their real value unless it actually decreases the total demand for output as a whole, and it cannot do this except by creating unemployment. A change in the money prices of factors is offset by a change in commodity prices and hence no change ensues in real factor incomes; the incidence is therefore not upon total real factor incomes and hence proportional, but upon that portion of income spent for consumption and hence regressive. Should, however, the tax be great enough to cause a fall in total demand of large proportions, it will create unemployment; a fall in total incomes and its incidence may very well be on profits and wages rather than on consumption. But short of such dislocations, this is a result not generally to be expected. We shall therefore assume that the sales tax is shifted to the consumer according to the principles already stated above; and since the proportion that consumption bears to income varies inversely with the size of income, the sales tax is a regressive tax.[15]

We must further bear in mind that a tax can be regressive without being repressive to economic activity under all conditions. Under the circumstances cited above, we have shown that a tax which transfers income can divert economic activity without repressing it. A progressive tax can have this result; so can a proportional or a regressive tax. None of these taxes, if spent, needs be repressive. The view that regressive taxes are necessarily repressive has its roots in the underconsumptionist philosophy of the business cycle. Since it was assumed that consumption taxes reduced consumption, they

were believed to hamper economic activity in an environment
where inadequate consumption was the factor limiting investment and hence other economic activity. A distinction
can, however, be made between an absolute tendency to repress and the relative repressivity of a tax compared to other
taxes. Again, assuming consumption to be the limiting and
strategic factor in a given underemployment situation, it is
quite likely that income taxes would be more stimulating
than sales or property taxes, even though the receipts from
each form of taxation were all spent. The spending of bor-
rowed money or newly created currency would, of course, be
more stimulating than the disbursal of taxed money. When
therefore we show that the sales tax plus expenditure of the
funds is not necessarily repressive under all conditions, we
do not thereby establish that it is a good tax. It is still regressive and, like the property tax, can be opposed on grounds
of justice alone. Of course, any tax whether on consumption
or property, if made high enough, may lose its diversionary
character and become repressive to economic activity. This,
however, is not only true of sales taxes but also of income
taxes. Just where this point is reached, and under what circumstances, is a problem which lies beyond our present interest. We conclude therefore that Professor Brown's analysis need not divert us from the view that the sales tax is regressive to income.

PROPORTIONALITY

By proportionality we mean the proportion that any tax
bears to the size of income or the value of property. A flat
percentage tax on all incomes is a proportional income tax.
A tax having rates varying directly with the size of income is
a progressive tax, and one having rates varying inversely
with the size of income is a regressive tax.

The proportionality of taxes may also be measured by the
manner in which they affect the distribution of income after
taxes. A proportional tax is one which leaves the relative distribution of income unchanged. Thus a 10 per cent tax on incomes of $100, $200, and $300 would make these incomes

respectively $90, $180, and $270, which is the same ratio. A progressive tax is one which makes the distribution of income more equal because it reduces the higher incomes by a greater percentage than the lower incomes. A regressive tax is one which makes the distribution of income more unequal because it reduces the lower incomes by a greater percentage than the higher incomes.

Property taxes are proportional to property, and sales taxes proportional to consumption; but, in effect, they both bear upon income inversely proportional to size and are therefore regressive taxes. It should be clear, however, that the proportionality of a tax is not inherent in its form. An income tax could be made proportional, progressive, or regressive just as sales taxes might be made progressive to income if they taxed consumption at steeply progressive rates.[16] This is, however, not to be expected for local taxation because the very purpose of sales taxes is to reach a broad base at a uniform rate.

A tax system could be made up of taxes of all three kinds and its net effects must be judged by the proportions that the system as a whole exacts from incomes of various sizes. Hence, a sales tax is regressive; but if it is combined with steeply graduated income and inheritance taxes with large exemptions, the net effect may be more progressive than another tax system composed solely of slowly rising progressive rates with small exemptions. What is significant, therefore, is not merely the type of tax but how steeply it is graded. For example, an income tax beginning with 1 per cent on low incomes and rising to 6 per cent on large may be less favorable to low-income groups than one with large exemptions that rises from 1 to 20 per cent, even if such a tax is combined with sales or excises taxes. No particular benefit accrues, therefore, to persons in low-income brackets simply by changing the type of tax unless the rate schedule is such that it alters the burden.

It is here that practical politics comes into conflict with scientific analysis. Liberal or progressive politicians are loath to espouse any form of the sales tax under any or all conditions because they find it impossible to explain their position to the electorate. So in practice they may argue against sales taxes and in favor of income taxes, even though what they will actually do is levy more property and excise taxes or even an income tax schedule that may be more burdensome to the small man than a combination of income, inheritance, and sales taxes might be. This is especially true since the war, when taxes on low incomes have been revised upwards drastically and have been supported by the very legislators who would never have consented to sales taxes even though the net burden of the latter might have been less. This being a question of practical politics and economic prejudice, we will let it rest there instead of proposing to legislators that they follow a program based upon an economic calculus that few will understand.

COMPARATIVE REGRESSIVITY OF SALES AND PROPERTY TAXES

A regressive tax may be looked upon as one that makes the distribution of income more unequal because it takes proportionately more from small than from large incomes. It is the degree of regressivity, or the slope of the tax curve, that determines whether one tax is more regressive than another.

The comparative or relative regressivity of property and sales taxes consequently is an empirical or statistical question. To make a comparison we must find the amounts paid by each income group, first by the levy of a sales tax, and second by the levy of a property tax, and then compare the two curves. In doing this, we are not concerned with the amounts now collected by each of these taxes. Obviously a 2.5 per cent sales tax would raise less revenue than a 2.5 per cent property tax and would therefore be less burdensome. If, however, we contemplate the two taxes with an eye to substitution of one for the other, we are faced by a different question: If the same amount of revenue is obtained by a taxing body by means of either a uniform property tax or a uniform sales tax, which of these taxes will be more regressive to income?

This is the question we shall examine statistically in the next two chapters. Before doing so, we may formulate in simple terms the nature of the problem. The proportion that a sales tax bears to any income is a function of the percentage of that income spent for consumption (propensity to consume) and hence subject to the tax. The propensity to consume varies inversely with the size of income and hence makes the tax regressive. The degree of regressivity regardless of the size of the tax will therefore be represented by a curve showing the percentage of income that each income group spends for consumption.

The regressivity of the tax on housing can be shown likewise by a curve showing the percentage of shelter tax costs to income, or more simply by the relation of income to the value of the dwelling used by that income class. Inasmuch as the size of the dwelling does not increase proportionately with income, this curve will also be regressive.

We may therefore accept two empirical laws of regressivity: (1) The proportion that a uniform sales tax on consumption bears to income varies inversely with the size of income and this tax is therefore regressive to income. (2) The proportion that a uniform tax on shelter bears to income varies inversely with the size of income and the housing tax is therefore regressive to income. This leaves the question: Which of these two taxes is more regressive?

8

The Relative Regressivity
of Property and
Sales Taxes on Homeowners

We are now ready to consider the burden of the property tax on persons of different incomes. Whereas the question of incidence and effects is of a qualitative and theoretical nature, difficult of direct empirical demonstration, the extent of the burden on income is clearly a statistical problem. Thus, it is generally known that the property tax is percentagewise more burdensome on low incomes than on very high incomes, likewise that a retail sales tax is more burdensome to the poor than to the rich; but it is not so obvious just how burdensome each of these taxes is to various groups. The percentage which any tax bears to income requires primarily only two data, income and the amount of the tax. Having obtained this information, we must next ask which of these is the more regressive, and the resulting comparison will give us the comparative regressivity of property taxes and sales taxes. This is the task which will occupy us in this chapter.

In 1950 total dwelling units were 45,875,000; of these 23,383,000, or more than one-half, were owner occupied.[1] A full study of tax burdens would have to take into account both homeowners and renters. The property tax itself is levied against the property, not against the person, but it must eventually rest either upon the owner-occupier or upon either or both the landlord and tenant. Although this study is primarily concerned with the levy on homeowners, a word may be said as to the data necessary to ascertain the burden on tenants. If the simplifying assumption is made that a tax on the building is shifted entirely to the tenant whereas the land

144

tax rests on the owner, consideration of the proportion that the tax bears to the tenant's income would require the following data: (1) the net income of the tenant; (2) the tax on that portion of the improved property used by the tenant.

From these two facts the proportion of the tax to the tenant's income could be calculated. Although this information would be desirable, it could be obtained only if the landlord computed and disclosed accurately the share of taxes paid by each tenant and if the tenant reported his income. These data are not, however, a matter of public record and must, therefore, be obtained by direct inquiry such as was made in the budgetary studies of the National Resources Committee for individuals and families in the United States.

Inquiry into the incidence of local rates on tenants and on homeowners in Great Britain has been made by Professor J. R. Hicks and Ursula K. Hicks on the basis of budget data gathered and made available by the Ministry of Labour, and rate data of the Ministry of Health.[2] This is possible in Great Britain because it is customary for tenants to pay the rates.

The data covered by this study, on the other hand, is confined solely to homeowners in the State of Wisconsin. Here the question of incidence is not raised because the owner is also the occupier, and whether he bears the tax in one capacity or the other would have no effect on its ratio to his income. It would, consequently, be frivolous to ask whether the tax is borne qua owner or qua occupier, though it would not be irrelevant to a decision whether it is wiser to own or to rent a home. For if the homeowner bears the tax as an owner, it means that he could have escaped it had he remained a tenant; if he bears it as an occupier, it means he would have paid an equal amount had he rented similar quarters as a tenant.

U. S. DATA OF NATIONAL RESOURCES COMMITTEE

The United States Department of Labor, in co-operation with the Works Progress Administration and the National Resources Committee, working through the United States Bureau of Home Economics and the United States Bureau of

Labor Statistics, made investigations regarding consumer income and expenditures in the United States for the year 1935/36.[3] In these studies consumer incomes consisted of money receipts plus an amount for the imputed value of an owner-occupied home. Expenditures were classified, and outlays for each item of consumption were shown by income classification in various parts of the United States. The items were then classified into groups, showing expenditures for food, clothing, housing, household operation, etc.

Housing expense for each person includes the money expense connected with the operation of a house, including rent for tenants and the imputed value of the home for homeowners. Housing expense (H) is then shown in two ways: as a percentage of the total expenditure (E) $\frac{H}{E}$ of each income group, and as a percentage of the income (Y) $\frac{H}{Y}$ of each group. The data is given for families, individuals, and institutions, and for all groups combined; but we shall confine ourselves to the family data.

Inasmuch as income consists of consumption expenditures plus savings, the ratio of housing expense to consumption will always be higher than the ratio to income except for those income groups which consume all or more of their income. It follows then that the ratio, $\frac{H}{E}$, for low-income groups will be about the same as $\frac{H}{Y}$. For higher income groups $\frac{H}{E}$ will always be higher than $\frac{H}{Y}$. It is not inconsistent, therefore, to say that $\frac{H}{E}$ is relatively constant for all income groups, whereas $\frac{H}{Y}$ diminishes as income rises, which is what the consumer expenditures study shows.

At income levels below $1,000, total consumer expenditure was greater than income, thus implying that these families were consuming savings, going into debt, receiving relief, or

TABLE 18

PERCENTAGE OF INCOME SPENT BY FAMILIES FOR ALL ITEMS AND FOR
HOUSING, FOR EACH INCOME GROUP

Income Level	All Items	Housing Money Expense	Imputed Value	Total
Under $500	149.3%	19.9%	9.0%	28.9%
$ 500–$ 700	112.7	13.5	6.4	19.9
750– 1,000	104.6	13.2	5.3	18.5
1,000– 1,250	100.6	12.7	5.4	18.1
1,250– 1,500	96.5	11.6	5.3	16.9
1,500– 1,750	93.8	11.5	5.1	16.6
1,750– 2,000	92.1	11.8	4.7	16.5
2,000– 2,500	88.6	10.9	4.8	15.7
2,500– 3,000	84.8	10.1	4.8	14.9
3,000– 4,000	80.4	9.6	4.7	14.3
4,000– 5,000	74.6	8.6	4.4	13.0
5,000– 10,000	64.8	7.5	3.9	11.4
10,000– 15,000	53.7	7.0	3.6	10.6
15,000– 20,000	52.7	5.2	3.4	8.6
20,000 and over	35.4	3.5	3.0	6.5
All levels	85.6	10.4	4.9	15.3

SOURCE: U.S. National Resources Committee, Industrial Committee, *Consumer Expenditures in the United States; Estimates for 1935–36* (Wash., 1939), Table 6A, p. 78.

being supported in part by friends or relatives. The proportion of current income going to housing declines from 28.9 per cent at the lowest income level to 6.5 per cent at the highest. The percentage expenditure for housing is thus inversely proportional to income, and it follows that a tax on the items entering into housing would necessary be regressive. The caution is necessary that the category of housing, as used in this report, is not, however, the same as we use it in our study, but includes many miscellaneous items necessary to housing maintenance and operation.[4]

Having shown in Table 18 that the sales tax and the housing tax are both regressive to income, we must now consider whether one is more regressive than the other. This can be seen from the comparative slope of the total expenditure-income curve compared to the slope of the housing expenditure-income curve.

If the proportion of income spent for housing and the proportion spent for consumption as a whole change at the same rate at all levels of income, the two curves will have the same slope. Consequently a tax raising a given amount of revenue on all consumption will have the same regressivity as a tax on housing expenditure alone. The data of the National Resources Committee show that housing as a percentage of total expenditure appears to be rather stable around 18 per cent on all income levels. If this were true, then sales and housing taxes would have the same degree of regressivity. (But compare this to our data below showing that the property tax is more regressive than the sales tax and remember that housing expenditure in the consumer study as mentioned in the previous paragraph includes "household operations.") Confirming Engel, these studies show also that all items of expenditure do not vary equally with income. Food expenditures bear a smaller proportion to total expenditure at higher-income levels; the proportion spent for housing, including household operations, remains about the same; and the proportion spent for practically all other items such as clothing, automobiles, medical care, recreation, furnishings, transportation, and education rises with income.[5]

Given this behavior of (1) consumption as a whole, (2) housing, (3) food, and (4) all other items, it follows: (1) a tax on all expenditure would be regressive to incomes; (2) a tax on housing expenditure including household operation would be proportionate to total expenditure at all income levels and, therefore, about equally regressive to income as (1); (3) a tax on food alone would be regressive to total expenditure and more regressive to income at all levels than any other consumption tax; whereas, (4) a tax on the remaining items of consumption (tobacco excepted) would be progressive to total expenditure and probably proportional to income; (5) a sales tax exempting food would be the least regressive of any sales tax. In fact, such a tax would be proportional.

The conclusion that the sales tax and a tax on housing and household operation would be equally regressive appears to conflict with our data indicating below that the property tax is more regressive than the sales tax. This conflict is only apparent and not real because the property tax is a tax on the value of the house, not on household operation. This being so, it leaves open the question of how housing costs as used in this book (Chapter 2) vary with total expenditure and with income. The general property tax is assessed only against real estate and not against household operation, and our calculations take this fact into account.

We turn now from general budgetary studies of housing costs as a whole to specific data showing the actual levies of property taxes by income groups. These data combine property taxes with special assessments for improvements in the belief that this method more accurately portrays tax costs.[6]

The average expenditures for current taxes and assessments are shown by income class for New York, Chicago, Providence, Columbus, Atlanta, Omaha–Council Bluffs, Denver, Portland, and for middle-sized and small east-central cities.[7] This study, like others of this series, was based on an expenditure schedule of persons who voluntarily gave information regarding their family budgets.[8] When the ratio of taxes is computed to the average income of each income class in these cities, it shows the property tax to be regressive. A comparison of relative regressivity of the property and sales tax based on these data furthermore shows the property tax to be more regressive for homeowners in the low-income brackets than the sales tax,[9] which agrees with the results of our study.

If, however, we compare Table 10, p. 31, of Housing Study No. 648 with our data, we find that the dollar amount of taxes levied in each income classification is less for these cities than we found for Milwaukee and Madison. The property tax–income ratio in Milwaukee and Madison accordingly appears to be much higher than in the other cities shown in the Con-

sumer Expenditures Study; whereas, the data for the small
towns is more similar.

Table 19 shows the average current taxes (special assessment omitted) by five different areas. The Chicago, Providence, and Denver data should be compared to our Milwaukee
results; that for the three "Middle-Sized East-Central Cities"
to our Madison results and the five "Small East-Central

TABLE 19

AVERAGE CURRENT TAXES ON OWNED FAMILY HOME AS A PERCENTAGE OF
AVERAGE ADJUSTED INCOME IN SELECTED CITIES, 1935–36
(WHITE NON-RELIEF FAMILIES INCLUDING HUSBAND AND WIFE,
BOTH NATIVE BORN)

	Chicago, Ill.	Providence, R. I.	Denver, Colo.	3 Middle-Sized East-Central Cities	5 Small East-Central Cities
$ 250–$ 499	......	.....	.....	12.05%	11.83%
500– 749	11.23%	.....	5.58%	6.65	5.91
750– 999	4.92	5.20%	6.38	5.85	5.06
1,000– 1,249	6.85	4.84	3.67	5.15	4.69
1,250– 1,499	4.92	5.66	2.98	4.57	3.60
1,500– 1,749	4.57	4.61	3.96	4.20	3.42
1,750– 1,999	4.23	4.83	3.80	3.49	3.60
2,000– 2,249	3.84	4.90	3.60	3.45	3.05
2,250– 2,499	3.77	4.35	3.28	2.94	2.66
2,500– 2,999	2.82	3.73	3.78	3.41	2.70
3,000– 3,499	2.69	4.23	3.96	3.31	2.39
3,500– 3,999	3.02	3.28	3.47	3.08	......
4,000– 4,999	2.45	4.81	3.15	2.78	......
5,000– 7,499	2.69	3.48	3.45	2.68	......
7,500– 9,999	2.29	3.52	2.63	......	......
10,000 and over	2.12	.....	.....	......	......

SOURCE: U.S. Bureau of Labor Statistics, *Family Expenditures in Selected
Cities, 1935–36*, Vol. I: *Housing* (Consumer Purchase Series Bull. No. 648;
Wash., 1940–41), Tabular Summary Tables 2 and 6.

Cities" to our ten small municipalities. All of these studies show the property tax to be regressive, although the percentages differ somewhat from those obtained in the Wisconsin study.

THE INCIDENCE OF LOCAL RATES IN GREAT BRITAIN

The statistical material for this study is found in the cost-of-living inquiry of the Ministry of Labour (1937–38) and in the inquiry into valuations of houses conducted by the Ministry of Health in 1938 for the Inter-Departmental Committee on Valuation for Rating.[10] A distinction is made between "formal incidence" and "effective incidence." The former term embodies the amount paid by the taxpayer without reference to the direct benefits he derives from local government by reason of the payment. "Effective incidence," on the other hand, is the general study of the effects of a tax including the benefits derived from it and the incidence on rentals, house prices, and the supply of houses. No "sub-normal" incomes because of prolonged unemployment, old age, or other disability are included in these data, and the incomes are restricted to a narrow range.[11]

The rates paid are shown as a percentage of expenditure which is a little less than income. For industrial households (cities) average family expenditure of renters varied between a low of $1,020 (£204 at $5.00 exchange rate) in the Southeast to $1,215 in London. The average rate payments varied between a low of $31 per annum in the Southwest to a high of $49.50 per year in London. (These amounts, it will be noted below, are for only one-third to one-fourth the property taxes paid by similar income groups in Wisconsin cities.) The highest percentage of rates to annual income is in London, 4.1 per cent; and the lowest is in the Southwest, 3.1 per cent.[12] The expenditures of agricultural households (renters) were much lower, rates ranging from $10 to $15 per year and about 2 per cent of income.[13] Thus the rural incidence of rates to income is about half that of urban areas, a result which is also found in the Wisconsin data shown below.

Homeowners, it is found, pay from 3 per cent to 4 per cent of their incomes in rates, the amount tending to be slightly higher everywhere than the ratio paid by tenants. The Hickses caution that these data are for the year 1938 and that during the war incomes rose without much change in rates, so that the "rate-expenditure proportion must now be far lower than in our calculations."[14]

They find, however, that the incidence of the rates is regressive in each of the areas and that the poorer the division the more steeply regressive the rates. The curves for all divisions showing the rate-expenditure proportion of working-class renters are, moreover, more steeply regressive at the lowest levels of income and tend to be less regressive at the higher levels.[15]

For middle-class households, the proportion paid by renters is about 3.8 per cent at an income of $1,750, falling to 3.5 per cent at $2,000 and to 3.1 per cent at $2,250, after which it appears to become proportional or even slightly progressive. For middle-class homeowners the rate proportion appears to be about 10 per cent higher than the renters' level.[16]

So much for "normal" incomes. The rates on subnormal incomes in York were double those shown above, running as high as 8.2 per cent of expenditures. In Bristol, based on independent sources, the incidence for renters with an income of $500 per year was 5.6 per cent. For homeowners the proportion was 8.5 per cent at an income of $500 per year. This would confirm the conclusion that the regressivity of rates is felt most severely by those in the lowest income brackets.

The higher proportion of homeowners' rates to income is attributed to the tendency of older people to remain in accommodations suitable to the period when they were more prosperous either because of inertia or because of the lack of suitable housing accommodations. When, however, a disproportionate part of income is spent for housing, other expenditures must be curtailed until such a time as the family reduces its outlays for house room to a level more in conformity with its income.

The regressivity of the rates by income classes in Great Britain is summarized as follows :[17]

Income	Proportion Paid in Rates
Under $1,250	3.8%
$1,250–$2,500	3.4
$2,500–$5,000	3.0
$5,000–$10,000	2.0
$10,000——	1.0

The Hickses' conclusions regarding regressivity agree with those of the Consumer Expenditure Study for the United States and with the Wisconsin data. But they show that the actual outlay for rates is lower in great Britain than in the United States by income class. The Hickses' data also are closer to the Consumer's Study than to the Wisconsin data, which show a much higher proportion of property tax expenditures to income.[18]

Except by inference, these authors make no comparisons of the relative regressivity of a tax on housing and one on other items of expenditure and, therefore, throw no light on the question whether a general sales tax is more or less regressive than a housing tax.[19]

THE WISCONSIN STUDY

The primary object of this investigation was to ascertain the relative regressivity of the property tax and the sales tax to homeowners in eighteen Wisconsin cities, villages, and towns. For this purpose, we obtained the net income of each homeowner and the property taxes levied on the home. (The tables containing the data obtained in this field research study are found in the Appendix.) Inasmuch as state income tax returns are open for public inspection in Wisconsin, income data were available in the offices of the Supervisors of Assessments of the Wisconsin Tax Commission.

After obtaining the income and property tax data, we computed the percentage of the property tax levied on the home to the owner's income and averaged for the three or five years for which the data were available. Each person was then classified by income, and the resulting data showed the ratio of property taxes levied to the income of homeowners in each income class. These data were computed for all of the homeowners in each community, except Milwaukee, where a one-third sample was used. The data were then combined to show the results for all towns together, for metropolitan Milwaukee, and for all of the cases studied. In each and every case they showed the property tax to be regressive and the shape of the regressivity curve was remarkably similar.

We were next interested in discovering whether a sales tax applied to the consumption of the same group so as to yield the same revenue as is supplied by the property taxes paid by this group would be more or less regressive. To obtain a schedule of the regressivity of the sales tax required data regarding the percentage of income spent for consumption of taxable commodities by each income group. Here we relied on the Consumer Expenditure Study of the National Resources Committee. Although this study did not cover the same areas as our data, we used the consumption-income ratios for comparable areas and applied them to Wisconsin municipalities. Applying these ratios to total income gave a total expenditure base to which a sales tax would apply.

Since our data showed the amount of property taxes levied, we could compute a hypothetical sales tax rate that would yield the same revenue from the same group of taxpayers. We then applied this rate to the expenditures of each income group and this gave the total sales tax that would have been paid by each group and the percentage that this tax would bear to income if it were levied in lieu of a property tax. This resulted in a schedule showing the sales tax–income ratio, which, as would be expected, was regressive. Inspection of the data for each case shows the relative regressivity of sales and property taxes.

We may anticipate our results by saying that in all cases this data showed that for the lowest-income groups the property tax took a larger percentage of their income than the sales tax, and that for high-income groups the sales tax took a larger portion of income than the property tax. For the middle-class group both property and sales taxes were less steeply regressive than at the top or at the bottom of the scale.

Another computation was then made to show the effect of a sales tax exempting food, which, of course, revealed that such a sales tax was relatively less burdensome to low incomes than a sales tax including this item.

The effect of homestead exemption was shown by deducting the amount of the exemption from the taxable property in each case and then computing the amount paid and its percentage to income. These matters will become more clear as we present the data below.

Throughout the study, we have assumed that the sales tax was borne by the purchaser and that the total property tax on both land and improvements was borne by the owner-occupier. The latter assumption is, of course, subject to the error that the tax on land may have been capitalized by the existing owner when he purchased the property; but the various properties in the sample were held for different periods of time, and it was impossible to measure the amount of the tax that may have been capitalized. It should be remembered, furthermore, that the capitalization of taxes merely reduces the price that the purchaser pays for a property. It does not alter the fact that, when he pays the taxes annually, they diminish his income.[20] It was, therefore, thought desirable to present and use for computation the total taxes levied on land and improvements, and then allow for modification of the results, so far as policy is concerned, by the probability that part of the land tax has been capitalized.

There is, however, another reason that it is desirable to include land taxes in computing the burden on income. The expenses of government are continually growing and, with them, the levies of property taxes. The increments of new taxes would be on both land and improvements and would not, of course, be capitalized unless present owners had already anticipated them when they purchased their properties years ago. All residential property consists of both the land and the structure. To eliminate the land tax for both high- and low-income groups would make little difference

in the degree of regressivity, since the land tax would be eliminated from the data throughout the income scale. The ratio
of land to the total value of residential property in Wisconsin is known to be about 25 per cent. However, as we have
shown, land values are a lower proportion of low-income
housing than of high-income housing. Therefore, if it be
assumed that land values are capitalized, the proportion of
income paid out as property taxes minus the increment capitalized is even greater for the low-income groups than for
the high. Regressivity is therefore possible even somewhat
greater than shown in our data.

Definitions

Before proceeding with the presentation of the Wisconsin
data, we shall define some of the terms used.

Income.—Income as used in this study is obtained from
Wisconsin state income tax returns. It is not identical with
taxable income, which includes exemptions, but is made up as
follows: gross income less deductions for (1) net loss from
the sale of securities, (2) interest paid, (3) net loss from
business or profession, (4) distributive shares of partnership
loss, and (5) other necessary expenses.

The income used was that of the family occupying the house
(usually the head of the family, either husband or wife or
both) and did not include that of children above eighteen
years of age who file independent returns. These were not
regarded as part of family income because children ordinarily
make a contribution for board (included in the income tax returns—minus expenses) but do not assume responsibility for
family maintenance. The error in these data probably lies in
the understatement of family income for several reasons.
The income of minor children is probably omitted from many
income tax returns. It is furthermore possible that the independently filed return of a husband or wife may have been
overlooked. And finally, income returns would tend to understate rather than exaggerate incomes. Since, however, the
last defect is inherent in all statistics of income, we saw no
reason to make any change in the official data.

The National Resources Committee, as we have already seen, has added to cash income the imputed rental value of a house in order to obtain the homeowner's total income. Income in this sense then consists of cash income as found in the income tax return plus net imputed value of the home. When this is done, total income is enlarged for all income classes, but the greatest percentage increase is on incomes below $1,000, and the extremely high percentages of taxes to income are diminished in this range, but the effect is relatively small for the balance and no substantial change is made in the general shape of regressivity curves or in the relative regressivity of sales and property taxes.[21]

The Indifference Point.—The burden of a tax on each income group varies with the type of tax levied. It is, accordingly, a matter of some importance at every income level whether revenues are raised by property or by sales taxes. At some levels of income, the property tax will be more burdensome, while at others the sales tax will bear more heavily. At some income level, however, the type of tax will be a matter of indifference to the taxpayer.

The indifference point is the income level at which it is a matter of indifference to the taxpayer whether the taxing authority raises the same amount of revenue by means of property taxes or by means of sales taxes. Incomes below the indifference point (low incomes) are, we shall find, burdened more heavily by property taxes. At the indifference point, both property and sales taxes take the same percentage of income. Above the indifference point (higher incomes), sales taxes take a larger portion of income than property taxes.[22]

Taxes.—By property taxes we mean the taxes levied on the home whether or not they are paid. This excludes special assessments of all kinds and personal property taxes.

By sales taxes we mean a uniform tax levied at the retail level on food, clothing, household operation, furnishings, equipment, and all other consumables except on gasoline, which is already subject to special excises. This is not an actual sales tax but merely a hypothetical sales tax that would

raise an equivalent revenue from the same group of taxpayers now being paid as property taxes.

Areas of Study

Madison.—Table A(1) shows the relative regressivity
of property and sales taxes in Madison, Wisconsin. The population of Madison (1940 census) was 67,447, and the number
of owner-occupied homes examined was 3,354. The data is not
a sample, but comprehends all owner-occupied homes in the
entire city.

Out of the 3,354 families owning homes, no income tax was
reported by 1,512 owners or their wives or husbands for any
of the five years 1933 to 1937. The average tax paid by this
group was $119. Under state law, all persons having an in-
come of $800 or more are required to report; and if they
report in any year, they are obliged to report in subsequent
years. It is possible that some of these persons had taxable
incomes and failed to report them and are, therefore, subject
to penalties under state law, but this seems improbable for
any large number. In order to ascertain something of the
economic status of persons reporting no taxable income, we
checked the city directory for the occupation of the owner-
occupants at a given address, with the following results in
the total of 1,512:

No occupation	633
Wage earner	502
Clerical	178
Business and professional	199

This group of "No Returns" has, accordingly, been eliminated from all of our calculations and, therefore, does not
affect the results. It seems apparent, however, that even if
some of them were tax evaders the average tax of levy of $119
on each of this group would bear a high ratio to their income.

The remaining cases consist of those who reported incomes
for the years under consideration. The tax payments of the
very lowest income groups actually reporting are an extremely high proportion of income, running from 23 per cent

to 88 per cent. Many of these people must have been spending more than they earned.

Table A(1) also shows the property tax to be more regressive than a sales tax raising an equal amount of revenue. The
property tax took a larger portion of the income of all taxpayers earning less than $1,871, whereas the sales tax burden
was heavier on incomes above this amount. We shall, therefore, designate $1,800 as the indifference point.

Although it is highly improbable that a sales tax would
ever be used to supplant the property tax entirely, it is inter-
esting to note that the average property tax rate of $0.02305
per dollar of assessed valuation would require a sales tax
rate of $0.1156 per dollar of sales to raise the same amount
of revenue.

Table F(2) shows that a sales tax exempting food would
have the same indifference point as the general sales tax, although it would take a smaller amount of money and a smaller
percentage of income of those below the $1,800 bracket and
a larger amount and a larger percentage of incomes above
this point. If then a sales tax were used in lieu of a property tax, as is done in some states, a tax exempting food
would be less regressive than a general retail sales tax on all
items.

Milwaukee.—The Milwaukee data shown in Table A(2)
differs from the rest because it is based upon a one-third
sample, whereas the rest of the data covers the entire statistical universe, all of the homes in the city or village under
consideration. The population of Milwaukee in 1940 was
587,472 and in 1950 it was 637,392.

Before undertaking the larger Milwaukee investigation
shown in the tables, we made a random sample of 123 homeowners. Out of this sample, half of the homeowners filed no
income tax returns in any of the three years 1935, 1936, and
1937, but paid an average tax of $116 on homes having an
average value of $3,863. For the remaining homeowners who
filed income tax returns, the average property tax ratio was
regressive to about the same degree as we later found in the
larger sample.

For our final Milwaukee investigation, we decided upon a sample of about one-third. The size and nature of the sample was primarily determined by the amount of funds and the availability of the data in the assessor's office. Because random sampling showed an inadequate number of high-income homeowners ($10,000 and over), we selected some districts in the city that we knew would give us an adequate sample of this group. As a result, we have a larger proportion of high-income groups in our data than would be found in the city. This does not greatly alter the representative character of the data, but it should not be used as an accurate sample of income distribution or of home ownership in Milwaukee. It must be confined to our purpose to show what portion of income is taken by each type of tax.

Of the 5,277 home-owning families investigated, 1,699 or roughly one-third filed no state income tax returns during the three years. They paid, however, an average property tax of $153. The breakdown of these will be discussed below for metropolitan Milwaukee.

As for Madison, the Milwaukee ratios show an extremely heavy burden on average incomes below $750 per year, 25 per cent to 144 per cent, thus implying that many taxpayers were spending more than their income.

The property–sales tax indifference point is reached in the area of average incomes of $1,628, just slightly lower than in Madison.

It is noteworthy that the property tax–income ratio shows little change between the $1,750 and $4,000 income level, while it is steeper below and above these levels. The same is true of the sales tax–income ratio.

The property tax rate used was $0.02997 per dollar of valuation, the equivalent of which in sales taxes would be a rate of $0.1284 per dollar of sales.

Suburbs of Milwaukee.—Table A contains the data for all homeowners in the following Milwaukee suburbs: Cudahy (Part 3 of Table A), population, 10,561; West Allis (Part 4), population, 36,364; South Milwaukee (Part 5), population, 11,134; Whitefish Bay (Part 6), population, 9,651; Wauwatosa (Part 7), population, 27,769. This table is on pages 207–19.

Cudahy, West Allis, and South Milwaukee are residential areas for factory workers, Wauwatosa for the upper middle class, and Whitefish Bay for the higher-income groups. Thus in Cudahy the highest income among the homeowners was one of $4,359; and in South Milwaukee, two had an average of $8,149. West Allis, however, had a larger percentage of high incomes; Whitefish Bay had 46 homeowners in the $10,000 and above bracket, with an average income of $32,453; and Wauwatosa had 30 in this bracket with an average of $18,469.

The point of indifference in each of these areas is as follows:

Cudahy	$1,367
West Allis	1,863
South Milwaukee	1,381
Whitefish Bay	2,353
Wauwatosa	1,873

The slope of regressivity in the low-income group and the tendency toward proportionately that we have thus far found in the middle groups holds true also for the wealthier Milwaukee suburbs, but not for those areas in which the lower-income groups reside.

In the less prosperous areas, Cudahy, West Allis, and South Milwaukee, the percentage of property tax to income continues to decline steadily at all income ranges with no exception for the middle groups as we found for Madison and Milwaukee. This probably indicates that the value of the homes among these taxpayers was adjusted to their incomes, whereas in Milwaukee and Madison many were living in homes purchased when they were on a higher-income level and consequently found the depression level of income quite disconcerting to them as property-tax payers. This appears to be true also of Whitefish Bay and Wauwatosa, both wealthier communities where the decline in the property tax–income ratio was at a slower rate in the middle-income levels.

Metropolitan Milwaukee.—By combining the sample of
Milwaukee with the suburbs, we derive Table A(8) for metropolitan Milwaukee. Out of a total of 8,087 families owning
homes in this area, 2,301 filed no income tax returns for the
years mentioned, but paid an average property tax of $148.
By use of city directories and other inquiry, we found the
economic status of a total of 2,301 of these "no returns" to be
as follows:

No occupation	1,282
Wage earner	659
Clerical	193
Business and professional	167

Random sampling also showed a considerable number of
widows and aged people among this group, and many of the
latter were probably prematurely retired during the depression years. This last statement, however, is merely an assumption based on general observation and not directly verified by our data.[23] We made attempts to find out whether
the "no return" had received any income from the State Department of Public Welfare in the form of old-age assistance,
aid for dependent children, relief, etc. But of 1,600 "no returns" for the City of Milwaukee proper examined for us by
the Department, they found only 85 who had received any
aid, thus indicating that the rest were living off capital, un-
disclosed income, or assistance from other sources. The burden of property taxes on this group must have been quite
heavy, but we have not included it in our calculations.

The regressivity of the property tax for the metropolitan
area is about the same as for the City of Milwaukee proper,
and the indifference point is the same as for Milwaukee
proper at about $1,628.

Table F(1) shows that a sales tax exempting food would
raise the indifference point slightly to $2,114, but that it
would also lighten the burden greatly on the lowest incomes
and increase it on the higher incomes as compared to the general sales tax.

Small Municipalities.—As examples of the tax burden in small communities, ten small cities in the area surrounding Madison were selected, as follows: Dodgeville (Part 9 of Table A), population, 2,269; Mineral Point (Part 10), population, 2,275; Evansville (Part 11), population, 2,321; Fennimore (Part 12), population, 1,592; Monroe (Part 13), population, 6,182; Cambridge (Part 14), population, 577; Edgerton (Part 15), population, 3,266; Mount Horeb (Part 16), population, 1,610; Stoughton (Part 17), population, 4,743; Sun Prairie (Part 18), population, 1,625. The data is combined in Part 19 of Table A.

The most significant thing about these data is the high number of "no returns," indicating that in these communities a substantial part of the homeowners had incomes too small to report (less than $800 per year). Out of a total of 3,715 homeowners, 2,757 who reported no income to the state tax authorities paid an average property tax of $61. This fact may be more significant than the ratios obtained from those who did report income.

In Table 20 we give the data on "no returns" for these ten communities. Out of the 2,757 cases for which no return was found, we were able to classify 2,240 by consulting with residents of the respective towns. This procedure is, of course, subject to some error in the sources of information, but it is the best that was available under the circumstances. The information obtained is as follows:

No occupation	1,514
Wage earner	342
Clerical	115
Business and professional	269
No information	517

The data for each municipality and for all of them combined show the burden of the property tax to be heavier on the lower-income groups than the sales tax. The point of indifference listed below is the income level at which it makes no difference whether the revenue is raised by the income tax

TABLE 20

"No Returns"—Small Communities

Municipality	Number of Families Owning Homes	"No Returns"	Av. Property Tax Paid by "No Returns"
Dodgeville	385	315	$43
Mineral Point	353	286	49
Evansville	382	231	51
Fennimore	317	251	65
Monroe	955	697	67
Cambridge	67	50	61
Edgerton	445	290	62
Mount Horeb	247	181	66
Stoughton	304	241	65
Sun Prairie	260	215	75
Combined	3,715	2,757	$61

or by the sales tax. Incomes below this point pay a heavier percentage under the property tax; incomes above it pay a heavier percenage under the sales tax.

Dodgeville	$1,397
Mineral Point	1,100
Evansville	1,137
Fennimore	1,561
Monroe	1,900
Cambridge	1,664
Edgerton	1,637
Mount Horeb	1,630
Stoughton	1,080
Sun Prairie	1,373
Combined municipalities	1,372

It is a significant fact that in these communities, quite unlike the larger cities, the use of a sales tax exempting food would hardly change the point of indifference. See Table F(3).

It is noticeable also that the average level of taxes by income groups in the small towns is only about one-half of that for cities like Madison and Milwaukee. This is due both to lower assessed values of home and to lower rates of taxation.[24]

All Communities Combined.—Table A(20) is for all communities combined. It shows that there were 6,570 families out of a total of 15,156 homeowners who reported no income for the period under consideration and presumably, therefore, had incomes less than $800 per year. They paid, however, an average property tax of $105. This group includes the aged, unemployed, sick, and indigent persons who lived on meager incomes or by using up savings and relying upon friends and relatives. We have seen that a disproportionately large portion of this number lived in the small municipalities and in the less prosperous suburbs of Milwaukee. Although the percentage of the property tax to income cannot be calculated for this group, it is, apparently, something above 12 per cent per year.

The amount of property taxes paid per family is relatively constant up to about $2,500, after which it begins to rise. This indicates the low-income groups must pay a disproportionate share of their incomes for housing and that the regressivity of property taxes is steepest at low-income levels.[25] The reason for this is apparently that house room cannot conveniently be reduced below a certain minimum regardless of income.

The average property tax levied for each income group is lower in the villages than in the cities, and the percentage of income paid in property taxes is also lower in the villages than in the cities. The point of indifference at which a sales tax becomes a heavier proportionate burden is also lower in the villages than in the cities.

On the whole, the data is remarkably consistent in this respect: In every community investigated, and in the average of all communities, the property tax bore more heavily on the low-income groups than a sales tax raising an equivalent amount of revenue; and a sales tax exempting food would push the point of indifference to higher levels of income, thus burdening the low-income communities proportionately less and the high-income proportionately more.[26]

Imputing Value of Home Ownership

All of the income figures used above are of cash income as reported to the income-tax assessor. A homeowner, of course, receives the shelter which his home affords, and this shelter has a cash value. Just what it is, we did not know and, consequently, did not include it in our estimates. Since this may underestimate the incomes and overstate the tax burden, we imputed to the value of Milwaukee homes an amount calculated from the Chicago study of the National Resources Committee. The following figures represent the income class and the proportion of non-money income from housing for all home-owning families:

Under $1,000	$150
$1,000–$1,999	174
$2,000–$2,999	221
$3,000–$4,999	306
$5,000 and over	534

When this is done, the heavy percentage of income taken from low-income groups is reduced, but the essential nature of the conclusions is unchanged. This can be seen by comparing Table A(2) with Table C. This procedure reduces the indifference point of property and sales taxes from $1,628 in Table A(2) with no imputed income to somewhere in the neighborhood of $1,400. What is true of Milwaukee would also be true of other communities, but the data was not completed for all of them. We conclude, therefore, that no important change in relative regressivity is made if the imputed value of homes is added to income.

Home Value by Income Groups[27]

The value of homes owned by income groups is shown in the Appendix by Table E: Part 1, combined towns; Part 2, metropolitan Milwaukee; Part 3, Madison.

Out of a total of 3,715 homes, in the small towns 3,384 or 91 per cent were assessed at less than $5,000, the greatest number (993) lying in the $2,000–$2,999 range.

Out of a total of 8,087 in metropolitan Milwaukee, 5,511 or 68 per cent were assessed at less than $5,000, the highest number (1,633) lying in the $3,000–$3,999 range.

Out of a total of 3,354 homes in Madison, 1,333 or 40 per cent were assessed at less than $5,000, the largest number being in the $5,000–$5,999 range.

This seems to show that the value of homes was lowest in the small towns, next in Milwaukee, the highest in Madison, and that persons having the same income had more valuable homes in the cities than in the towns.

Sales Tax Exempting Food

The effect upon relative regressivity of property taxes and sales taxes exempting food is shown in Table F in the Appendix: Part 1, metropolitan Milwaukee; Part 2, Madison; Part 3, combined towns; Part 4, all communities combined.

By comparing these tables with those showing the relative burden of these taxes with a sales tax including food, we get the following changes in the indifference points:

	General Sales Tax	Sales Tax Exempting Food
Metropolitan Milwaukee:		
Tables A(8) and F(1)	$1,628 income	$1,871 income
Madison:		
Tables A(1) and F(2)	1,871 income	2,200 income
Small towns:		
Tables A(19) and F(3)	1,372 income	1,372 income
All communities:		
Tables A(20) and F(4)	1,600 est. income	2,000 est. income

In presenting the proportions which various items in the budget bear to total expenditure, we saw that food bore a decreasing proportion as income increased. It followed then that a sales tax exempting food would be much less regressive than a general sales tax. This is borne out by our conclusions. It will be noted that the sales tax exempting food is almost proportional to income for all of the four groups for which calculations were made. The rate bears a constant percentage to incomes all the way from $500 a year to $10,000, after which it becomes regressive.

The conclusion follows that a sales tax exempting food behaves, for most income groups below $10,000 a year, much the same as a proportional tax on income. It is, therefore, less regressive than both the property tax and the general sales tax. For reasons of administration and broader considerations of fiscal policy, it should not, however, be considered the equivalent for all purposes of a proportional income tax. Income taxes, moreover, when levied are made progressive, thus avoiding any possible tendency toward regressivity.

Homestead Exemption

In recent years a number of states have passed homestead exemption laws which exempt a portion of the value of owner-occupied homes from taxation. Rental residential property and that used for mercantile or manufacturing purposes continues to be taxed without exemption. The effect of the law is, therefore, to favor one group—homeowners—and to discriminate against all other taxpayers with the avowed intention of encouraging home ownership.

Residential property comprises about 25 per cent of the total of all physical assets, and about 40 per cent of the total realty in the United States. In Wisconsin, residential property is roughly half the total real estate. According to the 1940 census, owner-occupied homes constituted 40 per cent of the United States total; in 1950 they constituted 51 per cent. It follows that such exemptions, therefore, affect about half the homes and probably less than one-fourth of all real estate. The immediate effect of an exemption of this kind is, therefore, to reduce the total tax yield. Regardless, however, of whether the total revenues stay smaller, are maintained at previous levels, or are even raised by the subequent levy of a higher rate, the portion of the total tax paid by homeowners is permanently decreased. If, furthermore, the exemption is a flat amount, it will reduce the burden of the small-home owner proportionately more than that of the owner of a larger house: an exemption of $1,000 will reduce the assessment on a $2,000 home by one-half, whereas it will reduce that on a $10,000 home by only one-tenth.

If the same total revenue must be raised from the same properties, the tax rate must be raised proportionately to the reduction in assessed values. To illustrate: Let us assume that before homestead exemption the tax base was $1,000,000, the rate was $25 per thousand, and total levies were $25,000. Now homestead exemptions reduce the tax base to $800,000, but the same total revenue of $25,000 must still be raised. This will require an increase of $6.25 in the rate to $31.25 per thousand.

The homeowner who formerly paid $25 per thousand on $2,000 assessment, or a total of $50, will now pay on a base of $2,000 with $1,000 exemption, leaving a net taxable base of $1,000. His tax will be reduced from $50 to $31.25, saving him $18.75. Compare this to the owner of the $10,000 home. He formerly paid $250 per year but will now pay on a valuation of $9,000 at the rate of $31.25 per thousand, a total of $281.25 or $31.25 more than previously. The effect of homestead exemption in a flat amount is then to increase the proportion of revenue collected from higher-priced homes, from rental properties, and from commercial and manufacturing real estate, and to decrease the proportion levied on lower-priced homes. In this sense, it directly favors the small-home owner.

Because homestead exemption decreases total revenues, it will produce a budgetary deficit if expenses are not decreased in proportion. If expenses are not reduced, either new, different types of taxes must be levied or the mill rate on general property must be increased.

Table G shows how homestead exemption would alter the amount paid by various income groups if the rates remained the same. The figures are hypothetical amounts showing how much this same group of taxpayers would pay if various amounts of exemption were applied to the properties they own. As might be expected, the lower-income groups would receive the greatest reduction in the amount of taxes levied and also the largest reduction as a percentage of their incomes. A $500 exemption would reduce the tax levy on properties owned by all those with incomes up to $2,500 by about 10 per cent; a $1,000 exemption by about 20 per cent; a $1,500 exemption by about 30 per cent; and $2,000 by about 40 per cent. The amount of reduction steadily decreases on homes of those with incomes above $2,500. At the $5,000 income level, a $500 exemption would reduce property taxes by about 5 per cent; a $1,000 exemption by about 10 per cent; a $1,500 exemption by about 15 per cent; and a $2,000 exemption by about 20 per cent. From this it seems apparent that homestead exemption would reduce taxation on homes owned by those with incomes below $2,500 about twice the percentage as on homes of those with incomes over $5,000.

Table H shows the effect upon total tax collections and the amount collected from each income group under various exemptions. These show that total collections on a $500 exemption would fall to 92.1 per cent; with a $1,000 exemption to 84.4 per cent; with a $1,500 exemption to 76.5 per cent; and with a $2,000 exemption to 68.6 per cent for the sample studied.

These data and analysis then show quite definitely that homestead exemption is a means of shifting the burden of property taxation from the lower- to the higher-income groups among homeowners and onto the shoulders of renters and commercial and industrial real estate. What, however, its total effect may be will depend upon what other forms of taxes are substituted for the revenues that have been lost.

PROPERTY TAXES AND NATIONAL INCOME

The ratio of the property tax to incomes would, no doubt, be considerably less at the present time than during the Depression when incomes fell drastically while property taxes fell somewhat less. Since that time, incomes have risen greatly and property taxes considerably.

The changing proportion of the national income taken by

property tax collections is shown by Table 21, Property Tax Collections and National Income, 1922–51. This table shows that, during the years of our data, 1935–37, the ratio of property taxes to income was in the neighborhood of 7 per cent. By 1951 it had fallen to about 3 per cent. This would indicate that the burden by income classes was on the average about twice as great during the years 1935–37 covered by our study as in recent years. The shift in incomes would, of course, not be proportional for all persons, being greatest for the lowest-income groups comprising part-time workers, unemployed, and those whose incomes have risen by more than the average. The ratios revised for present incomes would, therefore, probably show the greatest decrease in the percentage burden among persons with the lowest incomes where we found the burden in the 1930's disproportionately high. Such a shift would be in the direction of proportionality, although the tax-income proportion would still most likely be regressive.

In the State of Wisconsin, the total property tax levy in the year 1936 was 6.8 per cent of income, which is almost exactly the same as the national average.[28]

It must also be remarked that, since a rise in the level of incomes decreases the proportion spent for food, the degree of regressivity of a sales tax would also be altered in the direction of proportionality from the depression years to the present time. The general sales tax would, however, still remain essentially regressive.

Beyond these generalizations, I doubt the wisdom of venturing any further. The best way to find out the effect of the new level of incomes is to get new data, not to extrapolate, to adjust, and to revise the old.

PROPERTY, SALES, AND INCOME TAX EQUIVALENTS

In computing the relative regressivity of the property tax, we used a hypothetical general sales tax rate in each community that would raise the same amount of revenue. A property tax rate of 25 mills per dollar of a true assessed valuation is considered quite reasonable in most American cities.

TABLE 21

PROPERTY TAX COLLECTIONS AND NATIONAL INCOME, 1922-51

Year	State and Local Property Tax Collections	National Income[a]	Tax Collections as Per Cent of National Income
1922	$3,321,000[b]	$ 59,706,000	5.56%
1927	4,431,000[c]	77,429,000	5.72
1928	4,695,000[c]	80,397,000	5.84
1932	4,685,000[b]	41,690,000	11.24
1933	4,180,000[c]	39,584,000	10.56
1934	4,130,000[d]	48,613,000	8.50
1935	4,260,000[d]	56,789,000	7.50
1936	4,486,000[e]	64,719,000	6.93
1937	4,500,000[f]	73,627,000	6.11
1938	4,745,000[f]	67,375,000	7.04
1939	4,366,000[g]	72,532,000	6.02
1940	4,685,000[h]	81,347,000	5.76
1941	4,474,000[b]	103,834,000	4.31
1942	4,593,000[j]	137,119,000	3.35
1943	........[k]	169,686,000	......
1944	........[k]	183,838,000	......
1945	4,802,000[m]	182,691,000	2.63
1946	4,990,000[m]	180,286,000	2.77
1947	5,507,000[m]	198,688,000	2.77
1948	6,128,000[m]	223,469,000	2.74
1949	6,842,000[m]	216,716,000	3.16
1950	7,349,000[m]	238,963,000	3.08
1951	7,926,000[m]	278,400,000	2.85

[a] All figures in the National Income column are from the following sources: 1922-28—Simon Kuznets, *National Income and Capital Formation, 1919-1935* (preliminary reports, National Bureau of Economic Research; N.Y., 1937), p. 8; 1932-51—National Income Supplement, U.S. Dept. of Commerce, *Survey of Current Business, 1951*, p. 1950, and from 1953 Supplement, p. 6. [b] U.S. Bureau of Census, *Property Taxation, 1941* (State and Local Government Special Study No. 22; Sept., 1942). [c] National Industrial Conference Board, *Cost of Government in the United States, 1928-29.* [d] Estimated. [e] Leo Day Woodworth, "Importance of Property Tax in State and Local Tax Systems," in L. D. Woodworth *et al., Property Taxes* (Tax Policy League; N.Y., 1940), p. 8. [f] The 1937 estimate was made by the Twentieth Century Fund and the 1938 figure was estimated by the Treasury. Quoted by Alfred G. Buehler, "Personal Property Taxation," *ibid.*, p. 119. [g] Tax Policy League, *Tax Yields, 1939.* [h] Tax Insti-

TABLE 22

SALES TAX EQUIVALENTS OF PROPERTY TAXES

Municipality	Actual Property Tax Rate (1935–37) per Dollar of Valuation	Hypothetically Equivalent Sales Tax Rate per Dollar of Sale
Madison (1933–37)	$0.02305	$0.1156
Milwaukee	0.02997	0.1284
Cudahy	0.03172	0.1141
West Allis	0.02972	0.0971
South Milwaukee	0.02774	0.0825
Whitefish Bay	0.02510	0.1145
Wauwatosa	0.02686	0.1097
Dodgeville	0.02127	0.0583
Mineral Point	0.02922	0.0939
Evansville	0.02048	0.0663
Fennimore	0.02589	0.1044
Monroe	0.02263	0.0841
Cambridge	0.03130	0.0740
Edgerton	0.02334	0.0798
Mount Horeb	0.02173	0.0822
Stoughton	0.02611	0.0832
Sun Prairie	0.02826	0.0946

When sales taxes are levied, they run between 2 and 3 per cent, and scarcely ever higher. Because of these facts, the public may be prone to compare the burden of sales taxes at such a low rate with the known burden of property taxes, and thereby fall into a serious error. A sales tax raising the same revenue now raised by the property tax would, however, have to be much higher than those now in use.

The average property tax rate and the equivalent sales tax rate for the communities considered is shown in Table 22. From this it will be seen that in the urban areas where total property taxes are high, a sales tax of around 10 per cent would be needed to raise the same amount of revenue;

tute, *Tax Yields, 1940*, p. 27. ᴶ U.S. Bureau of Census, *Governmental Finances in the United States, 1942* (Wash., 1945), p. 27. ᵏ Data not available. ᵐ U.S. Bureau of Census, *Governmental Finances in the United States, 1951* (G–GF51-No. 2).

whereas in the small towns where property taxes are low, the sales tax rate would be somewhat, though not much, lower.

How does this compare to national estimates? In the year 1935/36, total property tax collections in the entire United States were about $4.3 billion. This was equivalent to a flat income tax (no exemptions) on all income of 7.38 per cent. We find that a general sales tax on all consumption except housing of 10.74 per cent would have raised the same revenues as the property tax,[29] and the sales tax would have been regressive according to the principles already known. These data tend to show the general reasonableness of the Wisconsin estimates of sales tax equivalents.

The families included in the Wisconsin data, omitting no returns and net losses, had a property tax levy as follows: All families earning from $0–$249 to $4,000–$4,999 annually, inclusive, paid a total property tax of $1,140,242 out of an income of $14,300,891, or 7.97 per cent. If we include the incomes above $5,000 (of which we have a disproportionately large sample), the percentage drops to 5.74 per cent. From this we may conclude that the property tax levy was equivalent to an average income tax of from 6 per cent to 8 per cent on all incomes without exemption.

TAXES AND THE SUPPLY OF HOUSES

Another way of computing the burden of the property tax is to ascertain its relation to the rental value of the homes for such property as is occupied by tenants, and the ratio of tax costs to the total housing costs for homeowners. Thus, if rentals or the cost of home ownership were $60 per month, the proportional tax expense would be 25 per cent. The question would then arise as to how such a tax would affect the demand for housing. Our Wisconsin data does not bear directly on this point, since it furnishes merely tax costs and not total housing costs. The Bureau of Labor Statistics budgetary studies do, however, furnish information on this score.

These show that the percentage of property taxes and assessments to the rental value of houses varies in different communities, although in all of them the curve is steeply regressive. Taxes took 18.3 per cent of the rental value of homes in twelve southern cities.[30] The average current taxes and assessments of a percentage of total rental value for sixteen different cities was 21.2 per cent. In New York City taxes represent roughly between 23 and 33 per cent of rental values. In Chicago the average was between 28.5 and 19 per cent; whereas in other cities it fell as low as 15–20 per cent.[31] In each of the cities there is a steep regression in the lower range of income.

In our analysis of housing costs, we showed that a property tax rate of 2.5 per cent on the value of realty was equivalent to about 25 per cent of the total annual cost of home ownership. Assuming a consonance between housing costs and the rental value of a house to the imputed income of the owner, we find that the property tax is equivalent to a 25 per cent sales tax on shelter.

We have already concluded that, if this tax were to be replaced by a general sales tax on all other items, it would require about a 10 per cent rate to raise the same revenues. There is little doubt that such a proposal would raise a great outcry; that a much greater tax on shelter does not do so we must attribute to custom, the failure of an adequate alternative source of revenue, and an apparent acceptance of the inevitable.

Some commodities, particularly alcoholic liquors and tobacco, already bear heavy taxes of this kind; but if it were proposed that a tax of even 10 per cent be levied on commodities in general, the objection would probably be made that it would be depressing to consumption and hence to the national income. Although we do not know the statistical coefficients of the elasticity of demand for housing, any more than we know it for other commodities or for consumption in general, it seems likely that an increase of 25 per cent in housing costs must have a depressing effect on the demand for housing accommodations. If this is true, then an increase in housing cost decreases the demand for space, lowers the volume of investment in housing, and, in addition to making

for low housing standards, probably has a depressing effect
on the national income.[32] In boom times or in periods of inflation after full employment has been reached, a reduction
in annual housing costs is less urgent than when material and
labor are available for abundant new construction. It would
seem, therefore, to be good policy to reduce the tax on shelter
at a time when resources are available in order to permit
such a reduction to stimulate the supply of new houses. This
would insure that reduced costs would be shared by the general population through lowered rentals, and it would create
increased demand for space at lower prices. As we have already mentioned above, tax reduction during periods of
extreme housing scarcity tends to increase the incomes of
property owners and the prices of real estate. When applied
to a good like housing that is subject to such a low increase
in total supply, the correct timing of tax policy may therefore be just as important as a policy correct in substance.

It follows then that a reduction in the tax on real estate
improvements during a period of high rents, material shortage, and heavy construction would inure to the benefit of
present owners of property, some of whom have already
capitalized the tax. It would not materially influence the
supply of homes or the level of rents. When, however, ample
material and labor are available, such reduction should stimulate new construction, increase total housing space, and benefit homeowners and tenants alike. It should, however, be
added that insofar as the tax reduction is made on land, it
will have no effect on construction, but will be capitalized by
landowners. When feasible, therefore, tax reductions should
be confined to real estate improvements if they are to have the
most favorable effect on construction activity. It is, however,
not certain on the basis of the data now available that a reduction limited to improvements would be in conformity to
"ability to pay," because it would probably increase the burden on farmers wherever they were taxed in the same tax
district as owners of other forms of property.

9
Methods of
Reducing the
Property Tax

It is now more than half a century since a consistent attack has been made upon the local property tax; and although other revenues have been used to supplement and even to displace it, this levy persists as the mainstay of local government. The vitality of the property tax in spite of its unpopularity, both among experts and the public, portends that it cannot be readily done away with. We may, however, examine various courses of action aimed at its mitigation and see which of them may be appropriate under present circumstances.

During the war, changes in the local tax structure deserved little attention; what was needed was more taxes of any kind. After the war new types of taxes were instituted in various states which diminished prospective property taxes. But this was also a period of intense demand for housing accompanied by general inflation and overfull use of resources. Since 1946 we have had a tremendous housing boom which has increased the total number of houses in the country by about 20 per cent. No change in tax structure during this period would have made physical production any greater because all resources were fully utilized. For a part of that time rent control existed in many areas and rents were below market equilibrium levels so that a reduction in property taxes would have inured to the owner rather than to the occupier of a house. Now, however, that the nation seems to be returning to a period when resources will be more freely available, consideration is also being given to the effect of the tax struc-

tures on the level of income and employment. Any diminution in the cost of housing may act as a stimulant to demand
and also be favorable to a higher national real income.

Regressivity and repressiveness are the two main disabilities of the property tax. Regressivity makes the tax inequitable and, under some circumstances, repressive to economic activity because it reduces consumption among the
lower-income groups. During periods of inflation when the
desire to consume outruns productive ability, a repressive
tax, though inequitable, may be useful. When, however, a
rising consumption standard is necessary to stimulate capital
formation, a tax which may reduce consumption retards economic progress.

The property tax, however, is repressive in the special
sense that it acts as a deterrent to the creation and use of
housing facilities, and this may have a depressing effect on
economic activity as a whole. How reduction in this tax would
affect total demand will depend upon the tax that is enacted in
its stead. If, for example, the property tax were displaced
by some other levy of equal regressivity, the change might
stimulate housing somewhat; but it would not change the class
distribution of disposable income. As a result, the repressive
effects would be shifted from housing to other commodities.
The elimination of some part of the property tax can have
favorable effects on housing regardless of its substitute, but
it can have the most favorable effects with respect to total
consumption only if it results in an increase in the progres-
siveness of the tax structure as a whole.[1]

The present tax probably diverts a potential demand for
housing into other commodities that are not taxed at all or
taxed at smaller rates. If, therefore, the same amount of
funds was collected through the use of an equally regressive
sales tax on commodities in general, it is likely that the demand for housing would be increased and that for other commodities would be diminished somewhat. While regressive
taxes are in themselves not desirable, if they must be used
something can be said for raising revenue by a small tax
on a great number of different commodities rather than by a

heavy tax on a single item because this is more likely to enable consumers to maximize their satisfactions. It is, however, not feasible to eliminate property taxes entirely; and
it would not be desirable even if it were possible, since that
portion of the tax resting on economic rent or quasi-rent
ought to be continued.

TAXES AND EXPENDITURES

The total amount of local taxes is governed primarily by
the volume of local government expenditure and can be diminished only if expenditures are cut proportionately. Waste,
inefficiency, and dishonest government are sources of unnecessary expense that ought to be constantly under attack, but
any considerable reduction in the tax load of municipalities
from these sources is quite unlikely.

Nor is it desirable to cut expenditures simply in order to
lower the tax load, for the services offered by a municipality
provide the necessities, luxuries, and amenities of community life. Drastic reduction of such expenditure regardless
of its consequences is just as foolish as a slashing of household expenses by a parsimonious housekeeper who has no end
in view other than the savings she can make. Adequate city
government, police and fire protection, health, education, and
recreation are forms of consumption provided for individuals
by the community and paid for by them collectively. Con-
tinual expansion of these services is prima-facie evidence that
they meet with a welcome response and are performed better
and more cheaply by the community than they could be by
individuals. Any attempt to reduce local taxes by slashing
such services indiscriminately is therefore unwise. It follows
accordingly that those who seek a reduction in property taxes
must provide some other means of procuring the wherewithal
for the conduct of local government. This may be done in
several ways.

New sources of revenue may be obtained by the municipality in lieu of the property tax. The state or federal government may levy new taxes which it shares with the local government in the form of shared taxes or grants-in-aid. Some

services, not shared by all citizens, might be paid for by fees. Or, finally, some of the functions now administered and paid for by local government may be transferred in whole or part to the state or federal government. Education, unemployment relief, aid to the blind, to dependent children, and to the aged are examples of functions now paid for jointly by the federal, state, and local governments. These and similar methods will be considered below.

Tax Limitation

Tax limitation is one of the procedures that violate the principle just described. It limits the amount that can be collected through property taxes without providing an alternative source of revenue. During the depression of the 1930's tax limitation by constitutional amendment was advocated in many states and adopted by Ohio and other states.

Tax limitation simply prohibits the levy of property taxes in excess of a certain specified rate. There is no doubt that such a policy effectively achieves its objective of reducing the levy on real estate. And if this were the only consideration of tax policy, the means used would achieve the end sought and no further thought would need to be given to the matter. But tax limitation drastically reduces tax yields and lowers the revenues of all governments dependent upon them. Governments then have the alternative of defaulting on obligations, impairing services, closing schools, wrecking the function of government, raising new sources of revenue, or going deeply into debt. In practice, each may happen to some extent. In Ohio, the revenues lost by tax limitation were made up chiefly by the levy of a state sales tax. Tax limitation accordingly is not a solution to the property tax question, but a radical device to force a solution. It is neither good economics nor political science to make decisions without contemplating alternatives.[2]

MUNICIPAL COSTS ALLOCATED TO HOUSING

The following list shows the proportions spent by 397 American cities on various functions during the year 1948:[3]

General control		8.0%
Public safety		23.9
Police	13.0%	
Fire	9.8	
Other	1.2	
Highways		7.6
Sanitation		8.1
Health		2.1
Hospitals		6.9
Public Welfare		11.2
Correction		1.0
Schools		22.2
Libraries		1.6
Recreation		4.5
Miscellaneous and unallocable		2.7

The bulk of these expenditures are, as we have already seen, paid for out of property taxes and are, accordingly, institutional costs not necessarily attributable to housing as such (see Chapter 2). It might be worthwhile, however, to see which of them might properly be attributed to shelter as an expense and which of them are only remotely related thereto. At a glance it would appear that, at most, the items included under public safety, highways, and sanitation are costs attributable to housing. Fire protection is wholly for the sake of property, whereas police protection is for the person as well. Garbage collection and some portion of highway maintenance are certainly an expense of living in the house. But these items, together, constitute about 40 per cent of the total municipal costs. From the viewpoint of cost accounting, there seems little reason to attribute to housing the cost of city government, hospitals, public welfare, and education. These are all desirable community services, but they are a part of community living costs and not a part of housing costs. It seems reasonable, therefore, to conclude that if housing were to be charged only with that portion of economic costs properly attributable to it, property taxes would be reduced very drastically.

It would, however, be misleading to conclude that realloca- tion of municipal costs can or should be made on the simple principle that the general property tax should bear only those costs attributable to shelter and that other taxes should pay for the balance. For, as we shall see, other considerations, chiefly governmental structure and administration, must de- termine the apportionment of the tax burden among various tax sources and governing units. Rather, we reach the nega- tive conclusion that the property tax ought to cover at least those costs properly attributable to housing, leaving open the question as to how the others ought to be financed.

Without attaching too much weight to this classification, we may allocate roughly about 40 per cent of municipal ex- penditures to inherent housing costs and the other 60 per cent to institutional costs which now rest on housing simply because the property tax happens to be the chief means of raising municipal revenues. If local taxes were allocated on this basis, the present property tax rate would be about 1 per cent rather than the existing 2.5 per cent.

LOCALISM VERSUS CENTRALIZATION

The origin and history of the property tax shows it never was intended as a device to tax property for those costs at- tributable to it; it was rather a means of taxing persons according to the ability theory (see Chapter 5). More re- cently, however, particularly after the extensive use of the income tax, it has been used because it is the only readily accessible and feasible source of revenue for local govern- ment. So long as local governments exist as independent, self- governing, administrative, and spending bodies, they must have sources of revenue. It is easily possible to devise schemes of taxation from the standpoint of pure economics that will eliminate the regressivity of the property tax and still provide ample sources of revenue. But it is not a simple matter to propose taxes that can be used by local govern- ments to accomplish these ends. Whenever, therefore, gen-

eral sales taxes, excise, or income taxes are proposed as substitutes for the property tax, it is usually necessary to move
to a higher governmental level where the states or the federal government makes the tax levies. After this is done,
administrative considerations and political pressure determine how the funds can best be returned to the local level.

But everywhere surrender of the taxing power by local
government to higher bodies destroys the independence of
these bodies and makes them dependent upon the will of
officials elected on a state-wide or national basis who may be
less heedful of the needs of local communities than local
aldermen or county boards. It also divorces the expenditure
of money from the process of raising it and may discourage
efficiency in local administration. When revenue and expenditure are completely divorced, in the absence of proper supervision, local government officials may make it their main objective not to do efficient work at home but to become able
lobbyists and manipulators aiming to wheedle larger funds
for their own communities out of state and federal governments. This tendency may be checked by making the basis
of distribution rest on some fixed rule of population or some
other accurately measurable need rather than at the discretion of some higher official. Even when this is done, however,
we must recognize the divorcement of revenue from expenditure, in itself, as an evil and not a good, a thing to be tolerated
only if other advantages are clearly apparent. Inefficiency
and lack of home rule, if not always a reality, are at least
fears that beset those who do not like to see local affairs
become too far removed from the grass roots which vitalize
them and make them responsive to the needs and values of
the people.

Local government is the closest resemblance to the ancient
Greek city-state and to the New England town-meeting, which
were the cradles of democracy. Many citizens look with appre-
hension at the centralization of government, its administration and finance, and fear that the evils attendant thereon are
greater than the presumed advantages of more efficient cen-
tralized bureaucracy. Local government is also a training

ground for democracy in which young men learn the arts of government, later to rise to higher stations in the state and nation. Local decisions regarding taxation and public expenditure are means of teaching the community how to choose among civic values; they enable citizens to be creative and active workers in a democracy rather than passive recipients of largesse from good government not of their own creation. Measures that would undermine local government or render local political life sterile are consequently abhorred by those who see a great value in this political institution.

The trend of the times has, however, been against local governments. The increasing complexity of economic life and the speed of transportation and communication have made the local community less provincial and less conscious of its prerogatives. The desire for better schools, roads, and municipal services has made local communities quite willing to accept state and federal aid and advice, much to their improvement. The most backward communities in the nation educationally, culturally, and physically appear to be those who have relied most on local government to pull them out of the morass.

A political or administrative invention is needed to perfect the instrumentalities of local government without destroying local initiative and responsibility, to enable the tax base to be broadened without making the new taxing power ruthless and the spenders heedless of the cost of raising the revenues. These are matters of administration that are now being worked out by experience in which central bodies set standards, give advice and guidance whilst leaving much initiative and detailed administration in local hands. There is no reason that human intelligence need be overwhelmed by such tasks of political adjustment. In fiscal terms our task is to devise efficient means which separate the planning and administration of expenditure from the raising of revenue. Inasmuch as combined state and federal income taxes are already high, and state governments are finding use for the taxes they now collect, it is needless to conjure up the fear that increased state and federal allocation of revenues might suddenly destroy the responsibility of local governments. With the lag in local tax rates behind other prices and costs, it seems probable that local taxes will rise again before they can be replaced by other sources, so that no sudden or catastrophic end of fiscal independence is in sight. Lower property taxes are likely to come very gradually, if at all, thus providing ample time to adjust the civic mind to its new responsibilities. There is, finally, no inherent reason that local governments must be reckless about spending money derived from other units, especially when they know that the funds obtained are limited and must be supplemented by local taxes if they are spent unwisely or extravagantly.[4]

New Sources of Local Revenue

The recent search for new sources of local revenue has grown out of the desire to maintain the fiscal independence of local government while at the same time displacing the property tax.[5] Efforts have been made to augment strictly local revenue sources to be collected by local authorities and requiring no approval by other governmental bodies.[6]

Table 23, which is based on census data,[7] shows the amount in millions (preliminary) and the percentage distribution of local government revenues in 481 cities in 1951.

TABLE 23

AMOUNT IN MILLIONS (PRELIMINARY) AND PERCENTAGE DISTRIBUTION
OF LOCAL GOVERNMENT REVENUES IN 481 CITIES IN 1951

Total general revenue	$4,813	100.00%
Collected by unit	3,843	79.84
Tax revenue	3,187	66.22
Property tax	2,416	50.20
Sales and gross receipts	466	9.68
Licenses and other	304	6.32
Charges and miscellaneous	656	13.63
Charges for current services	376	7.81
Special assessments	69	1.43
Other and unallocable	211	4.38
Aid received from other governments	971	20.17
From state governments only	872	18.12
From other sources	99	2.05

The difficulty of replacing any substantial part of the property tax is apparent from the small portion of revenue now raised by other sources. The bulk of nontax revenues now goes to special districts (school, sewer, water, etc.) which perform specific services for fees, whereas the special taxes go largely to counties and municipalities. In 1951, out of the total locally collected taxes of 481 cities, 76 per cent were from property and only 24 per cent from other sources.[8]

The thorough examination made by Hillhouse and Magelssen shows the nature of miscellaneous local revenue sources. Local taxes other than property taxes consist of income taxes, general sales and excise taxes, and many small items such as amusement taxes, licenses, motorists' taxes, parking meters, chain store taxes, occupiers' taxes, and special charges such as sewer rental, garbage and refuse collection service charges, and similar items.

In general, then, the search for new sources of revenue has been a great disappointment, and the failure to find such sources cannot be attributed to lack of diligence on the part of the searchers. Indeed such a search was foredoomed to failure because there are really only three common sources of tax revenue: property, income, or expenditure. All of the miscellaneous taxes mentioned fall into one of these three categories; and although the specific type of levy can find a multitude of variations, they all come in the end to one of these three forms.

Some have proposed the payment of special charges for each type of city service, such as sewer rentals, garbage and refuse collection. While these charges would then not be technically property taxes, in effect they would be costs of owning or using property and would have the same economic effect as property taxes. Nothing is gained therefore by substituting an indirect property tax for a direct property tax; what is wanted is an economic change, not one that is purely semantic.

Special local excises on individual items of consumption, such as amusement taxes and liquor taxes, also raise only small revenues and have less to recommend them than a general tax on consumption spread over a large number of arti-

cles. They are, furthermore, regressive taxes and open to the
same objections as the sales tax no matter what they may
be called. Thus the new sources of revenue used by municipalities outside of the income tax come in the end to special
forms of property taxes or sales taxes which raise only a
small amount of revenue. Their use consequently tends to
obfuscate and confuse the issues of regressivity and repressiveness without contributing anything to their solution.[9]

Some city taxes aim to tax the fluid population moving in
and out of the cities. These consist of travelers and tourists,
but predominantly of those living in the suburbs surrounding so many cities. These people use city facilities but generally make little or no contribution toward city revenues.[10]
In principle, any tax on these parasitical practices is to be
commended, although it would be better to integrate the city
and its suburbs.

Individual levies, such as those on theater admissions,
earned income taxes, gross receipts taxes, sales taxes, and
hotel room taxes, may serve the function of collecting revenue in the city from transients and those living in the suburbs.
Sewer taxes, on the other hand, may be used to raise funds
from tax-exempt property. But an admission tax is obviously
a sales tax, and a sewer tax is an addition to the property
tax. Except for their tendency to raise revenue from the
suburbanites and tax-exempt property, many of these miscellaneous taxes (sewer tax excepted) have little to recommend them, and their use can have little net effect in reducing the burden on shelter. Miscellaneous taxes, moreover, may
be classed as nuisances and are therefore undesirable administratively. It does not seem wise governmental policy for a
municipality to increase its tax collections by a few per cent by
imposing a host of local specialized nuisance taxes.

Local Income and Sales Taxes

If it be true that most of the so-called new sources of local
revenue are inadequate in amount and in the end are an
indirect or concealed property or sales tax, we may consider
next the levy of local income tax or a local sales tax.

Whenever the local income tax has been proposed by local government, it has usually met with opposition from wage earners and other low-salaried groups because it is usually made proportional or only very slightly progressive. The low-income groups (accustomed to the highly progressive rates of federal income tax schedules) do not seem to realize that the property tax is a regressive tax and therefore more burdensome to themselves than even a proportional income tax would be. When local income taxes were proposed in Madison, Wisconsin, for example, such an outcry was raised against them that the Wisconsin State Legislature prohibited their levy in 1947.

We have already seen that an income tax, which might have been levied during the 1930's as a complete substitute for property taxes, would have required rates between 4 per cent and 7 per cent of the national income. It would be nearer the lower figure during periods of prosperity and nearer the higher when the national income was low. Local expenditure has not risen as fast as the national income, so that the tax would now probably be closer to 3 per cent of disposable income.

Highly progressive local income taxes are not widely advocated because each local community fears that a progressive local tax would cause higher-income groups to move out of the city; and if such a tax were continued long enough, it might even encourage industrial establishments to locate elsewhere. These tendencies would not, of course, be as strong if every local community adopted like taxes; in that case, the incentive to move in order to escape tax payments would be only as great as the difference in the rate of assessment in the different communities—a minor matter. But should one community make a 1 to 5 per cent levy on incomes and adjacent or nearby communities none at all, mobility of large-income receivers would cease to be a negligible consideration. Since, in the beginning at least, uniform rates and assessments in all local communities are quite unlikely, rates on any local income tax must be kept quite low.[11]

Because of mobility factors and the fact that the income

tax is used by both the state and federal governments which can share their receipts with localities or make grants-in-aid, it seems unnecessary to use this device locally. Moveover, there seems to be no special merit to a local income tax as a means of preserving local independence when the same revenues can be obtained more simply through the same tax from other levels of government. If, however, this is impossible, the local proportional income tax remains superior to the property tax or the sales tax because it is not regressive and is certainly less repressive to construction activity. It furthermore ceases to be a burden upon those without income or with only meager incomes during depression or after they have reached old age and are living in retirement.

If both progressive and proportional taxes are impossible for local purposes and a regressive tax must be adopted, we may consider the relative advantages of local sales taxes and property taxes.[12]

Retail sales and use taxes ranging from less than 1 per cent to 3 per cent are imposed by New York City, New Orleans, Syracuse, and fifty-four California cities. A local sales tax has many of the same limitations as the local income tax, the chief of which is the mobility of the taxpayer: a heavy local sales tax would be burdensome to local merchants if other shopping areas were readily accessible. Since many cities are surrounded by suburbs that are fiscally independent and that would not join in a metropolitan area sales tax, those customers possessing automobiles would gravitate toward outlying communities for their purchases and thus escape the tax. In view of the probable adverse effect on local merchants and the administrative problem, it seems much wiser to have such a tax, if used at all, collected on a state-wide basis and then returned by some sharing system to the local communities.

If the sales tax is to be levied on a state-wide basis to replace a local property tax levy, we must return to the relative equity of the two taxes. What we have already said tends to show that a sales tax exempting food is probably less regressive than the property tax and would also be less repres-

sive to construction and to business activity. On the basis
of the information at hand, the burden on income of a sales
tax including food is probably not much different from that of
a property tax.[13] If, therefore, a sales tax is levied, it should
exempt food, and the proceeds should be used furthermore to
lower the levy on real estate improvements and not on the
site value of land. In practice a legislator may be forced to
choose, as he has been doing for two decades, between general
sales taxes and property taxes. In that case, he is likely to
compromise by levying a little of each.

TAX-EXEMPT PROPERTY

The laws of the various states specify which property is
free from taxation. Tax exemption narrows the tax base and
makes it necessary to raise the tax rate on property remaining
on the tax rolls. Tax-exempt property generally consists of
that devoted to charitable, educational, and religious purposes, and the property of the federal, state, and local governments.[14]

Putting tax-exempt property back on the tax roll would
require those administering these properties to raise greater
revenues. Churches would have to collect more from their
members; private schools would have to curtail activities,
raise tuition, or obtain greater funds from donors. Such institutions as the YMCA and YWCA would be forced to raise
rates or curtail services. Reducing tax exemption would not
alter the total tax load, but would merely change its distribution; taxes on housing and on business property would be
lowered, and those citizens who are interested in the churches,
schools, and charities now tax exempt would be obliged to contribute more for their support. It does not seem that this
change would alter the burden of property taxes away from
regressivity because the mass of people support the agencies
that now go tax free.[15] Removing the present public subsidy
to these activities might force curtailment of services and
make for a worse rather than a better community life. Balanced against this consideration is the tendency for large
concentrations of wealth to obtain tax exemption through

creation of charitable trusts, but what may be said on this score is just as true for income taxes.

It would be desirable if federal and state property located in municipalities made a contribution in lieu of property taxes levied at the full value of the property. It does not seem reasonable, however, that a local community should collect heavy taxes, far beyond the cost of service rendered, from such institutions as the state capitol, the state university, and other institutions which partake of the character of public monuments. Public housing should be assessed and taxed the same as private housing. Since state and federal tax sources are now predominantly income, corporation, excise, and sales taxes, payments in lieu of taxes would shift the burden to these other forms and thereby lessen the repressiveness of property taxes. On the whole, the tendency would be also toward less regressivity.

Homestead Exemptions

During the 1930's a number of states passed homestead exemption acts. These acts exempted all or part of the value of a homestead from taxation. A homestead was defined as a home occupied by its owner. It does not include rental property. Some of the acts exempted homesteads from state taxes; others, from both state and local taxes. In 1930, Vermont was the only state exempting homesteads from taxation: the exemption was limited to $5,000 and was applied to all taxation with the exception of state taxes on dwelling houses erected after April 1, 1929. By 1937, fourteen states had passed laws providing for exemptions, and two had passed constitutional amendments.

A flat exemption of $1,000 to $2,000 per homestead will reduce the tax base; and if the lost revenue is not obtained from other sources, a higher rate is needed on the rest of the tax base. As we have already shown, a flat exemption will benefit the small-income homeowner proportionately more than the large-income owner. It will also shift a larger portion of the tax to rental property and to commercial and industrial property. Assuming that the latter forms of property can carry the additional load, it still leaves open the question whether this form of discrimination against rental property is equitable to the tenant who must pay increased rentals.

Homestead exemption is furthermore undesirable because it discriminates against multi-family dwelling units occupied by tenants which can be erected at decreasing costs per unit of living space. Under these laws, multiple units of this kind would bear a heavier tax and would therefore be discouraged as against single-family, owner-occupied small houses. Homestead exemption thus militates against adequate housing for low-income groups on two grounds: it discourages the type of dwelling construction that can be erected at lowest unit cost; and, since it discriminates against rental properties, it burdens the tenants who must live in them. In general, it is a means of favoring those in moderate circumstances who own their own homes at the expense of both the lower-income groups who rent their homes and of the higher-income groups who own more expensive establishments. Since the latter result is one of its objectives and would reduce the regressivity of the tax as well, only the burden on renters and the inhibition to large-scale building remain as decisive objections to this procedure. Homestead exemption is not a desirable method of eliminating regressivity in the tax system. A better result can be achieved by a flat exemption on each dwelling unit, which we shall now describe.

A Dwelling-Unit Exemption

A dwelling-unit exemption is better than homestead exemption. It should be a flat exemption on every residential unit regardless of the size of the building, ownership, or occupancy. With this type of exemption, the discrimination against renters and multi-family dwellings implicit in homestead exemption would be removed. At the same time, the regressivity of the property would be lessened because a larger proportion of the tax load would be carried by owners of large residences and by commercial and industrial real estate (as described in Chapter 8).

A dwelling-unit exemption would also be stimulating to

residential construction for the lower-income groups. If, for example, the exemption for a single-family dwelling were $1,000, the exemption for a two-family dwelling could be $2,000, and for multi-family apartments of a given size the exemption would be computed by the unit exemption multiplied by the number of units. Apartment exemptions could be made on a sliding scale, increasing with the size of the apartment but at a decreasing rate. All residential property would thus benefit in proportion to the number of dwelling units contained, and no penalty would be placed on large-scale building. It should be noted that a dwelling-unit exemption would diminish the regressivity of the property tax; but since it would merely redistribute the tax load on housing without diminishing the total, the property tax would still remain as repressive to new construction. The device here under consideration would therefore diminish the regressivity but not the repressiveness of the property tax. If, however, the loss of revenue from the initial exemption were made up by other forms of taxation, the total burden on all property would also be decreased.

In order to encourage construction, some states have exempted new construction from taxation for a limited number of years. Exemptions on new buildings and other special financial encouragements to new construction are unfair and discriminatory against existing property. For municipal expenses must be paid; and if the owners of new construction make no contribution, the owners of old property must pay so much more. This discrimination will stimulate new building temporarily; but since it depresses the value of existing property, it constitutes a transfer of wealth from old to new owners as a bonus to encourage new construction. Viewed in another light, such transfers are a subsidy to new building paid by the owners of existing buildings. Such policies must, by their very nature, be a temporary rather than a permanent part of the tax structure because their continuation would be self-destructive; old property would be permitted to depreciate and deteriorate and eventually become unavailable as a tax base, while the new valuable property would be tax exempt. The only exemption that can be recommended, therefore, is one based on the dwelling unit regardless of whether it be owner-occupied or rental property, or whether it be old or new.

REDISTRIBUTION OF GOVERNMENTAL FUNCTIONS AND COSTS

Higher levels of government have been assuming an increasing proportion of costs that would otherwise have fallen on local government by three devices: (1) the reallocation of functions, (2) the use of shared taxes, and (3) grants-in-aid.[16]

Reallocation of Functions

Both our federal and local systems of government were created before many of their present-day functions existed, and the allocation of costs and responsibilities for these functions is largely a historical or traditional matter. Still they can be examined on rational grounds to determine who ought to be responsible for each function under present-day conditions and who ought to bear their cost. If a function can best be performed by local authorities, its actual execution should remain with them; whereas if it can better be performed by state or federal agencies, there are prima-facie grounds for making this transfer. Even though the financial burden usually has gone along with the making of policy and its administration, this relation need not always exist; one authority may execute the function, another raise the taxes to pay for it. This is the general principle which may serve as a guide to action—subject, of course, to the limitations arising from the separation of taxing from spending already adverted to above.

Reallocation of financial responsibility sometimes has, sometimes has not, moved together with changes in administrative responsibility. Some states now assume the main burden of assistance to the indigent but leave administration in local hands. During the Depression the federal government inaugurated the Works Progress Administration with federally supervised aid used jointly with local contributions to finances and administration. Some states have made assistance to the aged, to the blind, and to dependent children a state financial responsibility, whereas others put both the administration and a large part of the cost upon local units of government. Similar changes have taken place regarding a part of highway expense.

Shared Taxes and Grants-In-Aid

Assistance to local governments can be provided through the instruments of shared taxes and grants-in-aid. Tax sharing is a device whereby the state collects a given tax and distributes the entire proceeds or, more commonly, shares the proceeds with local units of government. The state may levy an income tax or a sales tax and redistribute the funds to the localities where the funds were collected. Some states return to municipalities a part of the income taxes collected in the locality as well as a portion of liquor and other excises. One of the objections found to this device is that some wealthy communities receive large returns from state-collected income taxes which enable them to reduce property taxes drastically, whilst other poorer communities receive little proportionate aid and are compelled to continue excessively high property tax rates.[17]

Grants-in-aid are appropriations made by the state and federal governments to lesser governmental units for the performance of specific service. These aids differ from shared taxes in that they are not dependent upon the yield of any specific tax but come out of the general revenues of the appropriating government. Thus federal grants-in-aid may be paid out of funds obtained from deficit financing when tax receipts are insufficient to defray expenditures. A grant-in-aid may be made directly to a state or local government without any standards of expenditure, or it may be accompanied by provisions detailing the type of expenditure and the standards of administration, depending upon whether its objective is primarily to provide financial aid or to improve the standards of local services and administration. Some federal aids are those for agricultural colleges, experiment stations, forest conservation work, highways, vocational education, vocational rehabilitation, unemployment relief, public unemployment service, public health and welfare service, aids to the aged, to the blind, and to dependents under the Social Security Act, and the administration of unemployment compensation.

The federal government is generally on the paying end and local governments on the receiving end of fiscal aids; the states are in between, participating both in paying and receiving, but they pay much more in aid than they receive, as shown by the following tabulation of fiscal aid in 1951:[18]

	Federal	State	Local
Aid paid	$2,393,000,000	$4,702,000,000	$ 514,000,000
Aid received	none	2,508,000,000	4,789,000,000

Compared with nineteen years earlier, federal aid has increased about seven times and state aid has quadrupled; and the tendency is continuing in this direction.

The aids to local government paid by the federal and state governments approximating $2,600,000,000 ($837,000,000, federal; $1,749,000,000, state) were paid primarily for three main categories of local expenditure: public assistance, highways, and education.[19]

Education.—The difference between financial responsibility and functional control is well illustrated by the response to the questions asked of a hundred or so professors of finance. When asked whether they favored an increase of federal control over education, 25 answered "Yes," and 82 said "No." When asked whether they favored an increase in financial support for education by the federal government and a decrease for states, 56 said "Yes," and 50 said "No."[20] That is, many favored increased federal financial aid without increased federal control. To decide where the functional responsibility for education shall lie as between the various levels of government is a broad question of political, administrative, and educational philosophy. Fortunately we need not answer it in order to decide whether local financial responsibility for education should be decreased.

Thus far the federal government has assumed very little responsibility for either the functions or finances of education, and whether it should do so is now a subject of much debate. Many educational leaders have proposed large federal aids to education, but thus far a number of questions remain undecided. Should this aid be extended only to public or as well to private schools? Should the distribution be made according to population, to wealth, to existing facilities, or to need? So far as the states are concerned the wisdom of separating financial responsibility and state control need not arise. Most states already supervise the educational system and lay down standards to be observed by local communities. They also render financial support to these schools out of funds collected by the state.

Property taxes levied for school purpose comprise the heaviest single item in most municipal budgets, and a substantial reduction in these taxes would be possible if the states concerned would increase their assistance to local communities according to already known principles. Payment by the states of all of the local school costs would reduce the property tax from 25 per cent to 40 per cent in many areas. Although such a heavy assumption of responsibility is not in prospect, yet it suggests that great progress in ameliorating the local tax burden could be achieved by having the state pay a large share of educational costs. The chief obstacle to this policy in this as in most other cases is, of course, the necessity of raising more revenues by the state legislature. Such a policy, it should be noted, would not, however, increase total revenues of state and local governments, but merely shift the source of revenue and the collecting agency. It would force the state legislatures to lay on taxes rather than councilmen and county boards.

Highways.—Federal highway construction and grants-in-aid for highway construction reach far back into American history; and by 1930, 75 per cent of all federal grants-in-aid were for highway purposes. Federal grants are made for new construction of through highways selected by state highway departments with the approval of the United States Bureau of Public Roads. These grants generally require matching by the state. Ordinarily this arrangement works satisfactorily, but it is ill adapted to cyclical business conditions. When materials and labor are scarce, it might be wise for states to delay new construction, but the threatened loss of federal aids causes them to expand activity (which might be carried on during less prosperous times) and thus contributes to inflationary pressure. In general, federal aids contribute to a decreased burden on the property owner chiefly in the country, where they provide ample highways that might not otherwise be available.

State gasoline and motor vehicle taxes are the main sources of support of local highway construction, maintenance, and repairs. These taxes are, however, largely allocated to through trunk highways such as state highways, county highways, and town roads which receive a larger share of gasoline tax and license revenues than is justified by their share of the total traffic. City and village streets consequently obtain a much smaller proportion than traffic warrants.

Present federal and state highway policies have given a disproportionate share of support to roads out in the country for both construction and maintenance. Since these costs would otherwise fall on local property, their elimination raises the net income of adjoining land and increases economic rent and land values. By giving inadequate support to cities and villages, this policy maintains the tax burden on urban real estate, which consists predominantly (about 75 per cent) of improvements. In sum, present highway policies tend to diminish the burden on land and to maintain it on housing. If, therefore, we desire to stimulate adequate housing, more support should be given to road construction and maintenance in cities and villages by the state governments. During the depressed period in agriculture, rural areas needed all the aid they could get; but now that agriculture has become more prosperous, a change may be propitious. Increased aids for urban areas have also been advocated for some time on the basis of traffic needs. The emphasis in the past upon the use of highway funds predominantly for new construction may have been warranted in the early development of our highway system, but it has less justification now that new construction in the country is less needed than the adequate maintenance and repair of existing highways and the creation of through routes in and around our cities.[21]

Public Welfare.—The activities of government now classified as public welfare, public assistance, or social security, although reaching back historically to the Elizabethan poor laws, came to be financially significant for local government chiefly after 1930. For the purposes here under consideration, we may divide the public welfare of social security programs in two general categories: first, social insurance, comprising that part of the program which is supported by payments under an insurance system and for which no direct appropriations are made by local governments; second, public assistance, which includes that part of assistance supported directly by public expenditure and paid for by taxes levied by federal, state, and local governments.

It is apparent that the existence of the old-age and unemployment insurance systems decreases the cost of public assistance. If the old-age insurance programs were extended to all citizens, old-age assistance based on need would largely disappear.[22] So also with unemployment compensation; at present these payments decrease the relief load which must now be borne by state and local governments, and any extension of unemployment compensation in coverage or in amount of benefits would tend to decrease this potential.

Prior to the Great Depression of the 1930's, local governments were responsible for the indigent poor, the blind, dependent children, and others in need of relief, and they maintained, as they still do, hospitals and other charitable agencies; but all of these functions together were only a small part of the total budget. They came to be financially burdensome with the Great Depression.[23] The percentage of total expenditure for charities jumped from around the

3 per cent which it held during the late 1920's to 9.8 per cent in 1930, reaching 17.5 per cent in 1939.[24]

Table 24 shows the expenditure of American cities for public welfare and for total operating expenses for the period 1926–45. (Because of non-comparability of some of the data, it is the proportions which are significant, not the total amounts.) These data show how welfare expenditures rose from small amounts to gigantic proportions from the early 1930's to the end of that decade. After the war began to absorb the unemployed, general relief expenditures gradually diminished until at present they are again on a very low level. Public assistance to the aged and to dependent children has also diminished, but not in the same proportion. The weight of the burden of general relief may then be said to be roughly

TABLE 24

PUBLIC WELFARE EXPENDITURES OF AMERICAN CITIES
(IN THOUSANDS OF DOLLARS)

Year	Total Operating Expenses	Welfare Total	General Relief	Old Age Assistance	Aid to Dependent Children
1926	$1,389,000	$ 43,507	......	......	......
1928	1,575,000	55,788	......	......	......
1930	1,737,000	67,524	......	......	......
1932	1,806,000	176,693	......	......	......
1934	1,745,000	287,972	$230,688	......	$15,093
1936	1,848,000	281,242	202,812	$11,545	17,239
1937	2,025,000	332,083	215,276	45,301	38,015
1938	2,167,459	380,910	240,904	57,793	46,314
1939	2,195,742	384,094	239,034	62,765	47,365
1940	2,193,915	367,101	222,087	67,139	47,091
1941	1,689,764	267,923	168,122	46,901	33,937
1942	1,914,243	263,814	133,757	49,431	32,021
1943	1,873,086	209,697	84,901	41,086	25,257
1944	1,904,844	185,729	56,293	47,978	26,239
1945	1,966,458	182,424	46,870	48,675	30,778

SOURCE: U.S. Bureau of Census, Financial Statistics of Cities, for the years 1939–45.

a function of the business cycle; where the aids to the aged and dependent children, though affected by economic conditions in general, are not directly related to them but to personal disabilities.

Public Assistance.—Under this category are classified old-age assistance, aid to dependent children, aid to the blind, and general assistance or relief. Payment under the first three programs began in 1936 and has been continued since. General relief was financed by the states and localities in 1930 and 1932. In 1932, the federal government made loans for relief through the Reconstruction Finance Corporation and from 1933 to 1936 aids were provided on a large scale for relief and work relief through the CWA, FERA, and the WPA.

Table 25 shows the percentage distribution of the cost of all assistance programs including relief and work relief for the period 1930–41, and for public assistance only, not including work relief, from 1942 to 1951.[25] The existing division of funds furnished by local and state governments varies rather widely. Some states furnish all the state-local share, and others divide the load equally between state and local governments. It seems to the writer that state governments should eventually carry the entire assistance load.

General Relief.—General relief or assistance includes the residual cases of needy persons and families not provided for by the other categories. Among these are the unemployables and the unemployed. General relief ran between 60 per cent and 80 per cent of the total cost of local expenditures for public assistance between 1930 and 1941, a period when unemployment was high.[26] In 1946, a year of high employment, general assistance was 39.5 per cent of the total.[27] The burden of general relief would not be oppressive if it were confined to the unemployables, but it becomes beyond the capacity of local communities to bear when large-scale unemployment exists. At such times, relief costs raise property taxes in some communities as much as 25 per cent.[28] It is, of course, now a matter of history that local relief broke down entirely during the Great Depression; and if it had not

TABLE 25

PERCENTAGE DISTRIBUTION OF PUBLIC EXPENDITURES FOR ASSISTANCE AND
WORK PROGRAM EARNINGS IN THE CONTINENTAL UNITED STATES, BY
SOURCE OF FUNDS, CALENDAR YEARS 1930–51

Year	Federal Funds	State Funds	Local Funds	Total
Expenditures for Assistance and Work Program Earnings				
1930	.....	8.7%	91.3%	100%
1931	.....	18.0	82.0	100
1932	17.5%	21.9	60.6	100
1933	63.9	11.7	24.4	100
1934	75.8	10.0	14.2	100
1935	73.3	13.1	13.6	100
1936	77.4	13.4	9.2	100
1937	71.0	18.2	10.8	100
1938	72.9	17.5	9.6	100
1939	69.4	20.1	10.5	100
1940	68.6	20.7	10.7	100
1941	66.5	22.6	10.9	100
Expenditures for Assistance Payments				
1942	38.2%	43.4%	18.4%	100%
1943	40.9	44.5	14.6	100
1944	41.4	45.8	12.8	100
1945	40.7	46.8	12.5	100
1946	40.6	48.2	11.3	100
1947	43.9	45.4	10.6	100
1948	43.9	45.6	10.6	100
1949	44.8	45.0	10.2	100
1950	44.6	45.5	9.9	100
1951	47.0	41.3	11.7	100

SOURCES: For 1930–41—"Trends in Financing Public Aid, 1930–41," *Social
Security Yearbook, 1941*, Table 14, p. 251. For 1942–47—"Public Assistance,"
ibid., 1946, Table 68. For 1948—*Ibid., 1948*, p. 55. For 1949—*Social Security
Bulletin, XIII* (Sept., 1950), 60. For 1950—*Ibid., XIV* (Feb., 1951), 28. For
1951—*Ibid.*, XV (Sept., 1952), 61.

been for direct federal assistance and work programs, local governments would have disorganized. At present, however, there is no provision for federal assistance in this category; and in the event of cyclical unemployment, local governments will be faced by an intolerable burden.

Legislation for sharing of relief loads varies among the states.[29] In 1946, for all states combined, more than half of all expenditures for this purpose came from state funds. In Arizona, Ohio, and Pennsylvania the state carried the entire load, and in nine other states more than three-fourths of the total came from state funds. On the other hand, local funds were the sole source of revenue in thirteen states, and at least three-fourths of the total in eight additional states.

It will be fortunate if nothing resembling mass unemployment again occurs; but if history should repeat itself and we are again faced with a severe depression, property taxes will be drastically increased. This contingency can be avoided if the states pay relief costs directly from sources of revenue other than the property tax. Should this be impossible because the state is either unable or unwilling to raise the necessary revenues, a part of the relief load might be carried by paying relief costs due to unemployment of eligible workers from compensation funds.

Unemployment compensation laws came too late in the 1930 decade to be of much help during this period. Since then all states have been accumulating funds; and, as a consequence of recent full employment, the number of workers eligible for unemployment compensation has reached about 46 million,[30] and the total funds available for the purpose of paying benefits in 1953 was about $9 billion. Hence any recession in employment would find unemployed workers receiving benefits of about $23 per week on the average for twenty-two weeks, depending upon the laws of the various states, and even this would not exhaust available funds. With four million unemployed, it is estimated the funds would last many years. The amount and duration of the payments is not, however, sufficient to protect hard-pressed workers for an extended period, and many might again be compelled to seek relief from local government.[31]

Any change in state laws increasing the duration or amount of benefits will by so much decrease the likelihood of the recipients' becoming the subject of local relief. Under present laws, however, there is no means of making provision for workers who may still be out of work after expiration of the period of the unemployment benefits. They must then go without income until such time as they become indigent, and then finally go on local relief. This is a rather inhuman procedure and seems entirely unnecessary. Nor does it seem desirable that the local community should be burdened with any share of the cost of cyclical employment. For, if we recognize, as we already have done, that it is the function of unemployment compensation to compensate the unemployed for a limited number of weeks, we should take the next step and see that, if as a consequence of their continued unemployment they become indigent, they should not become a burden upon local government. It is therefore desirable to lengthen the duration of benefits; or, if this does not seem feasible, provision should be made for having unemployment compensation continue to support needy eligible workers.

There is, furthermore, no good reason why, in the immediate future, we should run the risk of decreasing the incentives to new construction by increasing local taxes during depression when housing expenditure should be stimulated. Unemployment compensation funds which are now ample to support the unemployed should not be hoarded whilst property owners are levied upon for increased taxes and, in some cases, forced to let their properties go delinquent. We conclude then that provision should be made to remove the burden of general relief, due to unemployment, entirely from the shoulders of the local taxpayer and to shift it to the state in general, or the federal government, or, where that is impossible, to the unemployment compensation funds which were created for this purpose.[32]

APPENDIX

NOTES

INDEX

Appendix

TABLE A

RELATIVE REGRESSIVITY OF PROPERTY TAX AND A SALES TAX YIELDING THE SAME TOTAL REVENUE, LEAVING OUT "NO RETURNS" AND "NET LOSSES" IN DETERMINING THE SALES TAX RATE

Income Group	Number of Families	Av. Income	Av. Property Tax	Av. Sales Tax	Ratio of Property Tax to Income	Ratio of Sales Tax to Income
1: MADISON (including Nakoma), based upon 1933–37 Averages Property tax rate $0.02305; sales tax rate $0.1156						
No returns	1,512	......	$119	....	....	......
Net loss	22	......	227	....	....	......
$ 0–$ 249	32	$ 161	143	$ 49	88.82%	30.43%
250– 499	71	388	134	49	34.54	12.63
500– 749	92	636	148	61	23.27	9.59
750– 999	95	894	137	79	15.32	8.84
1,000– 1,249	141	1,131	135	95	11.94	8.40
1,250– 1,499	177	1,388	134	109	9.65	7.85
1,500– 1,749	168	1,621	153	122	9.44	7.53
1,750– 1,999	167	1,871	142	139	7.59	7.43
2,000– 2,249	150	2,122	139	155	6.55	7.30
2,250– 2,499	106	2,367	163	164	6.89	6.93
2,500– 2,999	150	2,751	176	184	6.40	6.69
3,000– 3,499	112	3,236	187	214	5.78	6.61
3,500– 3,999	82	3,753	181	230	4.82	6.13
4,000– 4,999	104	4,472	218	253	4.87	5.66
5,000– 7,499	105	5,991	248	322	4.14	5.37
7,500– 9,999	31	8,376	272	461	3.25	5.50
10,000 and over	37	16,775	325	606	1.94	3.61
Total	3,354					

TABLE A—Continued

Income Group	Number of Families	Av. Income	Av. Property Tax	Av. Sales Tax	Ratio of Property Tax to Income	Ratio of Sales Tax to Income
2: MILWAUKEE, based upon 1933–37 Averages Property tax rate $0.02997; sales tax rate $0.1284						
No returns	1,699	....	$153	....	....	......
Net loss	31	......	292	....	....	......
$ 0–$ 249	31	$ 120	173	$ 60	144.17%	50.00%
250– 499	105	359	152	60	42.34	16.71
500– 749	151	639	165	76	25.82	11.89
750– 999	221	883	157	92	17.78	10.42
1,000– 1,249	305	1,124	140	108	12.45	9.61
1,250– 1,499	406	1,377	137	125	9.95	9.08
1,500– 1,749	466	1,628	143	145	8.78	8.91
1,750– 1,999	382	1,870	152	160	8.13	8.56
2,000– 2,249	275	2,112	158	179	7.48	8.47
2,250– 2,499	202	2,365	178	202	7.53	8.54
2,500– 2,999	206	2,722	214	222	7.86	8.15
3,000– 3,499	149	3,245	233	246	7.18	7.58
3,500– 3,999	86	3,784	278	278	7.35	7.35
4,000– 4,999	131	4,478	295	324	6.59	7.23
5,000– 7,499	162	6,005	329	372	5.48	6.19
7,500– 9,999	84	8,505	402	531	4.73	6.24
10,000 and over	185	25,187	615	699	2.44	2.77
Total	5,277					
3: CUDAHY, based upon 1935–37 Averages Property tax rate $0.03172; sales tax rate $0.1141						
No returns	59	......	$106	....	....	......
Net loss	0	....	....	....	....	......
$ 0–$ 249	5	$ 211	132	$ 54	62.57%	25.59%
250– 499	2	387	123	54	31.78	13.95
500– 749	2	699	113	67	16.17	9.59
750– 999	11	890	103	82	11.57	9.21
1,000– 1,249	19	1,092	120	96	10.99	8.79
1,250– 1,499	20	1,367	103	111	7.53	8.12

TABLE A—Continued

Income Group	Number of Families	Av. Income	Av. Property Tax	Av. Sales Tax	Ratio of Property Tax to Income	Ratio of Sales Tax to Income
1,500– 1,749	9	$1,634	$123	$128	7.53%	7.83%
1,750– 1,999	11	1,873	127	143	6.78	7.63
2,000– 2,249	9	2,121	115	159	5.42	7.50
2,250– 2,499	4	2,339	138	179	5.90	7.65
2,500– 2,999	3	2,698	190	197	7.04	7.30
3,000– 3,499	2	3,412	126	219	3.69	6.42
3,500– 3,999	....	....	....	....	....	......
4,000– 4,999	1	4,359	122	288	2.80	6.61
Total	157					

4: WEST ALLIS, based upon 1935–37 Averages
Property tax rate $0.02972; sales tax rate $0.0971

Income Group	Number of Families	Av. Income	Av. Property Tax	Av. Sales Tax	Ratio of Property Tax to Income	Ratio of Sales Tax to Income
No returns	313	......	$118	....	....	......
Net loss	1	......	126	....	....	......
$ 0–$ 249	4	$ 171	107	$ 46	62.57%	26.90%
250– 499	19	404	119	46	29.45	11.39
500– 749	34	654	103	57	15.75	8.71
750– 999	64	885	117	70	13.22	7.91
1,000– 1,249	88	1,144	120	82	10.49	7.17
1,250– 1,499	109	1,395	117	95	8.39	6.81
1,500– 1,749	163	1,625	118	109	7.26	6.71
1,750– 1,999	148	1,863	119	121	6.39	6.49
2,000– 2,249	101	2,115	120	136	5.67	6.43
2,250– 2,499	74	2,372	127	153	5.35	6.45
2,500– 2,999	52	2,707	129	168	4.77	6.21
3,000– 3,499	24	3,201	135	186	4.22	5.81
3,500– 3,999	8	3,703	125	210	3.37	5.67
4,000– 4,999	19	4,429	170	245	3.84	5.53
5,000– 7,499	13	5,709	164	282	2.87	4.94
7,500– 9,999	7	8,778	163	401	1.86	4.57
10,000 and over	3	17,261	197	529	1.14	3.06
Total	1,244					

TABLE A—Continued

Income Group	Number of Families	Av. Income	Av. Property Tax	Av. Sales Tax	Ratio of Property Tax to Income	Ratio of Sales Tax to Income
5: SOUTH MILWAUKEE, based upon 1935–37 Averages Property tax rate $0.02774; sales tax rate $0.0825						
No returns	64	......	$ 92	....	....	......
Net loss	0	......	....	....	....	......
$ 0–$ 249	3	$ 175	109	$ 39	62.29%	22.29%
250– 499	4	357	103	39	28.85	10.92
500– 749	4	585	97	49	16.58	8.38
750– 999	12	861	103	59	11.96	6.85
1,000– 1,249	25	1,122	88	69	7.84	6.15
1,250– 1,499	36	1,381	83	80	6.01	5.79
1,500– 1,749	21	1,635	87	92	5.32	5.63
1,750– 1,999	34	1,904	97	103	5.09	5.41
2,000– 2,249	17	2,101	111	115	5.28	5.47
2,250– 2,499	10	2,381	103	130	4.33	5.46
2,500– 2,999	6	2,714	98	143	3.61	5.27
3,000– 3,499	5	3,133	131	158	4.18	5.04
3,500– 3,999	3	3,751	149	179	3.97	4.77
4,000– 4,999	6	4,515	165	209	3.65	4.63
5,000– 7,499	1	6,304	275	239	4.36	3.79
7,500– 9,999	2	8,149	159	341	1.95	4.18
Total	253					
6: WHITEFISH BAY, based upon 1935–37 Averages Property tax rate $0.02510; sales tax rate $0.1145						
No returns	84	......	$233	....	....	......
Net loss	3	......	316	....	....	......
$ 0–$ 249	4	$ 125	249	$ 54	199.20%	43.20%
250– 499	4	354	301	54	85.03	15.25
500– 749	11	623	305	67	48.96	10.75
750– 999	12	846	197	82	23.29	9.69
1,000– 1,249	24	1,113	181	96	16.26	8.63
1,250– 1,499	30	1,373	180	112	13.11	8.16
1,500– 1,749	30	1,637	152	129	9.29	7.88
1,750– 1,999	31	1,872	181	143	9.67	7.64

TABLE A—Continued

Income Group	Number of Families	Av. Income	Av. Property Tax	Av. Sales Tax	Ratio of Property Tax to Income	Ratio of Sales Tax to Income
2,000– 2,249	30	$2,123	$176	$160	8.29%	7.54%
2,250– 2,499	26	2,353	175	180	7.44	7.65
2,500– 2,999	48	2,736	199	198	7.27	7.24
3,000– 3,499	40	3,246	221	220	6.81	6.78
3,500– 3,999	24	3,693	211	248	5.71	6.71
4,000– 4,999	57	4,384	262	289	5.98	6.59
5,000– 7,499	70	6,075	275	332	4.53	5.47
7,500– 9,999	29	8,604	323	473	3.75	5.50
10,000 and over	46	32,453	594	623	1.83	1.92
Total	603					

7: WAUWATOSA, based upon 1935–37 Averages
Property tax rate $0.02686; sales tax rate $0.1097

Income Group	Number of Families	Av. Income	Av. Property Tax	Av. Sales Tax	Ratio of Property Tax to Income	Ratio of Sales Tax to Income
No returns	82	......	$142	....	....	......
Net loss	7	......	230	....	....	......
$ 0–$ 249	3	$ 168	182	$ 52	108.33%	30.95%
250– 499	13	379	150	52	39.58	13.72
500– 749	6	631	203	65	32.17	10.30
750– 999	17	891	147	79	16.50	8.87
1,000– 1,249	25	1,125	170	92	15.11	8.18
1,250– 1,499	36	1,382	162	107	11.72	7.74
1,500– 1,749	37	1,617	150	123	9.28	7.61
1,750– 1,999	44	1,873	140	137	7.47	7.31
2,000– 2,249	36	2,124	171	153	8.05	7.20
2,250– 2,499	34	2,361	172	173	7.29	7.33
2,500– 2,999	41	2,727	210	190	7.70	6.97
3,000– 3,499	31	3,259	242	211	7.43	6.47
3,500– 3,999	19	3,766	232	238	6.16	6.32
4,000– 4,999	34	4,485	271	277	6.04	6.18
5,000– 7,499	40	6,010	292	318	4.86	5.29
7,500– 9,999	18	8,526	288	453	3.38	5.31
10,000 and over	30	18,469	371	597	2.01	3.23
Total	553					

TABLE A—Continued

Income Group	Number of Families	Av. Income	Av. Property Tax	Av. Sales Tax	Ratio of Property Tax to Income	Ratio of Sales Tax to Income
8: METROPOLITAN MILWAUKEE, based upon 1935–37 averages						
No returns	2,301	......	$148	....	....	......
Net loss	42	......	280	....	....	......
$ 0–$ 249	50	$ 140	166	$ 56	118.57%	40.00%
250– 499	147	367	150	56	40.87	15.25
500– 749	208	640	162	70	25.31	10.94
750– 999	337	882	146	86	16.55	9.75
1,000– 1,249	486	1,126	137	101	12.17	8.97
1,250– 1,499	637	1,380	133	117	9.64	8.48
1,500– 1,749	726	1,628	136	135	8.35	8.29
1,750– 1,999	650	1,871	142	149	7.59	7.96
2,000– 2,249	468	2,114	150	167	7.09	7.90
2,250– 2,499	350	2,365	164	188	6.93	7.95
2,500– 2,999	356	2,722	197	207	7.24	7.60
3,000– 3,499	251	3,242	220	229	6.79	7.06
3,500– 3,999	140	3,761	247	259	6.62	6.89
4,000– 4,999	248	4,454	271	302	6.08	6.78
5,000– 7,499	286	6,010	303	347	5.04	5.77
7,500– 9,999	140	8,537	356	494	4.17	5.79
10,000 and over	264	25,599	579	651	2.26	2.54
Total	8,087					
9: DODGEVILLE, based upon 1935–37 Averages Property tax rate $0.02127; sales tax rate $0.0583						
No returns	315	......	$ 43	....	....	......
Net loss	1	......	73	....	....	......
$ 0–$ 249	1	$ 249	47	$ 19	18.87%	7.63%
250– 499	2	357	67	19	18.77	5.32
500– 749	8	597	56	29	9.38	4.86
750– 999	7	871	67	38	7.69	4.36
1,000– 1,249	2	1,073	55	47	5.13	4.38
1,250– 1,499	13	1,397	55	55	3.94	3.94

TABLE A—Continued

Income Group	Number of Families	Av. Income	Av. Property Tax	Av. Sales Tax	Ratio of Property Tax to Income	Ratio of Sales Tax to Income
1,500– 1,749	7	$1,636	$ 73	$ 62	4.46%	3.79%
1,750– 1,999	6	1,865	65	69	3.49	3.70
2,000– 2,499	9	2,259	67	79	3.97	3.50
2,500– 2,999	2	2,823	73	94	2.59	3.33
3,000– 3,999	4	3,435	58	107	1.69	3.11
4,000– 4,999	5	4,478	78	126	1.74	2.81
5,000– 9,999	3	6,393	117	125	1.83	1.95
Total	385					

10: MINERAL POINT, based upon 1935–37 Averages
Property tax rate $0.2922; sales tax rate $0.0939

Income Group	Number of Families	Av. Income	Av. Property Tax	Av. Sales Tax	Ratio of Property Tax to Income	Ratio of Sales Tax to Income
No returns	286	......	$ 49	....	....	......
Net loss	0	......	....	....	....	......
$ 0–$ 249	6	$ 153	49	$ 30	32.03%	19.61%
250– 499	5	329	89	30	27.05	9.12
500– 749	8	563	101	46	17.94	8.17
750– 999	12	895	72	61	8.05	6.83
1,000– 1,249	10	1,100	72	75	6.54	6.82
1,250– 1,499	5	1,395	82	89	5.88	6.38
1,500– 1,749	6	1,617	67	100	4.14	6.18
1,750– 1,999	....	......	....	....	....	......
2,000– 2,499	9	2,254	82	127	3.64	5.63
2,500– 2,999	2	2,881	128	151	4.44	5.24
3,000– 3,999	2	3,605	123	172	3.41	4.77
4,000– 4,999	....	......	....	....	....	......
5,000– 9,999	2	5,890	115	201	1.95	3.41
Total	353					

11: EVANSVILLE, based upon 1935–37 Averages
Property tax rate $0.02048; sales tax rate $0.0663

Income Group	Number of Families	Av. Income	Av. Property Tax	Av. Sales Tax	Ratio of Property Tax to Income	Ratio of Sales Tax to Income
No returns	231	......	$ 51	....	....	......
Net loss	3	......	97	....	....	......

TABLE A—Continued

Income Group	Number of Families	Av. Income	Av. Property Tax	Av. Sales Tax	Ratio of Property Tax to Income	Ratio of Sales Tax to Income
$ 0–$ 249	2	$ 86	$ 65	$ 21	75.58%	24.42%
250– 499	9	380	74	21	19.47	5.53
500– 749	9	636	61	33	9.59	5.19
750– 999	19	886	76	43	8.58	4.85
1,000– 1,249	21	1,137	61	53	5.36	4.66
1,250– 1,499	19	1,348	45	63	3.34	4.67
1,500– 1,749	21	1,600	56	71	3.50	4.44
1,750– 1,999	18	1,859	67	78	3.60	4.19
2,000– 2,499	12	2,208	70	90	3.17	4.08
2,500– 2,999	7	2,647	72	107	2.72	4.04
3,000– 3,999	6	3,546	88	122	2.48	3.44
4,000– 4,999	2	4,333	135	142	3.11	3.28
5,000– 9,999	3	6,238	120	142	1.92	2.28
Total	382					

12: FENNIMORE, based upon 1935–37 Averages
Property tax rate $0.02589; sales tax rate $0.1044

Income Group	Number of Families	Av. Income	Av. Property Tax	Av. Sales Tax	Ratio of Property Tax to Income	Ratio of Sales Tax to Income
No returns	251	......	$ 65	....	....	......
Net loss	1	......	93	....	....	......
$ 0–$ 249	2	$ 142	79	$ 34	55.63%	23.94%
250– 499	4	401	84	34	20.95	8.48
500– 749	5	710	131	52	18.45	7.32
750– 999	4	895	102	67	11.40	7.49
1,000– 1,249	10	1,161	100	83	8.61	7.15
1,250– 1,499	6	1,329	115	100	8.65	7.52
1,500– 1,749	11	1,561	109	112	6.98	7.17
1,750– 1,999	7	1,875	103	123	5.49	6.56
2,000– 2,499	7	2,286	112	141	4.90	6.17
2,500– 2,999	4	2,659	109	168	4.10	6.32
3,000– 3,999	3	3,391	128	192	3.77	5.66
4,000– 4,999	2	4,380	129	225	2.95	5.16
Total	317					

TABLE A—Continued

Income Group	Number of Families	Av. Income	Av. Property Tax	Av. Sales Tax	Ratio of Property Tax to Income	Ratio of Sales Tax to Income

13: MONROE, based upon 1935–37 Averages
Property tax rate $0.02263; sales tax rate $0.0841

Income Group	Number of Families	Av. Income	Av. Property Tax	Av. Sales Tax	Ratio of Property Tax to Income	Ratio of Sales Tax to Income
No returns	697	......	$ 67	....	....	......
Net loss	3	......	133	....	....	......
$ 0–$ 249	1	$ 90	125	$ 27	138.89%	30.00%
250– 499	10	379	96	27	25.33	7.12
500– 749	18	615	97	41	15.77	6.67
750– 999	18	885	87	54	9.83	6.10
1,000– 1,249	34	1,140	79	67	6.93	5.88
1,250– 1,499	29	1,371	99	80	7.22	5.83
1,500– 1,749	22	1,632	96	90	5.88	5.51
1,750– 1,999	18	1,900	104	99	5.47	5.21
2,000– 2,499	40	2,216	89	114	4.02	5.14
2,500– 2,999	17	2,758	99	135	3.59	4.89
3,000– 3,999	14	3,370	125	154	3.71	4.57
4,000– 4,999	17	4,553	122	181	2.68	3.97
5,000– 9,999	17	8,090	149	180	1.84	2.22
Total	955					

14: CAMBRIDGE, based upon 1935–37 Averages
Property tax rate $0.03130; sales tax rate $0.0740

Income Group	Number of Families	Av. Income	Av. Property Tax	Av. Sales Tax	Ratio of Property Tax to Income	Ratio of Sales Tax to Income
No returns	50	......	$ 61	....	....	......
Net loss	....	......	....	....	....	......
$ 0–$ 249	1	$ 237	61	$ 24	25.74%	10.13%
250– 499	....	......	....	....	....	......
500– 749	1	541	113	37	20.89	6.84
750– 999	....	......	....	....	....	......
1,000– 1,249	2	1,223	43	59	3.51	4.82
1,250– 1,499	1	1,484	74	71	4.99	4.78
1,500– 1,749	3	1,664	77	79	4.63	4.75
1,750– 1,999	....	......	....	....	....	......

TABLE A—Continued

Income Group	Number of Families	Av. Income	Av. Property Tax	Av. Sales Tax	Ratio of Property Tax to Income	Ratio of Sales Tax to Income
2,000– 2,499	3	$2,334	$135	$100	5.78%	4.28%
2,500– 2,999	1	2,729	172	119	6.30	4.37
3,000– 4,999	....	......	....	....	....	......
5,000– 9,999	5	9,942	112	159	1.13	1.60
Total	67					

15: EDGERTON, based upon 1935–37 Averages
Property tax rate $0.02334; sales tax rate $0.0798

Income Group	Number of Families	Av. Income	Av. Property Tax	Av. Sales Tax	Ratio of Property Tax to Income	Ratio of Sales Tax to Income
No returns	290	......	$ 62	....	....	......
Net loss	1	......	151	....	....	......
$ 0–$ 249	3	$ 201	83	$ 26	41.29%	12.93%
250– 499	8	417	74	26	17.75	6.23
500– 749	11	648	83	39	12.81	6.02
750– 999	20	862	75	52	8.70	6.03
1,000– 1,249	24	1,141	58	63	5.08	5.52
1,250– 1,499	25	1,377	64	76	4.65	5.52
1,500– 1,749	18	1,637	75	85	4.58	5.19
1,750– 1,999	9	1,887	83	94	4.40	4.98
2,000– 2,499	19	2,199	97	108	4.41	4.91
2,500– 2,999	5	2,827	82	128	2.90	4.53
3,000– 3,999	5	3,500	117	147	3.34	4.20
4,000– 4,999	4	4,239	134	172	3.16	4.06
5,000– 9,999	3	8,887	154	171	1.73	1.92
Total	445					

16: MOUNT HOREB, based upon 1935–37 Averages
Property tax rate $0.02173; sales tax rate $0.0822

Income Group	Number of Families	Av. Income	Av. Property Tax	Av. Sales Tax	Ratio of Property Tax to Income	Ratio of Sales Tax to Income
No returns	181	......	$ 66	....	....	......
Net loss	1	......	124	....	....	......
$ 0–$ 249	2	$ 174	118	$ 27	67.82%	15.52%
250– 499	1	412	70	27	16.99	6.55
500– 749	4	696	77	41	11.06	5.89

TABLE A—Continued

Income Group	Number of Families	Av. Income	Av. Property Tax	Av. Sales Tax	Ratio of Property Tax to Income	Ratio of Sales Tax to Income
750– 999	7	$ 866	$ 76	$ 53	8.77%	6.12%
1,000– 1,249	12	1,153	86	65	7.46	5.64
1,250– 1,499	8	1,378	88	78	6.39	5.66
1,500– 1,749	9	1,630	84	88	5.15	5.40
1,750– 1,999	6	1,869	78	96	4.17	5.14
2,000– 2,499	6	2,286	112	111	4.90	4.85
2,500– 2,999	4	2,757	85	132	3.08	4.79
3,000– 3,999	3	3,300	92	151	2.79	4.57
4,000– 4,999	1	4,428	94	177	2.12	4.00
5,000– 9,999	2	7,912	89	176	1.12	2.22
Total	247					

17: STOUGHTON, based upon 1935–37 Averages
Property tax rate $0.02611; sales tax rate $0.0832

Income Group	Number of Families	Av. Income	Av. Property Tax	Av. Sales Tax	Ratio of Property Tax to Income	Ratio of Sales Tax to Income
No returns	241	......	$ 65	....	....	......
Net loss	0	......	....	....	....	......
$ 0–$ 249	0	......	....	....	....	......
250– 499	4	$ 324	43	$ 27	13.27%	8.33%
500– 749	4	589	90	41	15.28	6.96
750– 999	10	895	97	54	10.84	6.03
1,000– 1,249	8	1,080	71	66	6.57	6.11
1,250– 1,499	13	1,376	76	79	5.52	5.74
1,500– 1,749	4	1,577	64	89	4.06	5.64
1,750– 1,999	7	1,889	79	98	4.18	5.19
2,000– 2,499	4	2,211	105	113	4.75	5.11
2,500– 2,999	3	2,878	86	134	2.99	4.66
3,000– 3,999	5	3,361	104	153	3.09	4.55
Total	304					

TABLE A—Continued

Income Group	Number of Families	Av. Income	Av. Property Tax	Av. Sales Tax	Ratio of Property Tax to Income	Ratio of Sales Tax to Income
18: SUN PRAIRIE, based upon 1935–37 Averages						
Property tax rate $0.02826; sales tax rate $0.0946						
No returns	215	......	$ 75	....	....	......
Net loss	1	......	81	....	....	......
$ 0–$ 249	1	$ 13	105	$ 31	807.69%	238.46%
250– 499	....	......	....	....	....	......
500– 749	4	661	103	47	15.58	7.11
750– 999	3	803	127	61	15.81	7.60
1,000– 1,249	3	1,046	75	75	7.17	7.17
1,250– 1,499	15	1,373	82	90	5.97	6.55
1,500– 1,749	4	1,640	128	101	7.80	6.16
1,750– 1,999	3	1,835	112	111	6.10	6.05
2,000– 2,499	5	2,366	108	128	4.56	5.41
2,500– 2,999	1	2,605	93	152	3.57	5.83
3,000– 3,999	2	3,418	107	173	3.13	5.06
4,000– 4,999	1	4,063	168	204	4.13	5.02
5,000– 9,999	2	6,659	127	203	1.91	3.05
Total	260					
19: COMBINED TOWNS, based upon 1935–37 Averages						
No returns	2,757	......	$ 61	....	....	......
Net loss	11	......	110	....	....	......
$ 0–$ 249	19	$ 153	74	$ 26	48.37%	16.99%
250– 499	43	377	78	26	20.69	6.90
500– 749	72	626	86	40	13.74	6.39
750– 999	100	878	81	52	9.23	5.92
1,000– 1,249	126	1,133	72	64	6.35	5.60
1,250– 1,499	134	1,372	76	77	5.54	5.61
1,500– 1,749	105	1,617	81	87	5.01	5.38
1,750– 1,999	74	1,877	85	95	4.53	5.06
2,000– 2,499	114	2,235	91	109	4.07	4.88
2,500– 2,999	46	2,752	93	130	3.38	4.72

TABLE A—Continued

Income Group	Number of Families	Av. Income	Av. Property Tax	Av. Sales Tax	Ratio of Property Tax to Income	Ratio of Sales Tax to Income
3,000– 3,999	44	$3,423	$107	$149	3.12%	4.35%
4,000– 4,999	32	4,458	119	175	2.67	3.92
5,000– 9,999	38	7,883	133	174	1.69	2.21
Total	3,715					

20: ALL COMMUNITIES COMBINED

Income Group	Number of Families	Av. Income	Av. Property Tax	Av. Sales Tax	Ratio of Property Tax to Income	Ratio of Sales Tax to Income
No returns	6,570	......	$105	....	....	......
Net loss	75	......	239	....	....	......
$ 0–$ 249	101	$ 149	141	48	94.63%	32.21%
250– 499	261	374	134	49	35.83	13.10
500– 749	372	637	136	62	21.35	9.73
750– 999	532	884	133	78	15.05	8.89
1,000– 1,249	753	1,128	126	93	14.61	8.24
1,250– 1,499	948	1,391	125	109	8.99	7.84
1,500– 1,749	999	1,625	133	128	8.18	7.88
1,750– 1,999	891	1,871	137	143	7.32	8.33
2,000– 2,499	1,188	2,223	148	166	6.66	7.47
2,500– 2,999	552	2,732	183	194	6.70	7.10
3,000– 3,999	629	3,436	208	228	6.05	6.64
4,000– 4,999	384	4,459	244	278	5.47	6.23
5,000 and over	901	12,743	378	463	2.97	3.63
Total	15,156					

TABLE B

ALL COMMUNITIES COMBINED: RELATIVE REGRESSIVITY OF PROPERTY TAX AND A SALES TAX YIELDING THE SAME TOTAL REVENUE, WHEN "NO RETURNS" AND "NET LOSSES" ARE INCLUDED IN COMPUTING THE SALES TAX RATE

Income Group	Number of Families	Av. Income	Av. Property Tax	Av. Sales Tax	Ratio of Property Tax to Income	Ratio of Sales Tax to Income
No returns	6,570	......	$105	....	....	......
Net loss	75	......	239	....	....	......
$ 0–$ 249	101	$ 149	141	$ 77	94.63%	51.74%
250– 499	261	374	134	77	35.83	20.59
500– 749	372	637	136	100	21.35	15.70
750– 999	532	884	133	125	15.05	14.14
1,000– 1,249	753	1,128	126	147	14.61	13.03
1,250– 1,499	948	1,391	125	170	8.99	12.22
1,500– 1,749	999	1,625	133	190	8.18	11.69
1,750– 1,999	891	1,871	137	210	7.32	11.22
2,000– 2,499	1,188	2,223	148	248	6.66	11.16
2,500– 2,999	552	2,732	183	290	6.70	10.61
3,000– 3,999	629	3,436	208	339	6.05	9.87
4,000– 4,999	384	4,459	244	413	5.47	9.26
5,000 and over	901	12,743	378	647	2.97	5.08
Total	15,156					

TABLE C

MILWAUKEE: RELATIVE REGRESSIVITY OF PROPERTY TAX AND A SALES TAX
YIELDING THE SAME TOTAL REVENUE, OWNERSHIP OF HOME
IMPUTED AND ADDED TO AVERAGE INCOMES

Income Class	Av. Income	Adjusted Av. Income (Imputed Home)	Ratio of Property Tax to Income	Ratio of Sales Tax to Income
No returns	......	......	.....	.....
Net loss	......	......	.....	.....
$ 0–$ 249	$ 120	$ 270	64.1%	22.2%
250– 499	359	509	29.9	14.9
500– 749	639	789	20.9	11.6
750– 999	883	1,033	15.2	10.5
1,000– 1,249	1,124	1,298	10.8	9.6
1,250– 1,499	1,377	1,551	8.8	9.3
1,500– 1,749	1,628	1,802	7.9	8.9
1,750– 1,999	1,870	2,044	7.4	8.8
2,000– 2,249	2,112	2,333	6.8	8.7
2,250– 2,499	2,365	2,586	6.9	8.8
2,500– 2,999	2,722	2,943	7.3	7.5
3,000– 3,499	3,245	3,551	6.6	7.8
3,500– 3,999	3,784	4,090	6.9	7.9
4,000– 4,999	4,478	4,784	6.2	6.8
5,000– 7,499	6,005	6,539	5.0	5.7
7,500– 9,999	8,505	9,039	4.4	5.9
10,000 and over	25,187	25,721	2.4	2.7

Amount imputed to incomes is based upon Consumer Purchases Study for
Chicago. The income of homeowners was adjusted by subtracting, from the
estimated rental value of the owned home, interest paid on mortgages, together
with the estimated expense of home ownership (taxes, interest, insurance, and
repairs).

TABLE D

ALL COMMUNITIES COMBINED: RELATIVE REGRESSIVITY OF GENERAL
PROPERTY TAX AND A SALES TAX YIELDING THE SAME TOTAL
REVENUE FOR PERSONS HAVING AN INCOME IN EACH YEAR

Income Group	Number of Families	Av. Income	Av. Property Tax	Av. Sales Tax	Ratio of Property Tax to Income	Ratio of Sales Tax to Income
$ 0–$ 249	40	$ 152	$151	$ 49	99.34%	32.24%
250– 499	103	398	138	49	34.67	12.31
500– 749	237	642	151	63	23.52	9.81
750– 999	424	887	133	77	14.99	8.68
1,000– 1,249	674	1,126	124	90	11.01	7.99
1,250– 1,499	904	1,381	125	124	9.05	8.98
1,500– 1,749	985	1,623	132	123	8.13	7.58
1,750– 1,999	878	1,871	136	136	7.27	7.27
2,000– 2,499	1,169	2,222	148	160	6.66	7.20
2,500– 2,999	550	2,736	183	187	6.69	6.83
3,000– 3,999	623	3,435	208	220	6.06	6.40
4,000– 4,999	382	4,459	243	266	5.45	5.97
5,000 and over	892	12,811	379	454	2.96	3.54
Total	7,861					

TABLE E
FREQUENCY TABLE SHOWING HOME VALUES BY INCOME GROUP

1: COMBINED TOWNS, 1935–37

Income Group	Home Values											Totals
	$0–$999	$1,000–$1,999	$2,000–$2,999	$3,000–$3,999	$4,000–$4,999	$5,000–$5,999	$6,000–$6,999	$7,000–$7,999	$8,000–$8,999	$9,000–$9,999	$10,000 & over	
No returns	334	758	774	486	261	91	35	12	2	1	3	2,757
Net loss	1	1	1	3	0	3	1	0	0	1	0	11
$ 0–$ 249	3	1	9	3	0	3	0	0	0	0	0	19
250– 499	1	6	9	20	2	2	1	1	0	1	0	43
500– 749	1	11	17	21	10	7	3	0	0	0	2	72
750– 999	2	11	31	25	16	8	5	2	0	0	0	100
1,000– 1,249	6	30	31	26	17	12	1	1	2	0	0	126
1,250– 1,499	6	29	29	28	26	8	6	1	1	0	0	134
1,500– 1,749	2	16	33	18	23	4	6	0	1	1	1	105
1,750– 1,999	2	6	19	20	15	6	2	2	2	0	0	74
2,000– 2,499	3	11	23	34	18	10	8	4	1	1	1	114
2,500– 2,999	0	1	12	12	9	9	3	0	0	0	0	46
3,000– 3,999	0	2	3	10	16	7	4	0	0	2	0	44
4,000– 4,999	0	0	2	4	7	11	5	2	1	0	0	32
5,000– 9,999	1	1	0	10	5	10	4	2	2	1	2	38
Totals	362	884	993	720	425	191	84	27	12	8	9	3,715

TABLE E (*Continued*)

Home Values

2: METROPOLITAN MILWAUKEE, 1935-37

Income Group	$0–$999	$1,000–$1,999	$2,000–$2,999	$3,000–$3,999	$4,000–$4,999	$5,000–$5,999	$6,000–$6,999	$7,000–$7,999	$8,000–$8,999	$9,000–$9,999	$10,000 & over	Totals
No returns	12	154	509	549	400	215	162	74	41	30	155	2,301
Net loss	0	2	1	3	2	0	9	6	4	0	15	42
$ 0–$ 249	0	1	7	14	4	3	8	5	2	1	5	50
250– 499	0	7	23	30	27	21	16	7	6	3	7	147
500– 749	1	14	32	48	32	16	20	14	8	4	19	208
750– 999	0	17	59	81	63	39	36	11	9	2	20	337
1,000– 1,249	0	25	89	126	105	45	35	17	14	12	18	486
1,250– 1,499	3	26	112	175	138	76	43	21	17	6	20	637
1,500– 1,749	1	26	107	186	181	89	67	32	12	7	18	726
1,750– 1,999	3	19	71	171	163	84	64	37	11	8	19	650
2,000– 2,249	0	6	54	109	104	75	45	26	18	10	21	468
2,250– 2,499	0	6	23	63	88	53	46	21	18	8	24	350
2,500– 2,999	1	0	15	36	69	62	48	40	28	15	43	356
3,000– 3,499	0	0	2	24	33	38	43	33	14	13	50	251
3,500– 3,999	0	0	2	7	8	11	26	22	11	15	38	140
4,000– 4,999	0	1	1	6	18	22	41	26	21	22	90	248
5,000– 7,499	0	0	1	5	4	25	28	32	28	35	128	286
7,500– 9,999	0	0	0	0	4	7	10	10	9	16	84	140
10,000 and over	0	0	0	0	2	6	9	10	17	10	210	264
Totals	21	304	1,108	1,633	1,445	887	756	444	288	217	984	8,087

TABLE E (*Continued*)

Home Values

3: MADISON (including Nakoma), 1933–37

Income Group	$0–$999	$1,000–$1,999	$2,000–$2,999	$3,000–$3,999	$4,000–$4,999	$5,000–$5,999	$6,000–$6,999	$7,000–$7,999	$8,000–$8,999	$9,000–$9,999	$10,000 & over	Totals
No returns	2	80	173	235	268	265	214	134	73	31	37	1,512
Net loss	0	0	1	1	0	2	1	4	3	2	8	22
$ 0–$ 249	0	1	2	5	9	4	3	4	2	0	2	32
250– 499	0	2	6	11	11	11	12	8	3	2	5	71
500– 749	0	0	12	6	12	15	19	11	4	0	13	92
750– 999	2	3	7	10	15	18	10	16	4	2	8	95
1,000– 1,249	0	2	8	16	29	27	27	12	7	4	9	141
1,250– 1,499	1	3	11	20	44	35	28	13	9	2	11	177
1,500– 1,749	0	3	6	14	25	37	40	15	8	4	16	168
1,750– 1,999	0	2	6	20	31	33	29	18	6	11	11	167
2,000– 2,249	0	2	8	14	25	28	27	20	15	4	7	150
2,250– 2,499	0	1	1	9	16	23	17	9	12	6	12	106
2,500– 2,999	0	0	0	10	7	27	29	26	20	13	18	150
3,000– 3,499	0	0	0	5	8	11	23	15	19	11	20	112
3,500– 3,999	0	0	0	1	1	12	14	26	14	5	9	82
4,000– 4,999	0	0	0	0	3	7	11	15	24	11	33	104
5,000– 7,499	0	0	1	0	4	8	9	12	15	11	45	105
7,500– 9,999	0	0	0	0	1	0	3	1	3	4	19	31
10,000 and over	0	0	0	1	0	1	1	2	0	1	31	37
Totals	5	99	242	378	509	564	517	361	241	124	314	3,354

TABLE F

RELATIVE REGRESSIVITY OF GENERAL PROPERTY TAX AND A SALES TAX EXEMPTING FOOD AND YIELDING THE SAME TOTAL REVENUE

Income Group	Number of Families	Av. Income	Av. Property Tax	Av. Sales Tax Exempting Food	Ratio of Property Tax to Income	Ratio of Sales Tax to Income
1: METROPOLITAN MILWAUKEE, based upon 1935–37 Averages						
No returns	2,301	......	$148	....	....	......
Net loss	42	......	280	....	....	......
$ 0–$ 249	50	$ 140	166	$ 30	118.57%	21.43%
250– 499	147	367	150	30	40.87	8.17
500– 749	208	640	162	45	25.31	7.03
750– 999	337	882	146	63	16.55	7.14
1,000– 1,249	486	1,126	137	74	12.17	6.57
1,250– 1,499	637	1,380	133	92	9.64	6.66
1,500– 1,749	726	1,628	136	121	8.35	7.43
1,750– 1,999	650	1,871	142	139	7.59	7.43
2,000– 2,249	468	2,114	150	150	7.09	7.10
2,250– 2,499	350	2,365	164	185	6.93	7.82
2,500– 2,999	356	2,722	197	204	7.24	7.49
3,000– 3,499	251	3,242	220	230	6.79	7.09
3,500– 3,999	140	3,761	249	260	6.62	6.92
4,000– 4,999	248	4,454	271	326	6.08	7.32
5,000– 7,499	286	6,010	303	342	5.04	5.69
7,500– 9,999	140	8,537	356	555	4.17	6.50
10,000 and over	264	25,599	579	881	2.26	3.44
Total	8,087					
2: MADISON (including Nakoma), based upon 1933–37 Averages						
No returns	1,512	......	$119	....	....	......
Net loss	22	......	227	....	....	......
$ 0–$ 249	32	$ 161	143	$ 36	88.82%	23.36%
250– 499	71	388	134	36	34.54	9.28
500– 749	92	636	143	41	23.27	6.45

TABLE F—Continued

Income Group	Number of Families	Av. Income	Av. Property Tax	Av. Sales Tax	Ratio of Property Tax to Income	Ratio of Sales Tax to Income
750– 999	95	$ 894	$137	$ 59	15.32%	6.60%
1,000– 1,249	141	1,131	135	78	11.94	6.90
1,250– 1,499	177	1,388	134	90	9.65	6.48
1,500– 1,749	168	1,621	153	106	9.44	6.54
1,750– 1,999	167	1,871	142	123	7.59	6.57
2,000– 2,249	150	2,122	139	145	6.55	6.88
2,250– 2,499	106	2,367	163	155	6.89	6.55
2,500– 2,999	150	2,751	176	183	6.40	6.65
3,000– 3,499	112	3,236	187	222	5.78	6.86
3,500– 3,999	82	3,753	181	242	4.82	6.45
4,000– 4,999	104	4,472	218	271	4.87	6.06
5,000– 7,499	105	5,991	248	361	4.14	6.03
7,500– 9,999	31	8,376	272	581	3.25	6.94
10,000 and over	37	16,775	325	810	1.94	4.83
Total	3,354					

3: COMBINED TOWNS, based upon 1935–37 Averages

Income Group	Number of Families	Av. Income	Av. Property Tax	Av. Sales Tax	Ratio of Property Tax to Income	Ratio of Sales Tax to Income
No returns	2,757	......	....	....	....	......
Net loss	11	......	....	....	....	......
$ 0– 249	19	$ 153	$ 74	$ 21	48.37%	13.7%
250– 499	43	377	78	20	20.69	5.3
500– 749	72	626	86	32	13.74	5.1
750– 999	100	878	81	44	9.23	5.0
1,000– 1,249	126	1,133	72	59	6.35	5.2
1,250– 1,499	134	1,372	76	73	5.54	5.3
1,500– 1,749	105	1,617	81	85	5.01	5.3
1,750– 1,999	74	1,877	85	95	4.53	5.1
2,000– 2,499	114	2,235	91	120	4.07	5.4
2,500– 2,999	46	2,752	93	144	3.38	5.2
3,000– 3,999	44	3,423	107	167	3.12	5.0
4,000– 4,999	32	4,558	119	201	2.67	4.4
5,000– 9,999	38	7,883	133	191	1.69	2.4
Total	3,715					

TABLE F—Continued

Income Group	Number of Families	Av. Income	Av. Property Tax	Av. Sales Tax	Ratio of Property Tax to Income	Ratio of Sales Tax to Income
4: ALL COMMUNITIES COMBINED, based upon 1935–37 Averages						
No returns	6,570	......	$105	....	....	......
Net loss	75	......	239	....	....	......
$ 0–$ 249	101	$ 149	141	$ 30	94.63%	20.0%
250– 499	261	374	134	30	35.83	8.0
500– 749	372	637	136	41	21.35	6.4
750– 999	532	884	133	58	15.05	6.6
1,000– 1,249	753	1,128	126	72	14.61	6.4
1,250– 1,499	948	1,391	125	89	8.99	6.4
1,500– 1,749	999	1,625	133	114	8.18	7.0
1,750– 1,999	891	1,871	137	132	7.32	7.1
2,000– 2,499	1,188	2,223	148	157	6.66	7.1
2,500– 2,999	552	2,732	183	193	6.70	7.1
3,000– 3,999	629	3,436	208	232	6.05	6.8
4,000– 4,999	384	4,459	244	301	5.47	6.8
5,000 and over	901	12,743	378	556	2.97	4.4
Total	15,156					

TABLE G

ALL COMMUNITIES COMBINED: Homestead Exemption*

Income Group	Number of Families	Av. Tax with $500 Exemption		Av. Tax with $1,000 Exemption		Av. Tax with $1,500 Exemption		Av. Tax with $2,000 Exemption		Ratios of Av. Taxes to Av. Incomes, Respectively			
$ 0-$ 249	101	$128	90.8%	$115	81.6%	$101	71.6%	$ 88	62.4%	85.9%	77.2%	67.8%	59.1%
250- 499	261	121	90.3	107	79.9	94	70.1	81	60.4	32.4	28.6	25.1	21.7
500- 749	372	123	90.4	111	81.6	97	71.3	85	62.5	19.3	17.4	15.2	13.3
750- 999	532	119	89.5	106	79.7	92	69.2	78	58.6	13.5	12.0	10.4	8.8
1,000- 1,249	753	112	88.9	99	78.8	85	67.5	71	56.3	9.9	8.8	7.5	6.3
1,250- 1,499	948	111	88.8	98	78.4	84	67.2	71	56.8	8.0	7.1	6.0	5.1
1,500- 1,749	999	119	89.5	105	78.9	91	68.4	77	57.9	7.3	6.5	5.6	4.7
1,750- 1,999	891	123	89.8	109	79.6	95	69.3	82	59.9	6.6	5.8	5.1	4.4
2,000- 2,499	1,188	134	90.5	121	81.8	107	72.3	94	63.5	6.0	5.4	4.8	4.2
2,500- 2,999	552	170	92.9	156	85.2	143	78.1	129	70.5	6.2	5.7	5.2	4.7
3,000- 3,999	629	195	93.7	181	87.0	168	80.8	155	74.5	5.7	5.3	4.9	4.5
4,000- 4,999	384	231	94.7	217	88.9	204	83.6	191	78.3	5.2	4.9	4.6	4.3
5,000 and over	901	364	96.3	350	92.6	337	89.2	323	85.4	2.9	2.8	2.6	2.5
Total	8,511												

* The percentage of tax after homestead exemption to the tax before exemption is shown by the percentage figure after each amount. The two income classes "No Returns" and "Net Loss" are omitted.

TABLE H

ALL COMMUNITIES COMBINED: Tax Yield with Homestead Exemptions*

Income Group	Number of Families	Total Taxes with Exemptions of			
		$500	$1,000	$1,500	$2,000
$ 0–$ 249	101	$ 12,928	$ 11,615	$ 10,201	$ 8,888
250– 499	261	31,581	27,927	24,534	21,141
500– 749	372	45,756	41,292	36,084	31,620
750– 999	532	63,308	56,392	48,944	41,496
1,000– 1,249	753	84,336	74,547	64,005	53,463
1,250– 1,499	948	105,228	92,904	79,632	67,308
1,500– 1,749	999	118,881	104,895	90,909	76,923
1,750– 1,999	891	109,593	97,119	84,645	73,062
2,000– 2,499	1,188	159,192	143,748	127,116	111,672
2,500– 2,999	552	93,840	86,112	78,936	71,208
3,000– 3,999	629	122,655	113,849	105,672	97,495
4,000– 4,999	384	88,704	83,328	78,336	73,344
5,000 and over	901	327,964	315,350	303,637	291,023
Totals	8,511	$1,363,966	$1,249,078	$1,132,651	$1,018,643
Per cent of taxable base remaining after exemptions	100.0%	92.1%	84.4%	76.5%	68.8%

*The two income classes "No Returns" and "Net Loss" are omitted.

TABLE J

CLASSIFICATION OF "NO RETURNS"

Income Group	Number of Families	Total Value of Homes	Total Property Taxes	Av. Property Tax
1: MADISON (including Nakoma)				
No occupation	633	$ 3,433,761	$ 79,148	$125
Wage earner	502	2,090,588	48,188	96
Clerical	178	996,231	22,963	129
Business & Professional	199	1,299,014	29,942	150
Total	1,512	$ 7,819,594	$180,241	
2: METROPOLITAN MILWAUKEE				
No occupation	1,282	$ 6,165,410	$182,486	$142
Wage earner	659	2,436,967	72,346	110
Clerical	193	1,137,180	33,078	171
Business & Professional	167	1,822,367	53,010	317
Total	2,301	$11,561,924	$340,920	
3: COMBINED TOWNS				
No occupation	1,514	$ 4,000,000	$ 94,851	$ 63
Wage earner	342	760,049	18,447	54
Clerical	115	320,835	7,655	67
Business & Professional	269	849,500	20,688	77
Total	2,240	$ 5,930,384	$141,641	

TABLE I

Classification of 50 Realtors

Income Group	Number of Families	Total Value of Homes	Total Property Taxes	Av. Property Tax

1. Marcos (including Nabana)

No occupation	875	$ 3,182,261	$ 70,118	$125
Wage earner	502	2,090,384	16,194	66
Clerical	178	806,371	22,061	120
Business & Professional	108	1,296,914	20,319	194
Total	1,713	$ 7,375,930	$150,241	

2. Metropolitan suburban

No occupation	1,282	$ 6,065,410	$98,450	$112
Wage earner	950	2,139,387	72,390	110
Clerical	191	1,531,150	35,674	171
Business & Professional	157	1,625,307	33,419	217
Total	2,701	$11,261,254	$240,720	

3. Country towns

No occupation	7,114	$ 4,000,000	$16,561	$ 85
Wage earner	849	730,040	18,117	91
Clerical	114	420,848	7,685	67
Business & Professional	243	849,590	20,355	77
Total	9,220	$ 5,960,554	$71,941	

Notes

Chapter 1

1 The mayor of a West Virginia city brought the financial issue to a focus in his community when he announced that he was dismissing all employees including himself on October 1, 1932, and that henceforth the city, without funds, would also be without schools, courts, judges, welfare service, garbage collections, fire and police protection, and the myriad of other services which the modern city offers.—Murray Seasongood and Clarence A. Dykstra in National Municipal League, *The Crisis in Municipal Finance* (N. Y., 1933), p. 1.

2 See Walter A. Morton, "Unemployment Relief and Local Taxation," *The Municipality*, June, 1946, p. 127.

Chapter 2

1 U. S. National Housing Agency, "Monthly Cost to Own" in *Housing Costs* (National Housing Bull. No. 2; Dec., 1944), pp. 16–19; and Albert Farwell Bemis, *The Economics of Shelter*. Vol. II of Bemis and Burchard, *The Evolving House* (3 vols.; Cambridge, Mass., 1934), Chapter 3: "The Annual Cost of Shelter."

2 Estimate of Jacob Crane, "Location Factors in Housing Programs," Part I of *Land, Materials, and Labor Costs* (U. S. National Resources Committee, Housing Monograph Series No. 3; Wash. 1939).

3 Bemis, *Economics of Shelter*, pp. 256 and 257. See also Miles L. Colean, *American Housing* (Twentieth Century Fund, Inc., Housing Committee; N. Y., 1944), pp. 25–30.

4 FHA, *Fourth Annual Report*, 1937, pp. 71–72. Raymond W. Goldsmith says: "Most current statistics and careful estimates agree that for about the last 20 years land under both 1 to 4 family and apartment houses has represented 15–20 percent of the total value of such real estate."—In National Bureau of Economic Research, Conference on Research, *Studies in Income and Wealth*, Vol. XIV: *Inventory of National Wealth* (N.Y., 1951), p. 30.

5 Wisconsin Dept. of Taxation, *Property Tax*, 1948 (Bull. No. 150; July, 1949), Table 3, p. 4.

6 U.S. National Housing Agency, *Land Assembly* (National Housing Bulletin B; Dec., 1945), pp. 17–19.

7 See Bemis, *Economics of Shelter*, p. 255, for list of items comprising cost of improving residential land. Also see Colean, *Am. Housing*, pp. 350 and 351.

8 Bemis, *Economics of Shelter*, p. 57.

9   The Bureau of Labor Statistics has found nevertheless that "the ratio of site wages to total construction cost remained fairly stable (from about 32 to 38 per cent) over the period 1931–32 to 1946–47."—*Monthly Labor Review*, LXVIII, No. 5 (May, 1949), 517.

10   According to *Housing Statistics* for Feb., 1953, p. 5, construction costs were as follows from 1939 to 1952.

1939	100.0	1942	118.1	1945	143.7	1948	214.7	1951	237.0
1940	103.7	1943	123.6	1946	159.2	1949	208.4	1952	244.0
1941	111.8	1944	134.7	1947	193.0	1950	219.9		

11   Theodore J. Kreps, "Building Materials and the Cost of Housing," Part IV of *Land, Materials and Labor Costs* (U. S. National Resources Committee, Housing Monograph Series No. 3; Wash., 1939). See Bemis *Economics of Shelter*, p. 58, and Table W, pp. 569–73 for data from the years 1840 to 1932; also pp. 274–87. For construction costs, see indexes under Construction and Real Estate in the *Survey of Current Business*, U. S. Dept. of Commerce monthly, and *Housing Statistics*, Housing and Home Finance Agency monthly.

12   Kreps in Part IV of *Land, Materials and Labor Costs*, pp. 58 and 59.

13   The rigidity of building materials prices has been attributed to monopoly and restrictive practices. On June 17, 1946, Attorney General Clark announced an anti-trust inquiry into housing and Wendell Berge, Assistant Attorney General, said "the whole construction industry has long been plagued with illegal trade restraints which keep prices high and resist the entrance of new processes and techniques. Mass production methods have not been utilized in the home construction industry. The anti-trust division's activity in lumber, masonry, cement and plumbing has revealed the existence of flagrantly restrictive practices. These four items represent more than two-thirds of the cost of materials in an average house. Consumers have been forced to bear elements of 'phantom freight;' products are distributed through a controlled system of jobbers selling at agreed-upon prices and building codes discriminate against cheaper and more efficient materials, such as prefabricated products."—Chicago *Sun,* June 18, 1946. See also Colean *Am. Housing*, pp. 394–98.

14   "Under present methods of production and distribution, the building industry is not geared to produce housing in such volume (one million per year) without increased costs and prices. It is characteristic of the building industry that prices have risen during periods of greatest activity and have fallen only when the volume of building was low."—U. S. National Housing Agency, *Housing Costs*, p. 5.

15   Bemis, *Economics of Shelter*, pp. 268–70. Colean, *Am. Housing,* Chapters 2 and 3 and Appendix B.

16 Bemis, *Economics of Shelter*, p. 226, Colean, *Am. Housing*, Table 8, p. 358.

17 U. S. National Housing Agency, *Housing Costs*, p. 24.

18 Paul H. Douglas, *Real Wages in the United States, 1890–1926* (Boston and N. Y., 1930), pp. 96, 101, 108, 135, 152, 182, 205. Shown in Bemis *Economics of Shelter*, Table X, p. 572, and Table Y, pp. 573–74. See Colean, *Am. Housing*, pp. 374–77.

19 Douglas, *Real Wages in U. S.*, pp. 271, 288, 287, 246, 472, 477, 391. Bemis, *Economics of Shelter*, p. 290.

20 Mercer G. Evans, "Labor and the Cost of Housing," Part V of *Land, Materials, and Labor Costs* (U. S. National Resources Committee, Housing Monograph Series No. 3; Wash., 1939), p. 80.

21 These measures do not appear, however, to be in the offing. Straus ventures: "I am inclined to doubt that improvements radical enough to effect substantial reductions in annual costs of housing are to be anticipated within any future that can now be foreseen."—Nathan Straus, *The Seven Myths of Housing* (N. Y., 1944).

22 Bemis, *Economics of Shelter*, p. 126.

23 John A. Zangerle (Auditor of Cuyahoga County, Ohio) in L. D. Woodworth *et al.*, *Property Taxes* (Tax Policy League; N. Y., 1940), p. 209.

24 This figure is used by the U. S. Housing Administration. But compare Bemis (*Economics of Shelter*, p. 129), who reports that the National Association of Real Estate Boards placed this allowance at 3 per cent.

25 The cost of maintenance on six projects in New York ranged from 21 to 38 per cent of total costs. "Operating expenses here include such items as fuel for heating, janitor service, painting, repairs, supplies, electricity for public spaces, advertising, insurance and such miscellaneous items as are necessary in the operation of a rental-housing project."—Peter A. Stone and Harold Denton, *Toward More Housing* (U. S. Temporary National Economic Committee, Monograph No. 8; Wash., 1940) p. 45.

26 This figure is widely used. See U. S. National Housing Agency, *Housing Costs*, and Dorothy Rosenman, *A Million Houses a Year* (N. Y., 1945).

27 For information of this type see U. S. Bureau of Labor, *Family Expenditures in Selected Cities, 1935–36*, I: *Housing* (Consumer Purchase Series Bull. No. 648; Wash., 1940–41), 35–37.

28 In 1931 the effective rate on all mortgages held by building and loan associations for the entire United States was 8 per cent, although nine states showed averages higher than 10 per cent, one being as high as 15 per cent.—Stone and Denton, *Toward More Housing*, p. 79.

29 "In addition to carrying interest rates as high as 10 per cent, a substantial commission was necessary to obtain . . . second-mortgage money" in the 1920's. The majority of these mortgages were on a monthly

amortizing basis, and failure to meet the regular payments subjected the property to foreclosure in order to wipe out the equity. It was found in some cases that, including the original commissions, fees and interest charges as high as 20 per cent were paid.—*Ibid.*

30 Compare: "Levels and trends of interest rates have always been of prime importance in evaluating conditions of the home-mortgage market. Up to the present time, however, little dependable information has been available on the structure of mortgage interest rates."—*Federal Home Loan Bank Review,* May, 1945, p. 231.

31 Commonwealth of Massachusetts, Department of Banking and Insurance, Public Document No. 8: Annual Reports of the Commissioner of Banks for the Commonwealth of Massachusetts for Years Ending on October 31, Part III relating to Co-operative Banks, Savings and Loan Associations.

32 The U. S. Census reports average interest rates on first mortgage loans made on owner-occupied, one- to four-family dwellings in 1920 at 6.22 per cent, and in 1940 at 5.54 per cent. The average effective interest rates (normal rate plus fees and service charges) charged in 1931 by Savings and Loan Associations was 8.0 per cent for the entire country. In 1936 the rate for Federal Savings and Loan Associations averaged 6.3 per cent in the United States.—*Federal Home Loan Bank Review,* IV, No. 3 (Dec., 1937), 80.

A questionnaire sent to 2629 building and loan associations gave the average annual interest rate for 1934 as 6.6 per cent for the United States.—*Federal Home Loan Bank Review,* I, No. 2 (Nov., 1934), 18.

33 The average current contract interest rate on 9452 mortgages recorded in New York from April to September, 1942, was 4.89 per cent; on 3831 mortgages recorded in St. Louis, May and June, 1942, it was 4.97 per cent. This average is composed of a range from under 4 per cent to 6 per cent. In St. Louis about a third of the borrowers paid 5 per cent and another third 6 per cent. In New York 57.1 per cent paid a rate of 5 per cent, and 20 per cent paid a rate of 4.5 per cent. The rate of interest decreased from 5.65 per cent on mortgages under $500 to 4.77 per cent on mortgages of $15,000 or over in St. Louis, and from 5.13 per cent on mortgages under $500 to 4.86 per cent on mortgages of $15,000 and over in New York.—*Federal Home Loan Bank Review,* May, 1943, pp. 231–32. See also *U. S. Census, 1940, Housing,* Vol. IV, Part I: *U. S. Summary,* p. 13.

34 Federal Home Loan Bank Board, *Eighth Annual Report,* for the period July 1, 1939, through June 30, 1940, pp. 35 and 36.

35 In a study of British housing Marian Bowley found that "rates [the British equivalent of American property taxes] added about thirty-three per cent of the cost of living in a house." She adds: "This is a very important addition to any price or cost. It is obvious that if rates

had not had to be paid a great part of the difficulty about the rents of houses built in the last ten years before the war would have disappeared."—Marian Bowley, *Housing and the State, 1919–1944* (London, 1945), p. 209.

36 For data on expenditures for general household operation, by income classes, see U. S. Dept. of Labor, Bureau of Labor Statistics (in cooperation with WPA), *Family Expenditures in Selected Cities, 1935–36* (Bull. No. 648; Wash., 1940–41). Vol. I: *Housing*, Chapter V.

37 Death rates and crime rates in areas of blight are about double the rates in other parts of the same communities. The centers of crime and disease are invariably the slum."—Straus, *Seven Myths of Housing*, p. 31. See the hearing before the Committee on Banking and Currency, U. S. Senate, 79th Congress, 1st Session (1945), Doc. No. S 1592, Part I, pp. 431–36.

38 Straus, *Seven Myths of Housing*, p. 34.

39 R. B. Navin, *An Analysis of a Slum Area in Cleveland* (report of a study made for the Cleveland Metropolitan Housing Authority in 1934), quoted in Alvin H. Hansen and Harvey S. Perloff, *State and Local Finance in the National Economy* (N. Y., 1944), pp. 109–12.

Chapter 3

1 Cheap food left a margin of income which stimulated the British housing boom in the 1930's. See Walter A. Morton, *British Finance, 1930–1940* (Madison, Wis., 1943), p. 323.

2 U. S. Bureau of Labor Statistics, *Family Expenditures in Selected Cities, 1935–36*, Vol. I: *Housing*.

3 In New York City the range of expenditure for housing was from 34.7 per cent of total expenditure for incomes of $500–$749, to 19.3 per cent for incomes of $10,000 and over. In Chicago the ratios for the same two classes were 34.9 and 17.9 per cent. In middle-sized cities, such as Providence, Columbus, Atlanta, Omaha, Council Bluffs, Denver, Portland, and others, the range was similar.—*Ibid.*, pp. 3, 4, and 5.

4 *Ibid.*, Tables I and II. See also U. S. National Resources Committee, Industrial Com., *Consumer Expenditures in the United States; Estimates for 1935–36* (Wash., 1939), p. 24. Referring to family expenditures: "In percentage terms, the proportion of income devoted to housing drops from 29 per cent at the lowest income level shown to 6.5 per cent at the highest. This is approximately the same rate of decline as that for all consumption categories combined, so that the percent of current consumption going to housing remains constant—approximating 18 per cent at all income levels." See also p. 46 of the National Resources Committee study, showing that the percentage expenditure for families and single individuals combined was 16 per cent.

John B. Blandford, Jr., Administrator of the National Housing Administration, showed household rent to be 15.4 per cent of consumer expenditure and household operation 13.4 per cent for the period 1930–39.—Hearings before the Committee on Banking and Currency, U. S. Senate, 79th Congress, 1st Session (1945), Doc. No. S 1592, Part I, p. 42.

5 Bemis, *Ecomonics of Shelter,* p. 33. In 1919 expenditures for housing were 17.5 per cent; 1921, 19.3 per cent; 1927, 17.9 per cent; 1929, 17.2 per cent: 1930, 18.0 per cent.—*Ibid.,* p. 30.

6 The average annual expenditure on housing accommodation was found by the Ministry of Labour to be 12.6 per cent of total expenditure in Sheffield, 16.2 per cent in Southampton and Plymouth, 12.6 per cent cent in York for renters.—J. R. Hicks and U. K. Hicks, *The Incidence of Local Rates in Great Britain* (Cambridge, Eng., 1945), pp. 28–29.

Gross rents in London for all households were 15.9 per cent of total expenditure. In the Southeast they were 13.7 per cent; Southwest, 13.0 per cent; Midlands, 10.8 per cent; Northeast, 11.8 per cent; Northwest, 12.2 per cent; North, 12.5 per cent; Wales, 11.6 per cent; Scotland, 9.2 per cent.—*Ibid.,* Table 4 of 24.

"It is commonly said, with what justification it is hard to discover, that an adequate and balanced provision for the needs of a family can be attained so long as (gross) rent payments do not exceed about 15% of income. . . . This safety line was reached in most Divisions by all save the lowest expenditure range."—*Ibid.,* p. 26.

7 Bemis, *Economics of Shelter,* p. 109, Table 20.

8 Annual reports of the Federal Housing Administration, 1938–41, and of the National Housing Administration thereafter.

9 The relationship between income-value elasticity and income-amenities elasticity is shown in Figure 2, drawn by Mr. P. L. Cheng.

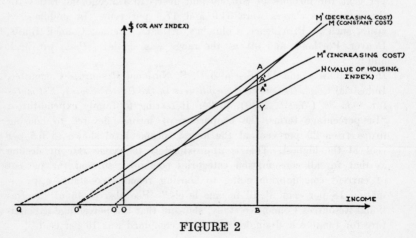

FIGURE 2

Let Line H be the Index of values of homes, which increases as income advances, but not as fast; Line M the index of amenities under constant cost, which must start from O", the point at which Line H starts; Line M' the index of amenities under decreasing cost, which starts at O'; and Line M" the index of amenities under increasing cost, which must start at Q or any point left of O". Therefore, at income level B, the following are the two groups of elasticity values under three cost conditions:

	Income-value elasticity		Income-amenities elasticity
Constant Cost	OB/O"B	$=$	OB/O"B
Decreasing Cost	OB/O"B	$<$	OB/O' B
Increasing Cost	OB/O"B	$>$	OB/ QB

10   See U. S. Housing Authority, *What the Housing Act Can Do for Your City* (1938) and *What Does the Housing Program Cost?* (March, 1940).

Chapter 4

1   Bemis, *Economics of Shelter,* pp. 177–78.

2   *Ibid.,* p. 184.

3   Production of houses from 1945 to 1951 was as follows: 1945, 225,700; 1946, 670,500; 1947, 849,000; 1948, 900,000; 1949, 1,000,000; 1950, 1,400,000; 1951, 1,100,000.—Figures for years 1945 and 1946 from U. S. National Housing Agency, *Fifth Annual Report,* p. 15; for years 1947–51, from Housing and Home Finance Agency, first to fifth annual reports.

4   Hearings before the Committee on Banking and Currency (John B. Blandford, Jr., Adm.) U. S. Senate, 79th Congress, 1st Session (1945), Doc. No. S 1592, Part I.

5   The following example will illustrate the relationship between housing amenities and housing costs. We assume that housing amenities are a function of housing space, and housing costs are a function of housing surface.

Housing Amenities (cubic feet)		Housing Surface (square feet)	
10 x 10 x 10 $=$	1,000	6 x 10 x 10 $=$	600
15 x 15 x 15 $=$	3,375	6 x 15 x 15 $=$	1,350
20 x 20 x 20 $=$	8,000	6 x 20 x 20 $=$	2,400
30 x 30 x 30 $=$	27,000	6 x 30 x 30 $=$	5,400

If building costs are $1 per square foot, according to the above hypothetical table, a house of 1,000 cubic feet will cost $600, or $0.60 per cubic foot. If a house of 8,000 cubic feet were built, the cost would be $2,400, or $0.30 cents per cubic foot. This is an eightfold increase of total amenities but with only a fourfold increase of total cost.

6 Speaking of housing, Bemis says: "Rectangularity is far more than a feature or a tendency; it is a predominant quality, a controlling fact. Fully nine tenths of the total residential building in this country is rectangular in form."—Bemis, *Evolving House*, III, 30.

7 *Ibid.*, p. 262.

8 *Ibid.*, p. 266.

9 The cost of wiring a six-room G. I. house in Madison is about $400, with an additional charge for fixtures of about $40, in 1953. The cost of wiring a larger house is not appreciably greater, say about 10 per cent including fixtures.

10 Using a system for a four-room house as a base (100), the retail cost of a cast-iron, hot-air, gravity furnace system including all piping is about 110 for a five-room house and 125 for a six-room house. A heavy welded steel furnace for a four-room house costing 100 is 110 for a five-room house, 135 for six rooms, and 165 for seven rooms. The cost to contractors of forced-air systems complete (not installed) is about as follows: 4–5 rooms, 100; 6 rooms, 114; 7–8 rooms, 140; 10–12 rooms, 172. Installation costs and profit to contractor average about 60 per cent and do not greatly change these relatives.

11 Contractors' costs for oil-burning boilers run about as follows: unit for 4–5 rooms, 100; unit for 6–7 rooms, 130; unit for 8–10 rooms, 190.

12 *U. S. Census, 1930. Population Bulletin. Families* (Wash., 1933); *U. S. Census, 1940. Housing*, Vol. II: *General Charcteristics*, Part I: *U. S. Summary*, pp. 1–5.

Chapter 5

1 Edwin R. A. Seligman, *Essays in Taxation* (8th ed.; London, 1913), Chapters 1 and 2. See also Gustav Cohn, *The Science of Finance* (trans. Thorstein Veblen; Chicago, 1895).

2 Jens Peter Jensen, *Property Taxation in the United States* (Chicago, 1931), p. 19.

3 Richard T. Ely, *Taxation in American States and Cities* (N. Y., 1888), Part II, Chapter 1; and Jensen, *Property Taxation*, Chapter 2.

4 Francis A. Walker, *Political Economy* (N. Y., 1888), p. 495.

5 David A. Wells *et al.*, *Local Taxations Being a Report of the Commission Appointed by the Governor of New York . . .* (N. Y., 1871).

6. *Ibid.*, p. 23.

7 *Ibid.*, p. 51.

8 F. C. Bastable, *Public Finance* (N. Y., 1892), pp. 418 and 419.

9 Ely, *Taxation in Am. States*, pp. 143–45.

10 *Ibid.*, p. 287.

11 "The property tax is faulty, because property is no longer a criterion

of faculty or tax-paying capacity. Two equal masses of property may be unequally productive, and hence unequally affect the margin of income from which public contributions are paid. The standard of ability has been shifted from property to product; the test now is not the extent, but the productivity of wealth. . . . The general property tax as actually administered is beyond all doubt one of the worst taxes known in the civilized world."—Seligman, *Essays in Taxation,* p. 62.

See also Jensen, *Property Taxation,* pp. 83 and 84.

12 On this point see the analysis of Amasa Walker *(Science of Wealth,* pp. 338 and 339) quoted in Wells *et al., Local Taxation,* p. 39.

13 In 1901 Professor Edwin R. A. Seligman said to the First National Conference on Taxation with reference to the demand of farmers to enforce the tax on intangibles: "The attempt to enforce the taxation of intangible personalty has been tried again and again. Its only result has been to produce not revenue but dishonesty. The enforcement of the personal property tax is converting us more and more into a nation of perjurers."—*National Conference on Taxation, under the Auspices of the National Civic Federation* (Buffalo, N. Y., 1901), p. 9.

14 After such a demand during the 1930's, New Jersey agreed to assess intangibles at only 6 per cent of their ratable value; but when this was done, holders of this form of property transferred it to jurisdictions where the tax would be negligible.—*Tax Policy,* July–August, 1945, pp. 11–13.

The reason for this can be readily seen in the case of government bonds. These are now subject to income taxes which for the wealthy run to a high percentage. If in addition they were to be taxed at 2.5 per cent each year, the tax would take all of the interest and part of the principal. Intangibles as a source of revenue under the general property tax are therefore out of the question as a source of local revenue.

15 U. S. Bureau of Census, *Property Taxation, 1941* (Special Study No. 22; Sept., 1942), pp. 27 and 39.

16 U. S. Bureau of Census, *Wealth, Public Debt and Taxation: 1922 Estimated National Wealth* (Wash., 1924), pp. 14, 28, 29.

17 Robert R. Doan, *The Anatomy of American Wealth* (N. Y. and London, 1940). Table facing p. 192 gives data for 1922; p. 220, for 1930; p. 248, for 1938.

18 U. S. Bureau of Census, *A Decade of Assessed Valuations: 1929–1938* (State and Local Government Special Study No. 14; Wash., 1941), p. 2. U. S. Bureau of Census, *Property Taxation, 1941.*

19 National Bureau of Economic Research, Conference on Research, *Studies in Income and Wealth,* Vol. XIV: *A Perpetual Inventory of National Wealth* (N. Y., 1951), p. 18.

20 The decline in the value of farm land between 1922 and 1938 reflects
    above all the fall in agricultural prices, in the economic rent of farms,
    and hence in the prices paid for farm land. Gross farm income dropped
    drastically from 1920 to 1922, made a partial recovery until 1929,
    and then sᴶumped to a new low in 1933. From this point on it made
    a gradual recovery to 1940, since which time it has more than doubled.
    Farm income in 1946 was almost four times that of 1933. The value
    per acre of farm real estate followed a steady downward trend from
    1921 to 1933, for a decline of about 50 per cent. Then it turned up-
    ward slowly until 1940, after which it has moved rapidly until by
    1946 it had almost reached the 1920 level at $147 per acre. In 1952
    it was $212 per acre.—U. S. Dept. of Agriculture, Bureau of Agricul-
    tural Economics Data, June, 1946; and *Agricultural Statistics, 1952:* p.
    627.

21 U. S. Bureau of Census, *Property Taxation, 1941,* p. 43.

22 *Ibid.*

23 Assessed valuations in the United States rose steadily from 1902 to
    1929, when they reached a high point of $165,000,000,000. By 1932 they
    had fallen 12.5 per cent from 1929; and by 1935, 22.7 per cent. The
    percentage drop from 1929 was as follows: 1930, —0.1; 1931, —5.5;
    1932, —12.5; 1933, —18.2; 1934, —21.4; 1935, —22.7; 1936, —22.7;
    1937, —21.5; 1938, —22.0.—U. S. Bureau of Census, *A Decade of As-
    sessed Valuations: 1929–1938,* p. 2.

24 This proved to be true during the 1930's when assessments were re-
    duced more slowly than the selling prices of real estate. The Home
    Owners' Loan Corporation during the first half of 1940 sold 100 prop-
    erties in Boston at an average of 73.5 per cent, and 80 properties in
    New York at an average of 79 per cent of assessed value. In Man-
    hattan, on the basis of 2,000 sales, assessed value was 20.7 per cent
    above market value in 1937 and 37.3 per cent above in 1940.—Robert
    H. Armstrong and Homer Hoyt, *Decentralization in New York City*
    (Preliminary Report to Urban Land Institute; Chicago, 1941), p. 182.
    Quoted in Colean, *Am. Housing,* p. 239.

    Land value in Chicago declined from $5,000,000,000 in 1928 to $2,-
    000,000,000 in 1933. Tax assessment of all buildings declined in Chi-
    cago by 44 per cent; in Cleveland by almost 40 per cent; in Philadel-
    phia, Los Angeles, and Baltimore by 30 per cent; and in New York
    by 11 per cent.—Homer Hoyt quoted in Colean, *Am. Housing,* p. 23.

25 John A. Zangerle, "Taxing Real Estate on Its Income," in L. D. Wood-
    worth *et al., Property Taxes,* pp. 205–17.

26 "The debt limit of the city of New York is 10 per cent of the assess-
    ment of its real estate. The outstanding debt is now within but a few
    million dollars of the entire debt limit and the legality of the debt is only

being held up by gross over-assessments."—Armstrong and Hoyt, *Decentralization in New York City*.

See, however, William Stanley Miller, President of New York City Tax Commission, in a letter to Mayor LaGuardia (printed in *American City*, March, 1940, pp. 35–36); "It never was intended that the tax structure of any great city should be predicated upon the ebb and flow of a distressed real-estate market. The main requisite of any tax structure is stability, because there must necessarily be a stable revenue to be derived from real property in order to meet the bills of the municipality.

"While the provision in the New York City charter specified value under ordinary circumstances, the difficulty in ascertaining what ordinary circumstances are, adds to the uncertainty of exactly what the low requires, and actual practices cannot be said to accept present market prices as the sole basis of appraisal."—Quoted by Colean, *Am. Housing*, pp. 23 and 24.

27 *National Municipal Review*, December issue showing investigation of Detroit Bureau of Governmental Research. Also Jensen, *Property Taxation*, p. 87.

28 *National Municipal Review*, December issues each year to 1945 and January issues, 1948–51.

29 In 1951 there was a total of 119,465 governmental units in the United States. These were made up as follows: counties, 3049; townships and towns, 17,338; municipalities, 16, 677; school districts, 70,452; and special districts, 11,900.—U. S. Bureau of Census, *Governmental Units in the United States in 1951* (Wash., 1951), p. 1.

Practically all of these units have the right to levy property taxes. The individual property tax rate is therefore a composite of the state tax, township or city tax, county tax, school district tax, and special district tax. Depending upon the number of special districts—sanitary, drainage, etc.—one property may be in as many as a dozen tax jurisdictions.

30 In 1927 the percentage was 27 per cent; 1932, 20 per cent; 1936, 7 per cent; 1946, 5.1 per cent.—Data for 1927, 1932, and 1936 was Woodworth *et al.*, *Property Taxes*, p. 8; for 1946, U. S. Bureau of Census, *Compendium of State Government Finances in 1947* (Wash., 1948), p. 2; for 1952, U. S. Bureau of Census, *State Tax Collections in 1952* (Wash., 1952), p. 3.

31 U. S. Bureau of Census, *State Tax Collections in 1952*.

32 In 1950 the figure was 96 per cent.—U. S. Bureau of Census, *Governmental Revenue in 1950* (Wash., Aug., 1951), p. 8.

33 In 1950 property taxes were 88 per cent of total tax collections.—*Ibid*.

34 State grants in aid to localities were $340,600,000 or 8.9 per cent of local tax collections in 1925, $773,100,000 or 18 per cent of local tax

collections in 1935.—Mueller in L. D. Woodworth *et al., Property Taxes,* p. 21.

In 1950 fiscal aids to counties, municipalities, and school districts were $4,166,352,000 or 52 per cent of total revenues.—U.S. Bureau of Census, *Governmental Revenue in 1950,* p. 9.

35 U. S. Bureau of Census, *Governmental Revenue in 1950* (Wash., Aug., 1951), p. 9.

36 *Ibid.,* p. 8.

37 *Ibid.*

38 U. S. Bureau of Census, *Property Taxation, 1941,* p. 13, and *Governmental Revenue in 1950,* p. 8.

39 In 1902 the property tax raised 43.7 per cent of the total revenues of state governments, in 1950 only 2.6 per cent. For county governments the corresponding figures are 72.8 per cent and 48.2 per cent. For municipal governments they are 71.2 per cent and 52.1 per cent.— U. S. Bureau of Census, *Property Taxation, 1941,* p. 9, and *Governmental Revenue in 1950,* pp. 8 and 9.

40 U. S. Bureau of Census, *Property Taxation,* 1941, p. 15.

41 Jensen, *Property Taxation,* pp 15–18.

42 *Tax Policy,* Feb., 1946, p. 2.

43 *Tax Policy,* annual issues, last July–August, 1952, p. 3.

44 Frederick L. Bird, *The Trend of Tax Delinquency, . . . Cities over 50,000 Population* (Dun and Bradstreet, Inc., Municipal Service Dept.; N. Y.). Published annually with cumulative information from 1930.

45 *Ibid., 1930–1940,* p. 7.

46 *Ibid., 1930–1944,* p. 7. Also see p. 12.

47 *Ibid.,* p. 13.

48 *Ibid., 1930–1939,* p. 16.

49 *Ibid., 1930–1944,* p. 14.

50 *Ibid.,* p. 9.

51 *Ibid., 1930–1937,* p. 13.

52 *Ibid., 1930–1934,* pp. 9 and 25.

53 *Ibid.,* annual issues, *1930–1934* through *1930–1944.*

54 U.S. Bureau of Census, *Realty Tax Delinquency* (Wash., 1934), Vol. II: *Urban Tax Delinquency,* Table D, p. 49. Computations of Colean, *Am. Housing,* p. 20.

55 Colean, *Am. Housing,* p. 21.

56 An outstanding study of this phenomenon can be found in B. H. Hibbard, John Swenehart, W. A. Hartman, and B. W. Allin, *Tax Delinquency in Northern Wisconsin* (Univ. of Wis., Agricultural Experiment Station Bull. 399; Madison, Wis., June, 1928).

57 Robert S. Ford, *Realty Tax Delinquency in Michigan* (Ann Arbor, Mich., 1937), p. 72. Also see Colean, *Am. Housing,* pp. 20–23, for discussion and further references.

58 William L. C. Wheaton, *Tax Delinquent Land in Cuyahoga County* (Regional Assoc. of Cleveland, Ohio, Pub. No. 13; Oct., 1941), p. 1.

59 *Ibid.*, p. 1.

60 *Ibid.*, Part III.

61 Alvin H. Hansen and Harvey S. Perloff, *State and Local Finance in the National Economy* (N.Y., 1944), pp. 56–62.

Chapter 6

1 See Otto Von Mering, *The Shifting and Incidence of Taxation* (Phila., 1943), p. 243.

2 See Jensen, *Property Taxation*, p. 64.

3 For an explanation of this theory, see: *ibid.*, pp. 63–75; Edwin R. A. Seligman, *The Shifting and Incidence of Taxation* (London, 1899), pp. 137–45 and 237; Carl Shoup, "Capitalization and Shifting of the Property Tax," in L. D. Woodworth *et al.*, *Property Taxes.*

4 Walter A. Morton in *The Municipality*, Feb., 1940, p. 25. Also his "Unemployment Relief and Local Taxation," *ibid.*, June, 1946, pp. 127–44.

5 See Jensen, *Property Taxation*, pp. 56–61. Jensen states this doctrine clearly on pp. 60–61: "Must the owners of capital goods in general finally bear the tax, or may they, after all, shift it to others? If they continue to furnish the same capital goods regardless of the reduction in the reward for their service resulting from the tax, they are bearing the tax. In other words, the question is, Will they save as much at a reduced rate of interest as before? . . . If the rate of saving is not affected by the reduced rate of interest, the owners of capital in general will bear the tax, and the incidence of the tax will tend to be proportionate to the return from capital."

Today we would add to Jensen's question the following: "Will they invest as much when the expected rate of profit is reduced?"

6 For a discussion of the incidence of British rates, see J. R. Hicks and U. K. Hicks, *The Incidence of Local Rates in Great Britain* (Cambridge, Eng., 1945), pp. 50–56.

7 See Walter A. Morton, *British Finance, 1930–1940* (Madison, Wis., 1943), pp. 331–34.

8 In this reference compare: "The failure of the general property tax adequately to reach the enormous volume of non-property income, and the frequent lack of correspondence between the market value of property and its income-yielding capacity contribute toward further violations of the ability formula. Since it is administratively impossible to determine the net worth of individuals, progressive taxation is ruled out." —Clarence Heer, "The Property Tax as a Measure of Ability," in L. P. Woodworth *et al.*, *Property Taxes*, p. 161.

Chapter 7

1   See Walter A. Morton, "Taxes and Loans in War Finance," *Bull. of National Tax Assoc.*, May, 1942, p. 226.
2   U. S. Bureau of Census, *Governmental Revenue in 1951* (Aug., 1952), p. 1.
3   The following states had general sales taxes in 1952: Alabama, Arizona, Arkansas, California, Colorado, Connecticut, Florida, Georgia, Illinois, Indiana, Iowa, Kansas, Louisiana, Maine, Maryland, Michigan, Mississippi, Missouri, New Mexico, North Carolina, North Dakota, Ohio, Oklahoma, Rhode Island, South Carolina, South Dakota, Tennessee, Utah, Washington, West Virginia, Wyoming.
4   Total revenues received from property taxes and sales taxes in the period 1945–51 (*ibid.*, p. 2) were:

Year	Total Taxes	Property Tax	% of Total	Sales Tax	% of Total
1945	$50,075,000	$4,802,000	9.59%	$ 775,795	1.55%
1946	46,128,000	4,990,000	10.82	899,757	1.95
1947	46,624,000	5,507,000	11.81	1,178,849	2.53
1948	51,123,000	6,128,000	11.99	1,477,726	2.89
1949	50,358,000	6,842,000	13.55	1,605,554	3.19
1950	50,967,000	7,349,000	14.42	1,678,571	3.29
1951	63,586,000	7,926,000	12.47	2,001,129	3.15

5   Gerhard Colm and Helen Tarasov, *Who Pays the Taxes?* (Temporary National Economic Committee, Monograph No. 3; Wash., 1940); and Helen Tarasov, *Who Does Pay the Taxes* (Temporary National Economic Committee, Social Research Supplement IV; Wash., 1942).
6   U.S. Bureau of Census, *State Tax Collections in 1952* (Wash., Aug., 1952), p. 3.
7   See, for example, A. M. Hillhouse and Muriel Magelssen, *Where Cities Get Their Money* (Municipal Finance Officers Assoc.; Chicago, 1945).
8   *The Municipality*, June, 1946, p. 144.
9   *New York Times*, Feb. 17, 1946, Section I, p. 8.
10 For the view that expenditure should be excluded in considering incidence, see Von Mering, *Shifting and Incidence of Taxation*, pp. 133–34.
11 This is a very brief summary of the conclusions regarding commodity taxes. For a detailed analysis, see John F. Due, *The Theory of Incidence of Sales Taxation* (N.Y., 1942), p. 32; and Von Mering, *Shifting and Incidence of Taxation*, pp. 173–78.
12 Harry Gunnison Brown, "The Incidence of a General Output or a General Sales Tax," *Journal of Political Economy*, XLVII, No. 2 (April, 1939), 254–62; amended in same volume, No. 3, pp. 418–20.
13 *Ibid.*, p. 255.
14 Strictly speaking, this statement would be true only if a tax were levied on all output, not as we here suppose on consumption goods only.

In the event of a general sales tax on consumption goods, factor incomes would fall by a little less than the amount of the tax—that is, by the tax multiplied by the consumption coefficient as will now be explained.

Assuming forward shifting, a sales tax on consumption goods would raise the price level of these goods by 2 per cent but would leave the price level of capital goods unchanged. Now if consumption goods were 90 per cent of the gross national product and the capital goods 10 per cent, the general price level which includes both these products would rise by the amount $T\left(\dfrac{C}{Y}\right)$, T being the amount of the tax and $\dfrac{C}{Y}$ being the average proportion of consumption goods to total output, or the average propensity to consume. This would give us (.02 x .9) or 1.8 per cent.

If, however, the tax were shifted backwards, the price level of all goods after the tax would remain the same, but all factor prices would fall by $T\left(\dfrac{C}{Y}\right)$ or 1.8 per cent, to 98.2 per cent of the pre-tax level.

That part of factor incomes (10 per cent) being spent for the untaxed capital goods would remain constant in real terms, and that spent for consumption (90 per cent) would fall in real value by 2 per cent below its previous level.

The concept of two price levels and the concept of the propensity to consume are both needed to simplify the analysis and to properly explain the incidence of a general consumption tax. They show that the tax is regressive to income regardless of the direction of the shifting. Some of those who fail to use these concepts tend to fall into the error that a sales tax is a proportional tax on income.

15 It should be cautioned here that the above analysis and the conclusions flowing from it have not taken into consideration the possibility that a general tax may have differential effects upon the supply of the various productive factors. Moreover, some of these factors have prices fixed by contract; labor unions may have escalator clauses which raise wages with the cost of living; other groups may have the necessary bargaining power to shift the tax. Such groups could, temporarily at least, push the entire burden of a tax upon the groups with lesser bargaining power. The tax might also have effects upon incentives to work, to save, and to invest. If it diminished the willingness to work, it would tend to raise wages relative to other factors. If it diminished the willingness to save and to invest, it might cause a rise in interest and profit relative to wages. We have neglected these effects because we are dealing here with a relatively small tax and because we really know very little about the incentive effects of sales and income taxes on the supply of the various factors of production. It does, however, seem possible to say

that the portion of labor operating under wage-escalation contracts might not bear any portion of a sales tax that was shifted forward, the entire burden resting on other sections of workers and the fixed-income groups. A tax shift backward might, however, be borne by union labor just as much as by other groups.

16 A progressive wartime consumption tax is discussed by Walter A. Morton, "A Progressive Consumption Tax," *National Tax Journal,* IV, No. 21 (June, 1951), 160–66; and by Pao Lun Cheng, "A Note on Progressive Consumption Tax," *Journal of Finance,* Sept., 1953, pp. 333–42.

Chapter 8

1 *U.S. Census, 1950. Housing, Preliminary Reports,* Series HC–5, No. 1, p. 1.

2 Hicks and Hicks, *Incidence of Local Rates,* pp. 2 and 3.

3 U.S. National Resources Committee, Industrial Committee, *Consumer Incomes in the United States; Their Distribution in 1935–36* (Wash., 1938), and *Consumer Expenditures in the United States; Estimates for 1935–36* (Wash., 1939); U.S. Bureau of Labor Statistics, *Family Expenditures in Selected Cities, 1935–36,* Vol. 1: *Housing* (Consumer Purchase Series Bull. No. 648; Wash. 1940–41).

4 U.S. National Resources Committee, *Consumer Expenditures in U.S.,* p. 24.

5 *Ibid.,* Table 7A, p. 79.

6 U.S. Bureau of Labor Statistics, *Family Expenditures in Selected Cities, 1935–36,* Vol. I: *Housing.*

7 *Ibid.,* Table 10, p. 31. The average income per income class is shown in the Appendix, Table 2, pp. 108–31, and housing expenditures for homeowners in Table 6, pp. 193–202.

8 *Ibid.,* pp. 396 ff.

9 See Jesse V. Burkhead, "Property Tax as a Burden on Shelter," *Journal of Land and Public Utility Economics,* Aug., 1944, pp. 255–63.

10 Hicks and Hicks, *Incidence of Local Rates,* p. vii.

11 *Ibid.,* p. 5.

12 *Ibid.,* Table 2, p. 12.

13 *Ibid.,* p. 13.

14 *Ibid.,* p. 37.

15 In the authors' own words: "The lower end of each Divisional curve is, therefore, rather steeply sloped, but as we move up the income scale the degree of regression declines, and rate incidence tends toward proportionality."—*Ibid.,* p. 39.

16 *Ibid.,* pp. 40–41.

17 *Ibid.,* p. 46.

18 Miss Marian Bowley, referring to Britain, comes to the same conclusions regarding the regressivity of property taxation. "The burden of

rates tended, therefore, to use up a larger proportion of the incomes of the poor than of the rather less poor, and so on up the scale of income."—Marian Bowley, *Housing and the State, 1919–1944*, p. 211.

19 "It is very evident that rent and rate payments increase as income rises, but not so quickly, so that the proportions which they bear to total expenditure declines as we move up the income scale."—Hicks and Hicks, *Incidence of Local Rates*, p. 25.

Compare this to the Consumer Expenditure data shown above, showing that in the United States housing remained at about the same proportion of expenditure for all levels of income, and the Wisconsin data showing that housing accommodation took a proportionate share of income in the middle brackets but a much smaller share as income rose above $5,000 per year.

20 However, if the tax had been capitalized by a reduction in the price paid for land, then the owner of the land is saving an amount of interest equivalent to the taxes being capitalized. We had no data to show which taxes had been capitalized and therefore omitted this factor in our calculation. The resulting figures accordingly may overstate the total burden of the property tax somewhat. As shown below, however, if the tax paid on land were deducted in the computation of the burden, it would make little difference in the degree of regressivity; if anything, the results might show the tax to be slightly more regressive than the figures we use.

21 This can be readily seen by comparing Table A(2) with Table C. It might be mentioned further that if what is desired is imputed income as a basis of calculation, all imputed income and not only a part of it should be used. Such a figure, for example, would include the services obtained from government and not paid for directly. This is generally avoided on the specious argument that taxes are a *quid pro quo*. Tax payments and tax benefits are, however, by no means coincidental. Total imputed income thus should include cash income, plus imputed income of home ownership, plus income from use of furniture, automobiles, plus the value of government services. This method would raise many low-income families to higher levels; a large but poor family sending all of its children to school has an imputed income in the form of education which brings its total income to a much higher level. But to carry this procedure to its logical conclusion, we should also need to value each and all of the services received from government, streets, sewers, justice, police and fire protection, army, navy, etc., a procedure which only needs mentioning to show its futility.

22 The determination of an indifference point can be shown graphically. In Figure 3, let CO' be the consumption line subject to sales tax; and HO'' be the house value line subject to property tax. CO' starts from base at O' and HO'' at O'', which means that a property tax would be

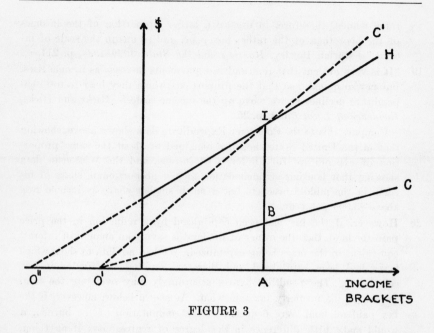

FIGURE 3

more regressive than a sales tax. Assume we know the size of tax base for both taxes and that the property tax base is three times larger than the sales tax base (or the total assessed value of houses is three times larger than the total consumption expenditures subject to sales tax), then the sales tax rate (to raise the same amount of revenues) must be three times as high as the property tax rate. So, if we make line O′ C three times as high (or O′ C′ is three times higher than O′ C from their horizontal base), we find the indifference point immediately at I, and A is the indifferent group. The income groups beyond A would be worse off with sales tax substituting for property tax, but the income groups among the OA would be better off.

23   The average age of heads of families who are homeowners in the United States is about ten years older than that of renters. The median age of homeowners was 47.5 years and of renters 37.8 years.—U.S. Bureau of Labor Statistics, Bull. No. 642, I, 86.

24   Urban tax rates are about 50 per cent above rural tax rates, as discussed below. Also compare to Hicks and Hicks, *Incidence of Rates,* p. 18.

25   See Hicks and Hicks for similar conclusions for Great Britain.

26   Table 21A shows the results of the sales tax burden when estimated income and consumption are imputed to the "no returns." This table is not used here because we believe it less reliable than the ones used, which are based only on cases where the income was shown.

In computing average income, we used income data for all persons whether they reported for one year or three years. Only a few, however, reported for less than three years. In order to check the results, we made a separate calculation of all persons showing income for each of the three years. This made practically no change in the results. These data are shown in Table D. It should be compared with Table A(20).

27 U.S. Bureau of Labor Statistics, *Family Expenditures in Selected Cities, 1935–36,* I: Housing, 19–23.

28 Total income received by individuals in Wisconsin in 1936 $1,451,236,000
    Tax levy on property in 1936.......................   98,991,277
    Tax as per cent of income received 6.8%

    Total Wisconsin income in 1936 is taken from the Report for the Conference on Research in National Income and Wealth, May, 1941, prepared under the direction of Frank A. Hanna, p. 2. Wisconsin's total tax levy for 1936 is from Bulletin No. 86 of the Wisconsin Tax Commission, Statistical Division, Dec., 1938, p. 3.

29 Computed from consumption data of U. S. National Resources Committee given in *Consumer Expenditures in U.S.*

30 U.S. Bureau of Labor Statistics, Bull. No. 640 (Wash., 1941), pp. 57, 417–40.

31 U.S. Bureau of Labor Statistics, *Family Expenditures in Selected Cities, 1935–36,* Vol. I: *Housing,* Table 11, p. 32.

32 Miss Marian Bowley estimated that in Britain rates added 33 per cent to the cost of living in a house, and that this payment diminished the demand for new housing and for other objects of expenditure.—Marian Bowley, *Housing and the State, 1919–1944,* pp. 209–12.

    Before the war, Professor Sumner H. Slichter said: "High real estate taxes are the next most important obstacle to cheap housing. The Detroit Bureau of Governmental Research estimates that the average tax rate based on true values in 274 cities in 1937 was $26.90 per thousand, or about 25 per cent of rent or rental value. This means that the present real estate taxes are equivalent to a 25 per cent sales tax on shelter. Everyone knows what an outcry would be provoked by a 25 per cent sales tax on food, fuel or clothing. When shelter is burdened with a sales tax of 25 per cent, is it surprising that people put up with old shelter and avoid heavy new tax liabilities by refusing to spend money on new housing. Surely, there is no reason why sources of local revenue should not be broadened to make it possible to cut real estate taxes in half."

Chapter 9

1 Or if (say, during depression) the funds now raised through it are obtained by borrowing or other means that do not diminish consumer incomes. We need not, however, consider the latter because we seek

permanent and not temporary policies, and borrowing in lieu of taxes is always a temporary expedient.

2 See Donovan F. Emch, "The Effect of Tax Limitation in Ohio," in L. D. Woodworth *et al.*, *Property Taxes*, pp. 56–69 and 277–78.

3 U.S. Bureau of Census, *Summary of City Government Finances in 1948* (Oct., 1949), p. 7.

4 For a summary of views on these matters, see "Federal, State and Local Government Fiscal Relations," U.S. Senate Document No. 69, 78th Congress, 1st Session (1943), pp. 84–94.

5 A thorough examination of the various forms of local taxation can be found in Hillhouse and Magelssen, *Where Cities Get Their Money*, and in the 1947 supplement to this book.

6 In the words of the Committee on Intergovernmental Fiscal Relations, "The major need is for a source of revenue which will enable the municipalities to tax their own resources independently. Much of the vitality of local government in the United States depends upon the discovery and utilization of such a source."—U.S. Senate Document No. 69, 78th Congress, 1st Session (1943), p. 413.

7 U.S. Bureau of Census, *Summary of City Government Finances in 1951* (1951).

8 Sources of total local collected taxes of 397 cities were:

	Property Taxes	Taxes from Other Sources
1944	88%	12%
1945	87	13
1946	85	15
1947	81	19
1948	78	22
1950	76	24
1951	76	24

All percentages were computed from U.S. Bureau of Census data, from the following sources: for 1944—*City Finances: 1944*, III: *Statistical Compendium* (1946), Table 2, 5; for 1945—*City Finances: 1945*, III: *Statistical Compendium* (1947), Table 2, 5; for 1946 and 1947—*Compendium of City Government Finances in 1947* (1949), Table 2, p. 6; for 1948—preliminary figures in *Summary of City Government Finances in 1948* (1949), Table 2, p. 5; for 1950 and 1951—*Summary of City Government Finances in 1951* (1951), p. 6.

9 For changes in miscellaneous taxes since the war see "City Tax Legislation, 1946," *Tax Policy*, Nov., 1946, and in succeeding years.

10 See "Taxing the Fluid Population," *Tax Policy*, Aug., 1947.

11 Philadelphia in 1944 raised 26.7 per cent of total local revenue by a 1 per cent income tax.—Hillhouse and Magelssen, *Where Cities Get Their Money*, p. 102.

12 While recognizing the undesirability of the sales tax, and after stating its limitations, the Committee on Intergovernmental Fiscal Relations said: "As against the steady and extensive surrender of local fiscal independence, the city sales tax might merit further consideration."—U.S. Treasury Dept., Committee on Intergovernmental Fiscal Relations (Harold M. Groves, Luther Gulick, Mabel Newcomer, and staff), *Federal, State and Local Government Fiscal Relations* (Wash., 1943), p. 11.

See also U. S. Senate Document No. 69, 78th Congress, 1st Session (1943), p. 413. This is a thoroughgoing study with extensive data on all aspects of local-state-federal fiscal relations.

13 This conclusion is based on the assumption that ordinarily a sales tax on food is paid by the consumer. During a period of inflation when the price of food seems to be higher than is necessary to bring forth the existing supply, a part of the price received by the grower represents costs and necessary profits and a part surplus profits, economic rent, or quasi-rent. A tax on food during the inflation might therefore be borne by the grower and result in a reduction in profits without impairing supply.

14 The National Association of Assessing Officers reported in 1947 that tax-exempt property in the United States has increased from 13 per cent in 1922 to 18 per cent of the total real estate. The property has escaped taxes largely because it has been acquired by churches, schools, charities, and local and federal government. Hospitals have changed from profit-making to nonprofit enterprises in order to escape local taxes.

A 1936 survey of tax-exempt real property in 52 cities (having a population of over 100,000) shows that 71.4 per cent of the total was owned by governmental units and the other 28.6 per cent was owned privately by educational, religious, charitable, and other groups. Of the publicly owned property, more than 85 per cent was owned by state and local governments and the balance by the federal government.—U.S. Bureau of Census, *Value of Exempt Real Property in Fifty-Two Cities* (Wash., 1936), p. 1.

A recent examination of this problem may be found in Mabel Newcomer, "The Growth of Property Tax Exemptions," *National Tax Journal*, VI, No. 2 (June, 1953), 116.

15 Although all Christians are admonished to contribute to the work of the Lord in proportion to their abilities and some sects advocate tithing, such data as are available show that church contributions are regressive to income, very much in the same way as property or sales taxes. The rich man may find it hard to enter the Kingdom of Heaven, but he still pays a smaller proportion of his income for support of religious activity than the poor man.

16 A history and description of these devices may be found in Henry J. Bitterman, *State and Federal Grants-In-Aid* (N.Y. and Chicago, 1938).

17 For shared taxes, see U.S. Treasury Dept., *Federal, State and Local Government Fiscal Relations*, pp. 155–59; for grants-in-aid, see pp. 159–73.

18 U.S. Bureau of Census, *Governmental Revenue in 1951*, p. 10.

19 U.S. Bureau of Census, *Governmental Finances in the United States, 1942. U.S. Summary* (Wash., 1945), p. 7.

20 U.S. Treasury Dept., *Federal, State and Local Government Fiscal Relations*, p. 87.

21 On this problem, see League of Wisconsin Municipalities, *How Should Wisconsin's City and Village Streets Be Financed?* (Madison, Wis., June, 1944). See also the report prepared for the U. S. Senate Committee on Postwar Economic Policy and Planning in 1944, entitled "The Role of the Federal Government in Highway Development."

22 When the Social Security Act was passed in 1935, it was realized that it would take some time to achieve its results and that old-age dependency and destitution might continue to require relief under old-age assistance programs. It was assumed that as old-age and survivors' insurance approached "maturity," and as it expanded in coverage and scope, the role of public assistance would gradually move in the direction of "residual responsibility." The Social Security Board data now show that old-age and survivors' insurance is carrying proportionately more of the aged at present than it did when inaugurated. It is found, however, that old-age insurance plays a larger part in the cities than in the rural districts where many of the aged are not covered. "Because the coverage of old age and survivors insurance is limited to industrial and commercial jobs, insurance benefits have replaced assistance to a greater extent in industrialized states than in places where agriculture predominates. Conversely, many farm states and communities—where per capita income is usually low and fiscal resources are limited—carry relatively heavier burdens for aid to needy old people and children than do richer areas."—Social Security Board, *Annual Report, 1946* (Wash., 1947), p. 436.

See also *Federal Old Age and Survivors Insurance in Wisconsin*, published by Region VI of the Social Security Administration in October, showing state and urban-rural comparisons.

"In January 1953, the organization members of the Chamber of Commerce of the United States voted 16 to 1 in favor of a sweeping expansion of the social security program to cover all working and all retired persons." They would bring all gainfully employed under social security and thus make unnecessary federal grants for old-age assistance. It is claimed that the present system is discriminatory because of the "unjustifiable exclusion of the 5 million senior citizens who get no benefits from the OASI system. To the extent that these people do not have sufficient resources of their own, they must depend on public charity via a 'means' test, otherwise known as public assistance."—Chamber of

Commerce of the U.S., *Economic Intelligence* (No. 59; Wash., June 1953).

Thus it seems agreed that care of the aged should no longer be a responsibility of local government.

23 See U.S. Bureau of Census, *Financial Statistics of Cities, 1927* (Wash., 1929), p. 49, for data from 1903 to 1927.

24 U.S. Bureau of Census, *Statistics of Cities, 1939,* p. 115, shows the per cent of expenditure for charities to total expenditure as follows: 1926, 3.1 per cent; 1928, 3.5 per cent; 1930, 3.9 per cent; 1932, 9.8 per cent; 1934, 16.5 per cent; 1936, 15.2 per cent; 1938, 17.6 per cent; 1939, 17.5 per cent.

25 In 1951, federal funds furnished 47 per cent, state funds 41.3 per cent, and local funds 11.7 per cent of expenditures for old-age assistance. Aid to dependent children and aid to the blind were financed likewise locally also by about 10 per cent of the total. Expenditures for general assistance (poor relief) have diminished greatly since the period of full employment.

26 *Social Security Yearbook, 1941,* Table 18, p. 255.

27 *Ibid., 1946,* Table 72, p. 59.

28 Walter A. Morton, "Unemployment Relief and Local Taxation," *The Municipality,* June, 1946, p. 144.

29 *Social Security Yearbook, 1946,* Table 71, p. 58.

30 *Ibid., 1951,* p. 21.

31 In a special report, *The U.S. News and World Report* of November 13, 1953, pp. 92–93, says: "Unemployment-insurance payments may replace close to a third of lost wages in the first two or three months of downturn. But, as the weeks roll by more and more workers exhaust their insurance and the percentage rapidly falls. The thin padding provided by the system tends to get thinner when most needed. . . . Unemployment insurance will bring a good deal of confusion and disappointment in a mild recession, unless recovery is quick—as it was in 1949. Jobless pay will help but not as much as was expected by those who framed the system in the first place."

32 I have discussed this problem more fully in "Unemployment Compensation in Wisconsin," *Social Service Review,* XX, No. 3 (Sept., 1946), 333–44; and in "Two Views of Unemployment Compensation," *ibid.,* XXI, No. 2 (June, 1947), 219–226. See also my "Unemployment Relief and Local Taxation," *The Municipality,* June, 1946, p. 127.

Index